"The inspiring story of a devoted mother's struggle to recover her son from autism. Emotional and moving, *A Real Boy* will strike a chord with all parents who have fought against the odds to get a proper diagnosis—and treatment—for their child."

—Chantal Sicile-Kira,
author of *Autism Spectrum Disorders*

# A Real Boy

*A True Story
of Autism,
Early Intervention,
and Recovery*

**Christina Adams**

BERKLEY BOOKS, NEW YORK

**THE BERKLEY PUBLISHING GROUP**
**Published by the Penguin Group**
**Penguin Group (USA) Inc.**
**375 Hudson Street, New York, New York 10014, USA**
Penguin Group (Canada), 10 Alcorn Avenue, Toronto, Ontario M4V 3B2, Canada (a division of Pearson Penguin Canada Inc.); Penguin Books Ltd., 80 Strand, London WC2R 0RL, England; Penguin Group Ireland, 25 St. Stephen's Green, Dublin 2, Ireland (a division of Penguin Books Ltd.); Penguin Group (Australia), 250 Camberwell Road, Camberwell, Victoria 3124, Australia (a division of Pearson Australia Group Pty. Ltd.); Penguin Books India Pvt. Ltd., 11 Community Centre, Panchsheel Park, New Delhi—110 017, India; Penguin Group (NZ), cnr. Airborne and Rosedale Roads, Albany, Auckland 1310, New Zealand (a division of Pearson New Zealand Ltd.); Penguin Books (South Africa) (Pty.) Ltd., 24 Sturdee Avenue, Rosebank, Johannesburg 2196, South Africa

Penguin Books Ltd., Registered Offices: 80 Strand, London WC2R 0RL, England

This book is an original publication of The Berkley Publishing Group.

The names and identifying characteristics of some people and places mentioned in this book have been changed.

Neither the publisher nor the author is engaged in rendering professional advice or services to the individual reader. The discussion or mention of any ideas, procedures, products, and suggestions in this book is not intended as a substitute for consulting with your physician and obtaining competent medical advice and/or medical care as to any situation, activity, procedure, or suggestion that might affect your health or the health of your child. Accordingly, individual readers must assume responsibility for their own actions, safety, and health and those of their children. Neither the author nor the publisher shall be liable or responsible for any loss, injury, or damage resulting from the reader's use, implementation, or imitation of any information or suggestion in this book.

PRINTING HISTORY
Berkley trade paperback edition / May 2005

Library of Congress Cataloging-in-Publication Data

Adams, Christina.
  A real boy : a true story of autism, early intervention, and recovery / by Christina Adams.—
Berkley Trade pbk. ed.
    p. cm.
  Includes bibliographical references.
  ISBN 0-425-20243-7
    1. Adams, Jonah. 2. Autistic children—United States—Biography. 3. Parents of autistic children—
United States—Biography. 4. Autistic children—Rehabilitation—United States. 5. Autistic children—United States—Family relationships. I. Title.

RJ506.A9A332 2005
618.92'85882'0092—dc22
[B]

2004062337

PRINTED IN THE UNITED STATES OF AMERICA

10  9  8  7  6  5  4  3  2  1

# Publisher's Note

*For my boy,*
*I'll always love you*

# Acknowledgments

In eighth grade in Virginia, I sat in a schoolyard trailer in a group of students handpicked to create a local public television show. I listened quietly as the others, loudly intelligent boys and girls, begged the teacher to tell them why they'd been chosen. Ms. Hedrick outlined their special traits: Glen had a talent for satirical humor, Karen had team-playing ability—everyone got short, pleasing answers that made me wonder why I was there. Then a boy asked, "What about Christina?" Ms. Hedrick smiled and said, "Christina has the ability to see through concepts." We were briefly awed but unnerved, as if she'd said I could translate ancient Greek or had the gift of prophesy. Later, I told my mother what the teacher had said, and she agreed—she understood me. I'd forgotten the incident, until it came time to publish this book.

I needed someone who could see through my concept—a book about a woman and man who struggle to recover their son from autism and reclaim their lives, without any widely recognized medical or educational guidelines, set against a panicky tide of autism spectrum disorders swamping the nation. Marcy Posner was such an agent. She read half the manuscript and picked up the phone. Marcy had faith in me, in the writing, and the importance of the story. She's a partner and a friend.

Best-selling novelist, teacher, and friend Jo-Ann Mapson and her agent Deborah Schneider, who pointed me to Marcy, also deserve thanks for their early belief in the book.

Editor Allison McCabe of Berkley Books understood the project immediately and refined it with deep editorial care and vision. Her support is deft, pervasive, and I can only speculate how fortunate I am to have her. Thanks also to Leslie Gelbman and her staff for their support.

The dreams and trials of the parents filled my head as I wrote and lived this book. Their honesty, agonies, and devotion to their children revealed courage known only to those who also live it. As one woman said to me and several other mothers, "We have an unbreakable bond."

For people on the spectrum—wherever lightly or heavily you find yourself on it—I cherish your unique intelligence, startling imagination, ability to synthesize information, and personal sweetness despite emotional and physical pain. The world is often unkind and displays a strong need for sameness in its populations. It needs help to function alongside its spectrum citizens, just as you live within its boundaries and contribute your talents to its worth.

Stephen Shore, thanks for your humor and your ability to neatly sum up the most challenging intellectual conundrum.

Thanks to everyone who, however briefly or steadfastly, taught my son. Your work enabled him to teach all of us with his trademark humor and gravity.

My mother, who read me poetry when I was a baby, is my role model. She provided a template for mothering and learning, so I could carry out the work of my son's early years and survive our battle with autism. Her patient indulgence of my own childhood intellect provided a foundation, which enabled me to figure out what my boy needed and let his mind flower.

My father, generous, good-humored, with a keen eye, never told his daughters they could not accomplish certain things because they were women—and showed us how by doing it himself.

My sisters, who grew and are still growing up with me—they are an important part of my son's heritage.

For the memory of my grandparents, great-grandparents, great-aunts, and great-uncles, and those ancestors further beyond; tough, stubborn, smart, honest, and loving people who worked hard all their days. They valued natural beauty, good manners, and, most of all, education. I hope their legacy is somewhere in me, and my child.

My husband Jack, also from a line of strong, determined people, has totally supported this book, and has given me so much to be grateful for.

As has my son.

Writing our story kept me going during recovery. But I am only publishing it in hope that it broadens the contemporary picture of the autism spectrum, helps families, and leads to better treatment and acceptance. I believe it will somehow benefit my son in ways I cannot yet see. I hope people do not prove me wrong, that the best parts of them will respond—and he will not experience discrimination, only admiration. That's the concept. I believe you see through it too.

Christina Adams

# Contents

# 1

## Strange New World

I am watching Jonah play. He is a boy of three, with hair like a ripe wheat field, blue lakes reflecting in his eyes. He sits peaceably on the smooth pale carpet of our home, putting small balls and toy parts into a little bus. The alabaster forehead above his pink cheeks is furrowed with concentration.

"Put it in there, take it out of there," he says, as if conversing with an invisible twin.

Again I note his perfect enunciation, often remarked upon by grocery-store strangers. Jonah smiles, the crescent of a dimple in one cheek, and lifts the bus. He spins its wheels, and my heart plummets, afraid to see the evidence of a mechanical fascination. Just as I start to label his fingers on the spinning wheels an autistic behavior, he pushes the bus into a wall. A measure of joy leaps in me.

"You can get it out," he encourages himself. His strong little hand opens the bus window and grasps the cluster of balls like a handful of loose change. The bus trundles off, Jonah pushing it like a devoted mechanic. His narrative floats down the hall, the short declarative sentences of a much younger child, and I am grateful.

Autism. Pervasive developmental disorder. What does it matter what they call it? On a darkened afternoon three months ago, these words enveloped my mind like a killing cloud, but now they mean nothing. His outcome is unpredictable. He might end up alone in his room, zoning out before a television. Or he could become an engineer in a cubicle, with sketchy social skills and an exasperated wife.

I can't see him anymore. "Jonah!" I call. I hear the odd rise and fall of his voice. My son doesn't care about the nuance of his sounds, he simply enjoys them, with an exuberant release. Since he's only just turned three, no one has done more than lift an eyebrow at them, but he grows taller every day.

"Jonah!" I call again. I rise from my swath of carpet by the fireplace and track him down the hall.

*Autism* is a strange and elusive word, soft, almost hollow in sound. It only becomes ugly when you find out what it means. Autism is a neurobiological disorder that affects social connection and intellectual comprehension, becoming apparent by age three, although many people are diagnosed years later. People with autism have unusual and repetitive behaviors, and absent or peculiar speech. They're often plagued by sensory overload, during which competing streams of thoughts, sounds, lights, and noises flash simultaneously through the brain. It can be like living in a casino, multiplied by fifty. It has no known cause, and no cure. Autism is a spectrum disorder, ranging from mild to profound disability, and we have no idea where Jonah will end up. The Childhood Autism Rating System (CARS) questionnaire I filled out scored him as moderate, with a scattering of traits both better and worse.

It's unreal that this is now our world.

Jonah was an early talker. "Dog," he said expertly at nine months, after the requisite "mama" and "dada," then "neck" for necklace as he played with my dangling beads on an Alaskan cruise ship that same month. He could recite the alphabet by eighteen months, count to twenty by way of skipping fifteen. He was the bright child my husband Jack and I silently assumed we would have.

From the baby book in my bad handwriting:

*You had a vaccine at two months, and when we took you back to the doctor for your six-month shots, you reacted when you saw the needle. "Look, he remembers the needle," said the doctor. "How smart are you?" she told you.*

After Jonah turned eighteen months, Jack, a soft-spoken lawyer, and I saw nothing unusual. We were too busy chasing him around the house. How quickly our once-calm child could fill a bathtub and drown three hand-signed music posters in the brimming waters—I'd just taken a moment to brush my hair. For nearly an hour, he'd placidly empty and refill cups at his sink, then suddenly squeeze toothpaste onto the marble counter, dump out three bottles of shampoo, put sunscreen in his hair, and festoon the toilet with rolls of paper. He refused to watch videos, scampering up to the massive television of Jack's bachelor days and shutting off the flickering images. Impulsively, he'd dash off to empty the linen closet, ransack the cleaning supplies, or pillage my makeup drawer.

At night in the rocker, nestled in my arms, he stared at my

face with adoration as I sang to the tune of an old Mexican lullaby: "I love my Jonah, I love my boy. I love my Jonah, he's my little joy." We thought he was bright, intense. His personality was not unlike our own.

What did we know, first-time parents with no family around to balance our observations? Jack's parents were deceased, his Midwest-raised brothers scattered around the country. I'd left my family in the mountains of Virginia for a career in Washington, D.C., seven days after college graduation. So at night, while Jonah played with water or paged through his books, I would sit in my white nightgown in his bedroom, poring over the simple-Simon parenting books offered by bookstores. I had checked that, yes, he could use a pincer grip to grasp a raisin between his two fingers. I noted his timely sit-up, his grasp of a spoon, his taste for Plums 'n Chicken baby food. I knew he could run into our outstretched arms, use a two-word phrase, dance to music. And it was clear that he loved us; from his big smile when we walked into a room, to his delight in Peek-a-Boo and other baby bonding games, his affection was evident in a hundred ways.

None of the books stacked by the changing table listed pointing as a milestone.

Pointing is a joint attention behavior, designed to share the object of one's interest with another person. Babies do it before they can even speak.

True: he never pointed. Also true: he cuddled, laughed, talked, and played.

So how could the lack of a tiny pointing finger change his life?

He defied the odds from the beginning. While pregnant, I'd learned about the wobbly heads and developing necks of babies, how they can't be expected to lift their heads for some time. But the moment he was born, to my surprise, he quite naturally lifted his head from my shoulder and looked straight into my eyes. He smiled the smile of my father when he was six days old. At four months old, his first big laugh filled the terminal of Atlanta's airport as neon lights caught his eye. At five months, his laugh pealed like fairy-bells at the sight of carrots dropping into a bag.

When Jonah was nine months old, I asked the doctor if the allergies and diabetes intertwined in our family trees indicated he should be on soy or non-milk formulas. She said no, so I kept the milk-based formula and added cheese and ice cream to his diet, in love with watching him eat foods that would strengthen his bones and fill his mouth with pleasure.

At twelve months old, the pediatrician plunged a needle into his thigh. This time it was the MMR vaccine, for measles, mumps, and rubella. At fifteen months, he went back for his fourth DTP/HIB vaccine, as recommended by the vaccine schedule, to protect him from diphtheria, tetanus, pertussis, and influenza. The doctor was charmed by his activity and the grin he flashed her as he looked into her eyes. The baby book remembers:

*"He's obviously bright," she said. "You might want to start toilet training right away." She said to get you a potty-training video for boys.*

Is a vaccination the stigmata of an autistic child?

Pointing, a hallmark of developing social interaction, often appears around one year of age. Did the MMR vaccine kill his chance to point, by injecting too many viruses at once into his immature immune system? In the years of Jonah's vaccinations, his other vaccines contained thimerosal, a preservative composed of nearly 50 percent mercury, one of the most toxic substances on earth. Was this enough to rob him of a predictable future?

As I walk, I hear him singing somewhere down the hall. "Happy birthday to you," Jonah sings. "Happy birthday to you. Happy"—he pauses and I hear the plastic bus window click close—"birthday, dear Jonah, happy birthday to you."

Or was it just some elusive swirl of genes? Or the strange rash during his first course of antibiotics for a post-vaccine ear infection, the water I drank from my childhood farmhouse well, my ride up the gondola on Aspen Mountain when I was pregnant? Or all of the above—vaccines and other factors colliding at a crucial intersection with the exquisite ballet timing of a five-car accident?

For the first time in my life, books let me down. None of the books aimed at the mass childrearing market mentioned the dozen tiny signposts that pointed to a large detour. None of them said, *If your child can keep himself occupied for forty minutes at a time and doesn't bring toys over to show you, something might be wrong.* They did not say, *If your child angrily refuses to look at you when you've returned from a weekend away, there might be a problem.* Or *If he cries at the sound of a blow-dryer or bursts into tears whenever "Twinkle, Twinkle Little Star" comes on the CD player, something might be badly wrong.*

None of them say, *If your child's family history is filled with intelligent people, some with immune-related problems like allergies, asthma, diabetes, and arthritis, and you load the child with fifteen vaccines by the time he is eighteen months old, you could be making a grave mistake.* Or *If your child doesn't point, all could be lost.*

Jonah's disappeared from the hall. Alone in the corridor, I peer into his room. He's lying on his back on the blue-trimmed maple bed, his square-toed toddler feet in the air. He's exploring his toes with total seriousness, like an unobserved intern with an imaginary patient.

"What are you doing?" I ask.

He doesn't turn. "He touching toes," he says earnestly.

I stroke his warm forehead, touch the small gilt widow's peak blending into his blond hair. I feel foolish for interrupting him when he's so busy.

Three months ago we got a diagnosis. Two days later, we started pulling him back to our world. We purged his diet of wheat and dairy products, in case they were gumming up his unusual brain. We made him ask for everything, every cup of juice, cracker, or object. Within two weeks, he started to change.

The new books I'm reading say 40 percent of kids with autism never speak. Most will never live alone, work, or have adult relationships. And a very few, found more often in first-person accounts than scientific books, are able to recover.

In the quiet bedroom, I watch Jonah's smooth contemplative face, the way he's figuring out his feet. I desperately want him to be one of the chosen. Every parent out there wants the same thing.

*People in hell want ice water,* whispers a bad voice.

I leave Jonah content on his bed, a rare thing, and return to the living room. The books say the rate of recovery is between 5 and 1 percent, odds better than a casino's one-armed bandits. Like gamblers with one last chance, we're staking our lives on our son.

# 2

# Dreamscapes

Our voyage to this foreign country began with a June trip to the Dordogne region of France, for a large joyous gathering of Jack's family. We took my mother along, her first time out of the United States. It had been a life's ambition for me, her far-flown California daughter, to take her to a place like this. Those shared moments with her remain as the good memories. There were others, but they are tinted now in the sepia tones of the olden days, before the crash. For in France it became apparent that Jonah was autistic.

I avoid thinking about it. When I do, I cringe at how our normality was stripped from us in what feels like a public, unbearable way. It helps if I don't picture it as something that really happened. After all, it was like a movie. The landscape of France. The flowers in the garden, the red linen dress my mother wore, the toasts drunk to brothers and cousins on the centuries-old terrace of a castle.

It helps if I don't remember how beautiful it all really was. How we were for a night the most lucky, favored people I knew and how there was even a real count at dinner, who was handsome and charming and owned many castles, including the two our families stayed in. It always helps to have aristocracy in a movie.

So: the plot. It was early June. There were six brothers and their families on a big vacation in France. The next-to-last brother, named Jack, had a wife, named me, who had just completed a graduate program in May. It was also their fourth anniversary, and they took their two-year-old son, named Jonah, and the wife's mother on this trip.

Jack's middle brother, who built movie theaters, had enjoyed a good year in an up-and-down business, and it was his fiftieth birthday. He and his wife arranged the trip. All the brothers and their families rode around together in big vans and visited castles and caves and drank wine and had a wonderful time.

Dinners were incredible, course after course around a vast carved table for twenty. The many children were amazingly well mannered despite being far away from hamburgers, computer games, and music. There was much joking and laughter and inquiries about college acceptance letters and various athletic honors.

Jack and his wife didn't have to be concerned about these things yet. They were having a hard time getting their son to eat during the vacation. They wanted him to stay seated for five minutes. They wanted him to not throw silverware across the table, or bite them in front of other family members. During the five-course dinners, he ate only bread and a handful of rice.

Everyone tried to help. The French cook, a warm, hearty woman, made special beef dishes, potatoes, and broth for the blond little boy. After the first dinner, the hostess disrupted her graceful seating plan to let each parent flank him at dinner so they could take turns eating. The boy's grandmother repeatedly rose from the table to entertain and console the child. The older kids dutifully walked him around the drafty castle halls and trailed him over the tender grass of the vine-draped lawn.

A special night came. The night designated to celebrate the brother's fiftieth birthday and Jack and his wife's fourth anniversary. The count who owned the castles arrived, and there was a magnificent dinner, with three birthday cakes flying thin candles, their sparks arcing down the castle halls. Afterward, the evening was fresh, the hour pale, as dark was still distant. The hovering dusk had a summer quality about it.

The beautiful little boy was happier outside. He walked over the lawn as the group raised their glasses again. His cousin, a young woman named Jane, who was Jack's niece, was visiting for one night only, as she was traveling across Europe for the summer. Authoritative, with a college degree belying her tattoo and belly ring, Jane played with the boy for half an hour after the lengthy dinner had ended. She flipped him and bounced him, and he took to her as he had to no one else. She chased him with a patience few others had shown. She watched as he held a butter knife to the corner of his eye, to catch the light. She saw him move his hands in a way that signaled to her.

The mother felt good about their play. She knew Jane worked with autistic kids and when the father approached her and asked, "What do you think of Jonah?" and she heard her say, "He's great," a small unspoken worry rolled from her shoulders. A whisper floated through her: *She knows a lot about kids—she wouldn't have said that if something was wrong.* The mother enjoyed the rest of the evening. She didn't know that in the far corner of the lawn, one brother had asked Jane, "So what do you think? Is Jonah autistic?" He was straining to make a joke, but the others had leaned in to hear the answer.

The evening ended. The small family, along with the grandmother, went back to their separate castle. Over the next few days, the boy found an island of calm in the ancient castle yard. He played with an old toy wheelbarrow he found in a shed. Once the mother heard him counting, "One flower, two flowers," as he picked some small white blooms. *How bright and considerate he is,* she thought, when, encouraged by his father, he presented her with the tiny blossoms. The trip wound on in a haze of wine and flowers and endless curling roads and fair summer landscapes. Dreamscapes, really.

The little boy and his family came home. His father went back to work. His grandmother went back to Virginia with travel stars in her eyes, and worry for her grandson in her heart. His mother proudly enrolled the little boy in the pre-school she had carefully selected from the sixteen she had visited. The little boy went off to school.

The movie should have ended here.

Instead, it became disjointed, a loosened film flapping and rolling in nightmarish frames as the rest of the tale unfurled.

# 3

# Hung Out to Dry

*Two Years and Eight Months Old*

It was Jonah's first day of preschool. We'd been back from France for three days, enough time to get over the jet lag. I dressed him in khakis, a thick blue cotton shirt, and new Stride Rite tennis shoes. Most of my friends' kids had started preschool, and I thought preschool activities would channel his high-energy curiosity. And without the nanny we'd had during my graduate school, I needed child care so I could handle the housework and tend to some freelance professional work. I felt so good about this perfect little school in a serene planned community. The place was surrounded by trees, and soft morning light dappled the parking lot. I remember the walk to the front door; Jonah's hand rested in mine, the strong baby hand that I loved. He was two and eight months old, and his world was opening up. A polished marble bunny stood in a friendly pose inside the door, marking the way to a toy-filled classroom near the generous backyard. I let Jonah go at the classroom door, planting a kiss between his big blue eyes as mine strained to hold back tears. "Bye, my boy," I whispered. "I'll be back very soon."

"Bye, Mommy," he said.

He didn't know what that meant until I walked toward the door. He ran after me, crying, grabbing my shirt with his hands. I left quickly, crying too. But I knew he was safe. I drove around town for two hours, my leather backpack stuffed with diapers. I wandered through a grocery store and a book-store, but I was too distracted to buy anything. I checked my watch every twenty minutes until I could pick him up.

---

His face was red and swollen from two hours of crying, but he was glad to see me. I took him home, made him French fries, soothed him to sleep. Afternoon came and we played in our backyard, rehearsing what to tell Jack about the first day of school.

The next day I came to get him again at two thirty, as planned.

"He wouldn't nap," said the director. "But we'll give it another day."

"Another day?" I said.

"Well, I mean, he'll settle in tomorrow. They always sleep fine by the third day."

The third day when I went to get him, his three teachers seemed quiet. "Did he have a good day?" I asked the director. "He ran around by himself," she said. "Wouldn't sleep. The teachers can't get anything done if he doesn't nap, so until he does, you have to pick him up early." I looked at her, shocked. "I'm paying for whole days and we only want him to stay until two thirty as it is!"

"He needs to sleep if he's going to stay here," she said. "You can call by one o'clock, but if he isn't asleep, you'll have to pick him up."

"But I *told* you he didn't sleep much," I said. "I wrote it on the application form, and I discussed it with the assistant director."

She just looked at me.

Jonah and I crossed the tree-lined parking lot to the Jeep. He climbed into his car seat and was asleep in three minutes. I called Jack. "They say he isn't sleeping, and he keeps walking around. They don't like what he's doing."

"What's he doing?"

"They just . . . I don't know, but they don't like the walking around and stuff." I started crying into the cell phone, confused and frustrated by the situation.

"He's a two-year-old. And he's not supposed to walk around?" Jack asks.

"They're making me pick him up early if he doesn't sleep."

"Well, don't cry. We'll talk when I get home. We'll figure something out."

---

That night, Jack sat Jonah on the couch beside him. His smooth happy face peeked from under Jack's strong arm. "I think," Jack said calmly, his gray-blue eyes resolute, "we should get him up early. That way, he'll sleep at the school from sheer exhaustion."

"All right," I said. Jonah looked peacefully at me, and I stared back at him, puzzled. He didn't look like a child who would have a hard time at preschool. Jack took Jonah on his lap. "Okay, little bug," he warned, "tomorrow, you are getting up early."

---

We woke Jonah at six fifteen the next morning, day four. He cried at the early wake-up hour, but laughed in the car, happy at the thought of school. "He slept today," said the director, when I came to get him.

"That's great," I said.

"But he woke up."

"Okay," I said. *Wasn't this a preschool,* I thought, *filled with kids and their various quirks?* "Where is he?"

"He's back in my office. I put him by the bookcase but he wouldn't sit still. He spun the chair, pulled the plugs from the wall, and took the books off the shelves."

"Oh, he won't stay in one place, ever, unless he's really interested in something."

"I want a psychologist to observe him. Have you considered hiring a shadow?"

*A shadow?* It turned out a "shadow" was a person that would follow him all day at school. I was dumbfounded. "Why in the world would I do that?" I asked her.

"He roams," she said. Her tone was hollow and strained, as if describing a restless ghost.

"The pediatrician says he's active. That he's bright."

"He's hitting his head against the wall."

"He does that at home sometimes, but only when he gets mad. The pediatrician says it's normal. Terrible twos."

"Pediatricians don't know anything," she said. "We see kids every day."

I was told I had to be on-call every day, and pick Jonah up the minute his nap ended. I was unnerved, and hurt. I knew from my friends that it took time for kids to adjust to pre-school, but I was certain he was content, that he cried a little but enjoyed his time at school. His enchanting little face and mischievous grin told me so. By now I'd noticed a red-haired boy in his class who sat on the floor with a blanket, thumb in his mouth, all day long. He smiled sometimes, a quick secret smile. Was that what they wanted?

Every day the next week, I made the fifteen-minute drive, past the yellow bulldozers adding to the ideal town, on the way to the perfect preschool. Every day I heard ominous things from the director, or a whispering teacher. "Jonah's roaming the classroom again." "He pinched another boy today." "He didn't sleep very long." "He's making noise while the other kids sleep."

Every day, I called Jack from the car, crying in the sunlight, halfway home.

"They said he's hitting his head again," I told him one day. That night, Jack picked us up and we drove to a business in a small office park. "I found this place because one of my clients, a kid with cerebral palsy, needed a padded helmet," he said. "If we get Jonah one, he won't hurt himself when he hits his head, and the school won't worry about liability." A man brought out a navy blue soft vinyl helmet, with a rainbow strap and perforated air holes. We put it on Jonah and he liked it. Jack ordered one as I surveyed the walls, with their framed picture of kids in wheelchairs and helmets. I felt strange to be in a store for disabled kids with my child, who was so healthy.

He was problematic, yes, but certainly he had no challenges like theirs.

––––––––––––

The phone rang one morning after I'd cleaned the kitchen. "He's awake," said the director. "We're trying to have a baby shower and he's in my office."

I flashed out of the house, imagining him wrecking the cake, stomping the presents, or something warranting the irritation in her voice. I walked quickly through the preschool door, only to find him the handsome stranger at a party, eating cookies, delighting the women, happy to be alive.

"Can I talk to you?" The director stopped me on my way in the next day.

I stood there warily, like a rabbit ready to run for its hole.

"This just isn't working for him," she said.

"What do you mean? He really likes it here. And the helmet came in; I'll put it on him tomorrow." She was younger than I was, but she looked at me with a hard face. "The helmet won't help. There are special schools for kids like him. I want some people from our local school to come over and see him. Then we can talk about his transferring."

"I don't plan to transfer him anywhere," I said. "Why should I?"

"Our school has a regular schedule. Jonah needs a place with a lot less structure."

"He's doing great!" I said. "He even naps now!"

"I want you to think about hiring a shadow or deciding who you want to see him. I'll let you know when the school people can come. They're pretty busy, but I'll tell them it's important."

Her phone rang and I left. *Special schools? Let unknown psychologists evaluate my child?* Why was she demanding this? I called Jonah's pediatrician. "You know him," I said. "He's always been high-energy, and the school doesn't like that. He's happy there, but they have a problem with him."

I could hear her sigh over the phone. "I'll tell you right now, you need to look for a new preschool."

"I hate to do that when he really likes it there."

"So let's wait and see what happens," she said.

But I knew they didn't love him. I knew he had to leave.

———

Monday morning, I called around to the preschools listed in the local parenting magazines and visited four of them. They all wanted their children to nap at least two hours. Then I called an unfamiliar school listed in the local phone book.

"Hello, Kid's House," said the warm-voiced woman who answered.

Hesitantly, I explained our situation, and it turned out that she liked little boys who didn't sleep that much. I drove over and found a modest school in a quiet old neighborhood. I entered the small front yard through a self-latching front gate. A cluster of sweet-faced children gathered by the fence. "It's trash-truck day," the director explained to me. "Heaven forbid they miss the garbage truck."

She had an opening for next week. I wrote her a check and left to pick Jonah up from the other preschool for the very last time. It was the end of our third week there.

"Can I see you for a minute?" the director called out when I arrived. "I've arranged for a psychologist to observe Jonah on Monday," she said. "Can you have him here at eight?"

"I'm taking him out," I said. "Today is his last day."

"Oh," she said. A quick expression crossed her face. "We think he's autistic."

I stared at her. I saw the white light of her office, her closed lips. The silver pendant of a child hung from her neck. "I'm sorry," she said. "That's why I wanted the psychologist to observe. I think you should talk to her."

*Talk to her. Autistic.*

"We're sorry it didn't work out. Good luck. Let us know how things go."

I said things I don't remember. I walked to the classroom. There he was, summer-flushed and handsome beside a small girl. They were listening to a teacher read from a book. "Come on, Jonah, Mommy's here," I said. "We're leaving." I was shaking, but I was damned if I'd let these people see it. One of his teachers came up to me. I hoisted Jonah on my hip, defensive. She put her face close to mine. "I saw hand-flapping today," she said.

An image from a television movie I'd seen as a child emerged from my mind, a rocking, hand-flapping boy isolated in a corner. *Hand-flapping is a classic autistic trait.* "Show me. Show me what he did," I said. I put my wrist in her hand.

She bent my hand back and forth. "We were on a nature walk," she whispered. "Some kids got excited, and he flapped his hands." She paused. "My son is autistic."

*I get it now!* I thought. *So mine must be too.*

"Bye-bye teacher," said Jonah. We left the classroom, passing the bunny's blank stone gaze, and headed for the door. The director motioned from her office. "Keep in touch. He's really a sweet boy."

"I know."

I buckled Jonah in the car and we drove through the planned community, past the bulldozers busily at work. I looked at his golden head, his sweet smile, and I began to melt like wax in a fire. *Could it be true? Could he be autistic?* I couldn't see. The sun was blinding me, and I willed myself to clutch the wheel and drive slowly home.

# 4

## Fruitless Ground

### Biting

Like most domestic violence, the biting started in the kitchen.

One night when Jonah was ten weeks old, I stood in the kitchen, holding him in my arms. The honey-toned maple of the cabinets cast a warm glow over his angry red face in his blue plaid baby blanket. He'd been unusually fussy for two hours. Jack and I had rocked, carried, and held him to no avail. On impulse, I reached inside his mouth and touched his pink lower gum. A tiny ridge of white tooth pressed itself into my fingertip. I was so happy at this ahead-of-schedule surprise. My precocious baby.

Six months later, in the same familiar kitchen, he bit me for the first time. I laughed, impressed and amused by the nip of baby teeth. I can't recall where that first bite landed, but it was either on my arm or breast, where I always held him.

He had been such an easy, social baby. I remember walking

the mall near our home with friends, our babies in strollers. Their babies would fuss and whine, while Jonah stayed calm, observing everything, holding a book, paging through it and then chewing on it. He was obviously intelligent. People had told me that Jack and I would have this kind of child—how could we not, they asked—as if hereditary traits were the sum total of it. Take Jack with his well-bred manners, analytical ways, and hidden playful streak, and add me, with my occasional wit, command of obscure facts, and natural ability to speed-read. Factor in our careers, his in law, mine in corporate communications, before motherhood and graduate school. What other outcome could there be? When Jonah was only two months old, I got my hair and makeup done for a New Year's Eve dinner. When I returned from the salon, he pulled away and cried as he examined the stranger with tall hair, colored eyes, and blush contouring her chubby postpartum cheeks. His rejection hurt, but I was proud of his powers of observation. As he grew, he loved to play with soft fuzzy blocks, musical toys, and rattles. He ate a stream of foods: crackers, chicken, peas, fruits. He was a delight, gasping with glee when we placed his little socks over his face and whisked them away to reveal our smiling faces.

Then around nine months of age, he started biting me constantly.

At first, my memory spaces the bites about a week apart. Then once, twice, three, and four times a day. The white tooth tip of his baby mouth had been the harbinger of an incredibly strong set of teeth—my chest, breasts, and upper arms sprouted a pattern of bruise flowers, purple, green, yellow, and blue. I talked to the pediatrician about it after his first birthday, during a well-baby checkup. "Bites a lot," she wrote in her notes, and handed me a sheet on how to do time-outs.

Months wore on, but Jonah's biting didn't stop. It would fade for a week or even two, but then return stronger than ever.

I called my sister. A veteran mom of two boys, she suggested everything in her mother's bag of tricks. Give him a time-out. Try not to react so he won't get rewarded with attention. Both of these approaches failed. I called her again. "Put soap on his tongue," she said reluctantly, "it worked for me. Or if you must, try hot pepper." I tried both, but he made little tasty sounds when I put them into his mouth, and smiled.

The mild California weather often left my arms bare, and as bruises shifted kaleidoscopically around my arms and chest, people began to notice. I kidded Jack that people would think he'd beaten me, and we'd laugh and joke about my possible sins, like failing to wash the car, or leaving wire hangers in the closet à la Joan Crawford. Then, a newly made friend told me she'd thought I *was* covering for Jack with the baby-biting excuse. This was a little startling, because Jack had always taken care of us. He baby-proofed the house in ingenious ways to protect Jonah, spent hours with him on weekends, and came home early sometimes, often with a little gift, so I could attend evening classes. But he could not stop Jonah's biting and the misery it caused me.

Come summer, legions of people, from the construction workers fixing our roof to the mothers of our adult friends, gave me advice. "Bite him back," they all said. "Best thing my mother ever did to me," said one. "I never bit anyone else again," said another. Yet all the books said that was off-limits.

One book suggested pressing his teeth firmly into his own arm so that he would feel the pain. "Here, Jonah," I said, after he had nipped me hard. I lifted his soft-fleshed little arm to his mouth and pressed his teeth into it. "See, it hurts. No bite!" I said.

He looked at the imprint of his two top teeth and laughed, seemingly unbothered by the pain. Then he rolled on the carpet and pressed my arm to his mouth. It was a game, and he preferred my flesh to anything else.

---

At his fifteen-month well-baby visit Jonah pattered around the examining room in his white diaper and socks, twirling the doctor's stool, opening cabinets, pulling out information sheets on diseases, climbing on the sink and running water from the faucets. Finally, she came in, and he looked up at her with a flirty grin.

"You're handsome, aren't you? Really cute," she said to me.

He leaned, smiling, on her knee as she placed her stethoscope on his chest.

"Gosh, I hate to stick him today . . . he's liking me, and I hate to ruin it . . . maybe I'll get a nurse to stick him instead," she muttered under her breath.

"Why do kids have to have so many shots so soon in life?" I asked her. "It wasn't like this when we were kids."

"HMO medicine," she answered. "They want you to get the shots now, because well-baby visits are only covered by insurance when the child is under the age of two. They're afraid you won't come back if it cost more."

But I would, I told her.

"All parents aren't like you."

She pulled out a long, dated-looking checklist. "How's he doing?" she asked. The list contained items like "walks well" and "drinks from a cup." I told her he'd taught himself to sit up and down on a stool, to our applause, that he had put on his socks and shoes, and could sing the alphabet song. She nodded.

I pointed out the rash-covered, scarlet-red cheeks he'd displayed since he was six months old, which I'd voiced concern about before. She dismissed my concerns.

"Head circumference is good, he certainly looks great." She mentioned how bright he was and urged me to start toilet training. She couldn't find a nurse to do the injection, so she held the syringe in her fist and plunged it in his thigh. His face turned even redder in shock, and he cried lustily as the DTP/HIB vaccine made its way into his system, for the fourth time.

Six days later, my son was back at the doctor's, for his first-ever ear infection.

His first course of antibiotics was prescribed, and after he took it at home that night, a strange purple red pinpoint rash spread over his arms and chest, prompting a chain reaction. The pediatric on-call nurse directed us to call 911, the 911 operator called for paramedics, and then the paramedics ordered us to drive him to the emergency room. "Mysterious rash, not a typical antibiotic allergy . . . we'll probably never know what it was," his pediatrician said the next day, writing a prescription for another drug.

Jonah, still a curious child who could always focus on a watch, keys, or anything new or different, began to grow more excitable and active. It became harder each month to capture his attention. Sometimes I wasn't sure what he was interested in or cared about anymore. He'd had a small stuffed white bear since he was a baby, and one night when I was cleaning his room I kicked it playfully into the air, pretending to make it fly. Jonah cried out in protest, and became upset with me, unable to stop his tears. I handed the bear to Jonah, apologized to them both, and silently berated myself for being so insensitive. But I was pleased with his empathy, since I had assumed he wouldn't mind. I'd unconsciously noted that his attachment to the bear, and his attention to my activities, had decreased lately.

When he turned eighteen months old, we went to our mountain cabin with a couple of friends. Parents of three grown sons, they flanked Jonah in the backseat of the Jeep as we drove to dinner. "One, two, three, four . . ." they heard him counting, and they shushed us quickly. We held our breath as he continued, "Sisteen, sebenteen, eighteen, nineteen . . . twenny!" We applauded with whoops of laughter. He beamed at us under the interior light and held my friends' hands, one in each of his.

The following week, Jonah and I met the mother and one of her sons in a Los Angeles mall. We sat down to eat dinner, but Jonah wouldn't settle in his high chair. He twisted and fought and wouldn't eat or sit as he usually did. "I don't see how I'm going to eat," I said, cramming bites of chicken in my mouth as I held him in the chair with the other arm. I tried to placate him with toys, then held him on my lap, but I gave up. After they had eaten, we entered a department store, but Jonah wouldn't stay in his stroller. He bucked and fought to get out, even screamed and howled right beside the jewelry counters. "I'm sorry," I kept saying. "He's *never* this bad."

"I know," said my friend, looking worried. "He just doesn't want to stay in."

Finally, I let him out and he ran, purposefully darting in and out of shops, as if seeking something he wanted but couldn't find. Finally, he found a display of lights in the front of a store, and he ran back and forth and gazed at it in a way I'd never seen before, gleeful for the first time that night.

We dropped my friend and her son off at their home, a place filled with art glass and collectibles. I could barely keep Jonah's hands in sight. He grabbed and snatched and ran through the house as if driven by an unrelenting engine. "I have to go," I told her, and we kissed quickly as Jonah sat down in the dog's water bowl. I called Jack and tried to tell him what a rough night it had been. "He was so wild and uncontrollable," I said. "You've never seen him like this before, and neither have I."

He never went back to the way he was.

---

As Jonah headed for his second birthday, his biting grew in intensity. He started biting other kids, even sinking his teeth into the tender backs of their necks, like a small happy vampire. All of the child-care books offered, "Wait for the child to outgrow it." Nowhere was there a chapter titled, "What to Do When Your Child Hurts People."

Two weeks after he turned two, I went back to the pediatrician just to discuss the biting. He'd bitten two kids at his party. I showed her two of my constant bruises and told her again of my unhappiness.

"Did you try time-out?" she asked. She handed me the same faint copy of the time-out sheet I'd received a year ago.

"But I've been doing this time-out thing, and it doesn't work."

"A child has to be a certain age before time-out is effective. He's getting old enough now that you should try it again."

Then why did she waste my time by giving me the time-out sheet back then?

"And try handing him to someone else when he bites," she added.

I felt crazy, like I was edging along a high ledge without a net, a place for crazy people, where no one could help me solve my problem.

———————————

As Jonah grew taller and more handsome, his energy and his will grew along with his frame. The biting became a permanent part of our lives.

Cuddling on the couch in the dark; holding him warm in a towel after his bath; his teeth would flash out and sink into me, a bramble, a fishhook, a needle. Playing patty-cake and hugging afterward, he would laugh with delight and then set his teeth into the muscle of my neck. I couldn't understand it. I couldn't track its pattern. I became afraid. Not of him as a person, but of his infernal impulse to bite. We stepped up our efforts, Jack and I. He told Jonah, "No, no," sharply, almost shouting, and took him immediately away from me when he was home. Sometimes Jonah's face would screw up and cry, but usually, he laughed or just looked at me. The biting, once a small, exotic habit, was now disturbing and unavoidable, like a peacock screeching in the front yard.

Then face-hitting began.

Jack's late father, a mild-mannered, cultured man, could break an apple in half with his compact, muscular hands. Those hands, I learned when Jonah started using his small sturdy hands to hit me between the eyes, had passed through Jack to Jonah. When I wore glasses, the hit would smash them into my nose or to the floor. Since he didn't watch television or videos or go to preschool, it was obvious that he had invented the hit-Mommy-in-the-face game himself.

One night we were in a Burger King play area with his friend Jordan, and Jordan's mother. Jonah bit Jordan for the third time in a month, and the mother took Jordan away, both of them in tears. When I picked Jonah up to scold him, he hit me right between the eyes. It hurt, a stinging, bruising, bone-ache kind of hurt. I took him outside, sat him down, and held his hands tight. I talked, clutching his hands, for fifteen minutes as he begged, "Want down." I wouldn't let go of him. "You are not going back in there until you learn your lesson," I said, crying.

Finally, a man sitting nearby said, "He is only a child. Do not do what you are doing. You should let him go." He left, and I sat there, shamed and despairing.

Along with hitting and biting for fun, Jonah started to bite in anger. He'd set an incisor and yank, so it left small inky pools of blood under the skin.

Cooking dinner, the kitchen became a defensive zone. My hands would be in raw meat, making meatballs or a hamburger for him, or cutting skin off chicken, and he'd zero in from behind. Or the stove would be on, water running in the sink, and he'd attack, a grinning maw headed for my legs and thighs. His teeth were strong and like the snapping turtles of my Southern childhood lore, he wouldn't let go. So I'd frantically run hot water over my germ-slicked hands, an anxious housewife in a leg-hold trap, slinging water through the air as I pried his jaws apart. Soon I was afraid to cook. A hot skillet and running water at five o'clock had become his siren song. It was a force stronger than hunger. Grapes, crackers, raisins; nothing held more allure than a bite of me. I started having Chinese food delivered, or waiting until Jack could come home so I could cook.

But Jack often worked late, as he was swamped with legal cases, and we became sick of Chinese food.

I was angry. Things were so hard for me, so hard, and nobody understood. Why couldn't I be like other mothers, cooking dinner as my child played charmingly with toys at my feet? I started escaping the house, taking Jonah anywhere for dinner. His behavior had deteriorated when eating out too, but flying forks and getting my head pounded in a booth became preferable to staying at home with his biting.

One night when Jack was home, we were seated around the kitchen table with Jonah in his new booster seat. I'd been able to make steak, grilled vegetables, polenta. Red wine for Jack, white for me. But Jonah had finished eating, and he wanted something. I don't remember what it was—a third cookie, a wineglass, a knife. Whatever it was, I said, "No," and took it from his hand. Quickly, like a fish darting through water, he got his sharp little teeth around my forefinger and bit hard. It hurt so badly I stopped breathing. The pain blasted forth a memory, how I'd read as a child that Spanish Inquisition torturers used to insert pins under their victims' fingernails. Such a small form of cruelty had always puzzled me, but now I understood. Jack took Jonah from the table, held him face to face, and scolded him harshly. I went to the freezer, put bare cubes of ice on the punctures bracketing my fingertip, and left for the bedroom. I fell on the bed, with the melting water dripping on my chest. I cried for twenty minutes as the pain swelled to a throb.

In the surreal quiet of the bedroom, I stared at the ceiling. I couldn't believe that my own child could do this. I curled up and closed my eyes, trying to ease away the pain, but I couldn't turn my mind away from my despair. Finally, the solitude and weeping helped my body produce the special "forgetting chemicals" mothers somehow develop. Thoughts of Jack and Jonah in the living room drew me out.

"Hey, look who's here!" said Jack softly. "It's Mommy!"

Jonah's worried face looked up. With a smile he reached his arms out to me.

I knew he had no knowledge of the pain he had inflicted. I sat with him on the long leather sofa, in the flickering light from a gentle new video, the lamps glowing low. I hugged him and kissed his head and encouraged him to watch the screen. But that night had broken something in me. I tried not to think about tomorrow, and the next day, and the long day after that.

In the morning, I couldn't shake my bad feelings. The biting, the hitting, one long year melting into another. Seven months had passed since my second visit to the pediatrician about his biting.

Jack came home, smiling to see us. After we'd eaten dinner, with Jonah's chair out of reach of the table, I started talking.

"Jack, somebody's got to help us with the biting. I want to take him to a psychologist," I said.

He frowned. "I don't know why," he answered.

I'd expected he wouldn't like the idea. Jack had a master's degree in psychology and had worked toward his PhD, but he'd chosen to practice law instead because he'd seen some heavy-handed professionals in the field.

"Well, what else can I do?" I said. "It's been going on for a year and a half. And now there's the hitting too. Maybe a psychologist can at least tell us what to expect."

"Can't you ask the pediatrician about it?"

"I've done that and I get nothing. She isn't qualified to handle this. There has to be somebody who can."

Jack looked unhappy. "I don't want them interfering with him," he said. "He's a perfect little boy."

"I won't let anyone mess with him, honey. I don't want that either."

I called the pediatrician the next day. I wanted a referral to a psychologist, and although she was reluctant, I got the name of a therapist.

———

The therapist wanted to see me alone the first time. He was a pleasant, dark-haired man who asked about our family structure, our former nanny, our marriage, what movies or videos we watched at home. I knew he was plumbing fruitless ground, but I described our quiet family life, and waited for him to ask about Jonah. Then his friendly face shifted from affability to sternness. "I must ask, is there any abuse or neglect in the home?"

"First of all, no. Second, I know it's not that simple a problem."

If all our attempts and determination hadn't stopped the biting, I was positive there was more to it than being a childhood phase.

After fifty minutes of talk about Jonah's brightness, his long attention span alternating with intense activity, and overall good health, plus the biting and hitting, he said everything sounded fine. He thought it would be a good idea to see Jonah, and I agreed, restraining myself from saying, "I could have told you that."

A month later, Jonah and I returned. After Jonah explored the entire office, compromised every light fixture, and attempted to poke objects into every electrical outlet, it was apparent he'd charmed the man. The psychologist looked at me and said, "He's a wonderful, normal boy. There's nothing wrong here at all. I'm not even going to write a diagnosis down in your file."

I hadn't expected anything as harsh as a diagnosis. But then came those terrible words again. "As for the biting—you'll just have to wait it out." He saw the dismay on my face and added, "I know, it's hard. My son bit until he was four years old."

———————

Nothing earns a child a bad name as quickly as a bite. My closest mom-friends continued to visit, but they didn't stay long. Jonah had bitten their children several times and they were backing off. It was as if he had scattered small land mines around our cozy living room, and when we turned our backs one would go off and leave a red ring of teethmarks on some child's leg or shoulder.

I took it on myself. It was my son who was the biter, my home, my responsibility. I was the keeper of an untamed child who knew not what he did. I didn't know how much longer I could make amends for his unfathomable nature, and the bites he inflicted. I knew all of our friends might fall away, so I assumed a grim patrol. I never sat down anymore, anywhere, when kids were present. I peered from the kitchen, stood over the children, carried my big boy on my hip, to keep his teeth out of other kids' flesh. It didn't always work. But I was trying to retain our friends, make us acceptable, not too dangerous to know.

Later, the danger became a symptom, and then all was understood.

# 5

## Summer Storm

### *July*

Like every summer before and since, the waning days of July seemed like a dream to me. The leaves of trees glittered greenly in the breeze. There was a Fourth of July celebration, with kids in red T-shirts and shorts showing their brown legs. Stillness hung in the evening air.

The afternoon we left our first preschool for good, I called Jack. He had known only one child with autism when he was in the psychology field, a child who had no speech. And in light of the pediatrician's and therapist's positive past comments, he thought there was no chance the school was right. But when I pumped him for professionals I could consult, he suggested speech therapists. So I got out the local phone book and called every speech therapist and educational expert I could find. By day's end, I'd spoken to three speech therapists, an educational consultant, and a person from the special school the preschool director had mentioned. I also called our pediatrician. As I described what the preschool's director and teacher had said about Jonah, each listener was alert and concerned. "Tell me about his language," they all said. "Does he talk?"

"Oh, yes," I'd said. I listed some of his recent phrases: *Want to go to the library. Want to go see the water. Want to go see Jordan. Mommy drinks Pepsi, Daddy drinks coffee. Ready for school. Want to see the vacuum cleaner. Want to go home and see Daddy. Say please, say please.* No one mentioned the possibility that these were phrases he'd copied, or wondered if he could ask or answer questions. "Oh, he's not autistic," they all said. "Language like that rules out autism."

"Does he line things up, like cars or toys?" a couple of them asked. *No.*

"Does he spin things, or flip his fingers in front of his eyes?" *No.*

"Is he affectionate? Does he like people?" *Yes.*

I told them about the biting, but no one took that seriously. "Perhaps the school wasn't a good fit for him," they said. "I'd be happy to look at him, but it seems certain he doesn't have autism."

Jonah's pediatrician didn't want to see him, just told me not to worry. Of the speech therapists, I booked an appointment with one who had mused that some of Jonah's behaviors, like the way he could already count things in twos and threes, his ability to notice the tiny details of a flower, and his amazing verbal and aural memory, indicated he might be gifted. That seemed more likely to me than a learning disorder, considering the bright people who inhabited both sides of his family tree. Perhaps he was both gifted *and* bothered by something? That was what I was hoping. That was what I could deal with.

———————

Jonah started his new preschool. Sally, the owner of Kid's House, had run the place for twenty-five years. She and Marci, the director, were caring and experienced. I'd told them about the biting, the hitting, and the no sleeping, and they thought they could vanquish those habits. He was welcomed into Room One, for the smallest kids, with open arms. "Oh, he's so cute! So handsome!" the teachers cried.

"Look at that cute shirt!" said Shari, his main teacher, approvingly. They could tell how much we doted on him. They helped him cry for the first day or two, then watched him grin later in the week as he entered the room and ran to his favorite toys.

As I waited for our speech therapy appointment to arrive, I went to the local library and found a book on gifted kids, a book on a boy with severe attention deficit hyperactivity disorder, and Lorna Wing's *Children with Autism*. It was one of only two books in the city library system on autism. The other was Temple Grandin's *Thinking in Pictures*. Temple was a high-functioning autistic woman who became an agricultural scientist and livestock facility designer. Although I'd read autistic writer Donna Williams's autobiography *Nobody Nowhere* on an Australian business trip the year I met Jack, I knew very little about autism and my curiosity was piqued by the school's comments. I also thought ADHD, a common boyhood malady according to the media, was worth researching. Plus, these were the only books on kids with learning differences.

I read the ADHD book first. The boy was wildly out of control. He hit, kicked, screamed, and ended up in special schools. But he had good speech and normal intelligence. After a few years, he had largely gotten himself under control with the help of medication and support. ADHD didn't sound unreasonable; my two sisters and I had been very willful and energetic as kids, and I had a mixed track record in elementary school. I could read when I was four and was bored to death until sixth grade. I wasn't good at listening to the teacher, and I always sat in the back of the classroom, looking out the window. But I'd never been labeled anything other than lazy. *Maybe it's ADHD?*

Next, I read the gifted-child book. Yes, Jonah spoke early and he was exceedingly curious, but some of the signs, like very early reading, sophisticated sentences, and asking abstract questions, weren't there. The sentence that stood out in my mind was, "Gifted boys are likely to be diagnosed as developmentally delayed in their early years."

Then, the Wing book.

I approached this one with trepidation, even though I was convinced that autism was not a possibility. After all, the professionals had been so certain. And after reading Wing's scholarly British book, I was sure that autism, for us, was as remote as the moon. The boys and girls portrayed in it had less similarity to Jonah than the Lost Boys of *Peter Pan*. They said bizarre and indiscriminate things; they screamed when the salt shaker was moved on the breakfast table; they took off their clothes in front of strangers and roamed the house. So remote was the disorder portrayed in the book that my whole picture of it took on a European, otherworldly quality; scones with butter, trains speeding through wet countryside, strange and enchantingly difficult little beings wandering English gardens like troubled fairies.

"Of all the things I've read," I told Jack, "the ADHD book

seems to come closest to describing him. I think he has it. I mean, maybe I had some of it when I was a kid. Not the aggression, but I always got bored in school."

"You're just looking for something to be wrong with him," Jack said. I was surprised, and then I realized he was upset.

"No, I am not!" I said. "But there's something that's not right."

"You get all these books, and with every different one, you say, maybe this is what's wrong with him. Look hard enough, and sure, you'll find something bad."

"So what am I supposed to do?" I said. My eyes filled with tears. "All the pediatrician ever says is, just wait and see. He's gotten so hyper I can't even take him to a park without chasing him for an hour straight. He keeps biting everyone all the time! What do you want me to do?"

"I don't know," he said. "I'm uncomfortable with you reading these books and diagnosing him. You're not a doctor."

"No, I'm not. But the doctor isn't helping. The therapist didn't help. So tell me—what am I supposed to do?"

"We have an appointment with the speech therapist coming up. Can't you wait and see what the medical professionals have to say?"

"I'll see what she has to say. But I'm not going to stop trying to find out what's going on with him. You're welcome to find out too."

He sighed. "Okay. I'll do that," he said.

There was really nothing more to say.

---

We were early, and the speech therapist was running a half hour late. The interview didn't start off well because she insisted that she and I get Jonah's history on paper, so Jack took Jonah outside. By the time we finished, an hour had passed. All that time, Jack and Jonah had been waiting. When they came in, they were both unhappy.

"I'm so sorry you had to wait," the therapist said.

"I can tell you now, he's in a bad mood," Jack said tersely. "He's been waiting for an *hour and a half.*"

"I'm sorry," she said. "Really."

I knew it couldn't have been easy to handle Jonah for that long, exploring every square foot of the place and cranky without his nap.

"Can you sit down, Jonah?" the therapist said. She pointed at a table in the corner. Atop it sat a tea set, a cat, and some action figures. He grabbed a toy airplane. "Tell me your name," she said. "How old are you?"

His round babyish face, flushed with the July heat, looked down at the airplane. Jack took the plane from him, and Jonah cried out angrily and slammed his own head atop the table. We were aghast. But he wasn't hurt, just mad. The therapist composed herself and continued. "Okay, Jonah. Give the cat a cup of tea. Can you pour the cat some tea? It's thirsty."

*A tea set? This is California,* I thought. *Nobody drinks hot tea.*

He ignored the tea set.

"Show me, Jonah. Like this. Meow, meow, the cat's thirsty. Poor kitty. Can you give the kitty a drink, like this?" She tilted the pitcher into a miniature cup, then made the cat drink from the cup. "Can you do that?"

He reluctantly touched the cat, then picked up the cup and banged it on the saucer. Finally he put the cat next to the cup and tilted its head toward the opening.

"Can you make the man get on his motorcycle and ride?" she said.

*He can do that,* I thought. But he ignored the man, going for a toy spoon instead. As I waited for her to cajole him into doing the task, I thought, *Surely he has done this, made a toy man ride a toy vehicle?* The idea of it seemed familiar, a simple thing, but when I looked for the memory, it was a phantasm, the memory of a boy I thought I had known but didn't. We sat there, waiting. He picked up the motorcycle and turned it over. Then he dropped it to the table. He started to cry angrily, then squirmed onto my lap and tried to bite me. "He's so tired—he does far better than this at home," I shouted to the therapist over his cries. "Really, he does. It's just that he had to wait so long—"

"I'm glad to hear he does better at home," she said. "Because what I see here doesn't look good. This is not the child you described over the phone. But if you are telling me he does better at home—"

"Yes, he does. The wait was just too much for him."

Jack pulled Jonah off me and they headed for the door. I felt a terrible tension as Jonah's voice faded down the corridor. The speech therapist looked nervous and serious.

"Bring him back next week. What time can you come in?"

There was no way Jack was going to let him come back. I could tell the therapist had not appealed to him.

"I'll call you," I said. "Let me check the calendar."

"I really think I could help him," she said. "But I need to get a clearer picture."

"Okay," I said, exiting the door. I paid the bill and went outside. Jonah was running up and down the sidewalk. When he saw me, he brightened and ran to me. I swept him up, and he put his hands gently on my face and then hugged me. As for Jack, two hours with an overwrought Jonah had gotten to him. "I hope you don't want me to come back here again," he said, "because there's no way I want her to treat him."

"Right now," I said, "all I want is to get him home."

# 6

## Darkness Falls

*Later in July*

The new school, Kid's House, was working out, although Jonah had started to exhibit some problems. He didn't sleep much during nap time, and he had bitten a two-year-old in his class. He also didn't like to listen to his teachers, but he was very attached to a couple of them. Shari, his main teacher, was determined that he would become a happy member of the school. "Don't worry, Mom, we're coming along fine!" she told me at the end of every day. "This place is like paradise, so helpful and caring," I told Jack.

Every day, I would drop Jonah at school, go home and clean the house, do errands, and work until around three P.M. I'd pick him up, his face shining with sun despite twice-daily ablutions with sunscreen, and he'd settle happily into the back of the Jeep and say, "Want to go to the library" or "Want to go home." He never answered my questions, but I thought that would come.

Nearly three weeks passed and I was running behind as I set off to pick him up from preschool. It was later than usual, around four P.M., when I got there. It had been a long day for him, and I walked in feeling guilty.

"Hi, Mommy," said Shari as I entered the big sandy back-yard. Jonah was on the swing, the one near the fence, where he nearly always was when I arrived, swinging away in his navy and yellow short set. He ran to me with raised arms, and clung to me with great joy as I picked him up, hunching his body into mine as he clutched my neck. Then he swerved away, so I let him down and he ran back to the swing.

Shari and I stood together as he swung. Watching him, Shari said, "You know, he reminds me a lot of my nephew. My nephew's autistic."

"Oh, really?" I said.

"Yes. Same rascal ways, although my nephew's a little older."

"Oh," I said. We stood there.

"I have to get busy now, gotta watch the kidlets," she said. "See you tomorrow."

I collected Jonah from the swing. Usually I made him say good-bye to his teachers, but this time I just took him by the hand and left. The gate shrieked as we pulled it open, and clanged behind us as I led Jonah to the car. I buckled him in and dialed Jack's cell phone. "Jack?"

"Yes?"

"Hi. I was just talking to Miss Shari at school. She said Jonah reminds her of her nephew, and her nephew is autistic."

"This is the second time we've heard that word from a

preschool. I'm going to call Ross. His daughter Jane works with autistic kids. Maybe he can put us in touch with her."

---

When I got home, Jack was already on the phone. He handed me the cordless so I could join in. I set Jonah in the middle of the hallway floor, and handed him my keys. He smiled and began examining them one by one. "I have Ross and Jane on the line," Jack said. "We've been talking about Jonah."

"Hi, Christina," said Ross's deep voice. "Jane happens to be home from college. So the timing is perfect. I wanted her to talk to you."

"Hi," said Jane. "Jack was telling me some things about Jonah."

"Yes. He's been having a hard time since the vacation in France," I said.

"Jane and Ross have wanted to tell us something," Jack said in a controlled voice. "They feel that Jonah is autistic."

"But I read a book about it, and he didn't fit it *at all*," I said. "And all the speech therapists said he isn't."

"Jane and Ross have known since they saw him in France," Jack said.

"We've been planning to talk to you," Ross said. "We wanted to fly out in person to tell you."

"But he can't be autistic," I said. "He talks too much, and autistic kids do weird things. He doesn't do any of those."

"He is definitely autistic," Jane said.

"But why do you say that?" I asked. Jonah was still playing with the keys at my feet. I saw his small finger push down the red alarm button.

"In France, behind the house, I saw him hold a butter knife

up to the corner of his eye, so the sun could reflect off the blade."

My memory showed me a picture of him in the green grass of the courtyard, alone among a dozen relatives. "What else did you see?"

"I saw him doing some hand-flapping."

"I have never seen that. Plus, the boy down the street does it. It's normal."

"I don't know about the boy down the street," Jane said.

"I've seen him do something like the butter knife thing," said Jack. "He held up a cookie baking sheet in the kitchen and flashed the ceiling lights off it."

"You never told me that," I said. Jonah rolled on the hallway floor with the keys. The alarm sounded distantly from the garage, then stopped. I sat down on the carpet, pressing the black phone to my head. My ear started to hurt.

"Let's stay on track," Ross said. "Jane and I have talked this thing out, and from what she saw in France, she thinks he's autistic. And she wouldn't say so if she wasn't sure."

"I work with autistic kids every day," Jane said calmly. "There's no doubt he's autistic."

The light was so strange. It was only late afternoon but darkness was already starting to fall. "So it's true," I said, bitterly, mournfully. "I'm the mother of an autistic child." The words came out of me, as a blood-colored stain filled my vision. Jane was only twenty years old, a student, not a doctor, but I knew she was right. The universe was rushing by in black and red. There was silence on the line, and I was plummeting into a dark new oblivion.

"But Ross and Jane say there is a program you can do," said Jack. "That kids can get much better with it."

"What program?" I said.

"It's called Lovaas therapy," Jane said. "Or ABA, applied behavioral analysis. Some of the kids can do much better. Some can recover and become almost like normal kids."

"How do you get this therapy?" I asked automatically. Everything in my mind was reforming, like chaos, birth, and death rushing by in a tunnel of blackness.

"Someone in your area can provide it. Ask around."

"Ask who?"

"Maybe the school, or other families," she said. "I'm not sure in your area, but there has to be somebody."

"Do you think this therapy works? That it could work for Jonah?" I asked.

"Yes," she said with complete assurance. "I think he would do great with it."

Jonah had become bored with the keys and had started shredding a new coloring book I'd bought him. I watched the torn scraps cover the hallway as he laughed in amusement. Then he started crawling on top of me, trampling my crossed legs with his small shoes. From the void I felt pressure but no pain.

"There are a couple of books you ought to read," Jane continued. "*Let Me Hear Your Voice* and *Behavioral Intervention for Young Children with Autism,* by Catherine Maurice. She was a mom whose kids recovered."

"Recovered?"

"Yes. They aren't autistic anymore."

"Is this the same program you do where you work?" I asked.

"We might do some things a bit differently, but it's basically the same."

"So could you come down here and work with him?"

"Well, I can try to come out for a visit. I mean, what do you want me to do?"

*I want you to recover him,* I wanted to say. *I want you to leave your job and live here and help us.* "I don't know," I said. "I just want to get this program started."

"Call UCLA. They have some people there, I think," she said.

"This program doesn't work overnight," Ross said. "It can take a while."

"Months? Years?" I asked.

"I would think you will see some great changes in a matter of months," Jane said. "But you have to get started. The program works best if started by the age of three."

He was two and ten months. We were still in the window. I would do this. I would fly anywhere, do anything. If I had to move to Los Angeles, to be near UCLA, just the two of us, I would. Jack could visit on weekends. *We would live in an apartment and I would work with Jonah in a clinic all day long if that were what it took.* "Okay. I'll start calling tomorrow," I said.

We moved into the kitchen after the phone call. I had thought we would come together, reach for each other, but Jack stood silently at the counter.

"He'll never be normal," I said at last. "Our lives are ruined."

Jack immediately got angry. "That is such a negative thing to say. How do you know that? That's fatalistic."

"It's true, isn't it?"

"I don't know that it's true."

I wanted us to hold each other, but he wasn't about to embrace me. I sat down and didn't know what to do. Was I supposed to get up and hug him? All I could feel was the weight of my body. After we put Jonah to sleep, I asked Jack to come to bed, but he refused, wanting to be alone. When he finally came to our dark bedroom, I begged him to share what he was feeling with me. The script of tragedy was going wrong. People are supposed to cry together, to choke out their pain to each other. I tried to get him to talk. I wanted comfort, and I wanted to hear that he was feeling terrible too.

"I don't think you want me to talk," he said.

"Why would you say that? I want to hear what you have to say."

"Okay. I think you're being self-pitying."

"Self-pitying! After what we found out, I'm self-pitying?"

"You said your life is ruined, and he's never going to be normal. What's the point of talking if that's what you think?"

"At least I said *something*. You haven't said anything about how you feel. This is it, Jack! This is the worst thing that can happen to a couple. I want you to talk to me!"

"Okay. I won't wallow in your self-pity with you. I won't accept that he'll never be normal. What else is there to talk about? Now I need to get some sleep," he said, turning away. "You should try to rest too."

Soon Jack had willed himself into sleep, but I tossed and turned, fighting bad dreams until the moon left the sky.

# 7

# A Rainbow with All the Right Colors

*Knowing*

The morning has barely begun, but I'm already red-eyed and wrecked as I start my tearful phone calls. The first is to the school district. "I've got a child we just found out is autistic," I choke out to a machine. "I need to get him signed up for services." Then I reach a speech therapist who cautions me against applied behavioral analysis, the program Jane spoke of, calling ABA "stuff for trained seals." She refers me to three of her clients. One, a father, has a daughter, which I learn is rare; he tells me four out of five kids with autism are boys. He lists the names of state and federal legal documents that guarantee Jonah an appropriate education, and cautions me not to lose our house as we search for treatment. "There's no end to how much you can spend," he says. It feels like suddenly the ground has shifted our house to the edge of a big cliff, poised to crash in a sea of expenses. Another of the speech therapist's clients, a former attorney who used ABA for her son, tells me her story, a very hopeful one, and then remarks, "I know a woman in your neighborhood. She must live within blocks of you. Call her."

I do, and the neighbor, Greta, is warm and welcoming over the phone. She invites us to see her son Mark's home ABA program, although she won't be there. "There are always therapists at my house, so just walk right in!" she says. I'd never met this family; I had no idea someone that close by was dealing with autism.

A school district employee calls back. I start to cry over the phone. She makes soothing sounds and promises to put us at the "top of the pile" when special education employees begin meeting in August. I repeat the spelling of our names for her, and hear her labored breathing over the phone as she affixes the proper label to our file. Then I call Jack at work and tell him of the opportunity to visit our neighbor's ABA program.

---

After a quiet dinner, we drive four blocks to Greta's home, but I approach the door of the large house like it is a foreign country. *This is a house with a disabled child in it,* says the sentence in my head. I am afraid to see Mark, afraid to see what might be Jonah's future.

"I think I'll wait with Jonah outside. You can look first," says Jack.

I walk through the house until I step inside a custom-built schoolroom. And there he is, a small, dark-haired boy who doesn't look up from his chair at the table. "Say hi, Mark," commands a young male therapist next to him, while a young woman watches. "Say hi."

"Hi," he says in a tiny clipped voice I can barely hear.

"No. Try again," says the therapist.

"Hi," says Mark again, a niche higher. His head turns my way but his eyes flutter oddly at an object over my shoulder. Jonah's direct eye contact has become fleeting, too, but it's not like this.

"Hi, Mark," I say. I want to run, escape, and deny this confusing glimpse into our future. But I can't.

"Mark, touch five," says the therapist in a flat voice. He holds up a flashcard. Mark averts his gaze and flicks his hands in the air.

"No. Try again. Touch five."

Mark touches the card quickly and looks up in the air.

"Good job!' says the therapist. He hugs Mark and roughs up his hair. "Go jump now," he says. Mark runs over to the bed in the corner of the room and jumps up and down on it. The therapist makes a mark in a notebook and shows it to the young woman. "This is a new drill for him, so he's not too happy about doing it right now," he tells her. "Time to work again," he says to Mark. "Come here."

Mark comes, but rebounds from the table area and wanders off to a basket of toys.

"No. Sit down," says the therapist.

Mark sits. "Good sitting!" the therapist says.

I walk around the room and gaze at the calendar on the wall and the pictures of Mark on his bulletin board, surrounded by smiling sisters, brother, and parents. Then I come back to the table, and allow myself to look at Mark. I see the neatness of his slim brown feet, the gleam of his clean hair. I walk around behind him and look over his shoulder. He is drawing a rainbow, a long clumsy arc with all the right colors. The fact that this boy can draw a rainbow flies like a dove into my fearful mind. It tells me that after my tears recede, my son and I can have the light of hope, the promise of a future.

# 8

# Tough Cookie

*An Early Diagnosis*

In a grim coincidence, *Newsweek* magazine has a cover story on autism this week. It's full of dire stories, kids who embody the worst of autism, with severe behavior problems and no speech. Their families, brave as they are, inhabit a barren plain of despair. Jack and I are both surprised to read about the high rate of pitocin, a drug given in labor, among a group of mothers of kids with autism. I had pitocin. I get a sick feeling, but comfort myself that the data is still being studied, and is unproven.

In bed at night, I try to get him to talk about what's happened. It isn't going any better than last night.

"Whatever your feelings, I want to hear them," I say.

"You may not like them," he says, lying stiffly in the dark.

"Go ahead."

He turns toward me and says, "I think it's your fault."

"What?" I say.

"You took pitocin when he was born to make your labor go faster."

"And you think that made him autistic," I say.

"Yes, I do."

"But Jack, four out of every five women I know had pitocin. Their kids aren't autistic—"

"I don't care what everyone does. You asked the doctor for it. You were impatient and you didn't want to wait."

"But my labor wasn't progressing. I had been in labor for two nights! She was the one who gave it to me. But I asked for it."

"Yes, you asked for it," he says.

"And you don't like what that says about me."

"That's right. I don't."

"I let you sleep both nights of my labor, so you wouldn't be tired at the birth. You have no right to judge me."

"Maybe not. But that's the way I feel. You had to know and I told you."

"You could have said something. I read everything I could about pregnancy and childbirth, and you only read one book. You were there when she gave it to me, and you didn't say a damn thing."

"You're right. I didn't," he says.

———

A child psychiatrist Jack knows, Dr. Gilbert Kliman, is in town. He is an eminent Harvard-trained clinician near seventy, whom Jack uses as an expert witness in foster-child court cases. I'm always nervous around him because I imagine that he can see right through me, brilliant Freudian that he is, and interpret my every gesture, every word. Jack wants him to look at Jonah.

He comes to our house around four. "Hi," he says quietly to Jonah. Jonah looks somewhere in his direction, then runs to the laundry room and says, "Want vacuum cleaners," pushing on the door.

"Not right now," I say. I pull him back to the living room, and he tries to bite my hand.

"Hey, Jonah," the doctor says, his wise eyes large behind their lenses. "You're wondering who this funny man is. I am a friend of your mom and dad's. I came to visit them, and you, in your house."

Jonah wanders away.

"Can you jump with me?" The doctor pretends to skip an imaginary rope. "Look, I'm jumping rope. Can you jump too?"

Jonah glances sideways and stops moving.

"Look. Can you jump like this?"

The doctor jumps again, his tie flying. I watch in despair. Jonah's never done anything like that before. We've pretended to camp out and roast a hot dog, to fly to the moon, but no jumping rope.

Jonah flexes his legs, the slightest trace of a jump, then looks away.

"Hey, I bet you like fire trucks. Can you be a fireman? Put water on this fire?" The doctor gets an imaginary fire hose. "This is heavy. I'll need your help," he says gently. "Can you help me put out the fire?"

Jonah watches him spray water on a pretend fire. He raises his arm like an unfamiliar tool and makes a vague motion.

"Good putting the water on the fire, Jonah!" says the doctor.

I follow them outside on the patio. The sun is bright but not terrible.

"Jonah, can you moo like a cow?" the doctor asks. "Can you do that?" he says to Jack and me. We are surprised by the request, but we do it. Jack and I moo in a loose circle around Jonah. He looks up, startled by such cacophony. The doctor joins in. "The cows are mooing, Jonah," he says. "Maybe the mama cow is looking for her baby cow. Can you moo too?"

Jonah runs out of the circle, but then he comes back. "Come on, moo," I say. I moo loudly, surprising myself. Jonah makes a small moo noise back.

"Whenever you can, sing your words to him," the doctor whispers to us. "Jonah, Jonah, I am going over here, and you can follow me, yes, you will. Now-how, look what I am doo-ing. I am pretending to be a cow-boy," he singsongs.

"Why are you doing that?" I ask.

"There's something about music and singing, there's a school of thought that this might make a change in his brain growth. Especially at his young age."

We watch as the doctor gets Jonah to make a siren noise like a fire truck. Jonah put his arms out and runs away, but the doctor turns that gesture into becoming an airplane, and the two of them are soon flying about in the backyard. Jonah seems confused but intrigued as the doctor works like a determined child, engaging his subterranean imagination.

"You two will need to learn to do this," Dr. Kliman says, panting a bit. "Find what he likes, follow his lead, and then build upon it. He's giving out cues that he wants to engage."

We've been reasonably fun parents. I acted out books with Jonah, played horsey with him, baked pretend cakes. But we don't normally moo, or sing our words to him. I realize we will have to change our whole parenting style.

"Don't let him focus too long without interaction," says the doctor. "Comment on what he's doing as he does it. This lets him know he is a self, a separate being."

---

Later we sit down to dinner, the four of us, Jonah at the end of the table.

Trying to be a hostess despite my turmoil, I place take-out Chinese food on the table and scoop it onto plates, and set the radio station to soft jazz. We begin to talk.

"So what is your diagnosis?" I ask.

"At this time, were I to make a diagnosis, although today is just a social call, not a formal diagnosis, I would say he has a pervasive developmental disorder, with autistic features."

"Is that autism? What does that *mean*?" I ask.

He frowns slightly. "This diagnostic labeling is a difficult matter. But the main issue is that autism is a spectrum. That means it encompasses severe cases to more mild cases like Asperger's syndrome. But all of those are PDDs, or pervasive developmental disorders. These can include Rett's syndrome or childhood disintegrative disorder, or fragile X."

"What are those?"

"They're related problems that often resemble autism, but are usually chromosomally caused."

"Could he have any of those?" I asked.

"Doubtful, but you should have him tested for fragile X, although he doesn't seem to have those physical features. The *DSM Manual* of psychiatric diagnoses is in the process of better defining these problems, but that will take a long time. So this is clumsy, but the best we have right now."

Jonah bangs his spoon and throws his rice. I grab his hand and say, "No, don't do that," and I look at the doctor with a face of dismay and frustration.

"He's extremely sensitive to sound." The doctor nods toward the radio. "Even that is too much for him."

"This dinner music?"

"Look at him. He's flinching and acting out because it's painful for him."

I turn it off. Jonah gets down from the table, sticky rice grains falling slowly from his clothes to the floor. He runs next to the sofa and hunches himself into the carpet.

"What do you think his outlook might be?" I ask.

"It's too soon to say," he says. "But he's so young, he has a lot of plasticity in his brain. That means it's still malleable, can still be retrained, and new neurological connections can be fostered with the proper stimulation."

"Even though the ABA program works best if started by the age of three, and he's two and ten months?" I ask.

"You may not feel this way, but you really do have an early diagnosis. He has time to develop, and we'll just wait and see what that leads to. I would also urge you to watch sugars, artificial colors, and keep his food very pure."

"We're going to look into the autism diet," I say. "Some kids improve on that."

He frowns. "I wouldn't pin a lot of hope on that, but it couldn't hurt."

"What about this ABA approach?" says Jack. "What is your opinion of it?"

"The behavior modification? Well, Lovaas certainly got very

good results in his 1987 study. But I would like to see Jonah up at my clinic. You'll need some sort of program here at home, and the school system can offer that. But I would like to do a complete evaluation at my school in San Francisco and train you in our Cornerstone method."

"What is that?"

"It's a method of three-way communication I developed. Two people take turns interacting with the child and then discuss the child's participation in front of him, and eventually with him. It helps the child develop a sense of self and existence. We've seen significant IQ rise in the children."

"We'll do that as soon as possible," Jack says.

Plasticity, neurons, mooing, disintegrative disorders, singing your words. A sense of self. I've lost mine right along with Jonah.

---

On a second visit I meet my neighbor, Mark's mother, Greta, in person. She is petite and amiable, and a vast portion of her world is dominated by autism. I'd never heard of a real-life kid with autism before being told my son has it; Greta says we're the fourth family she's heard of within a few blocks, all of us unhappy newcomers to a dismal party. Greta advises me to try the special diet found in Karyn Seroussi's *Unraveling the Mystery of Autism and PDD*. Greta buys these books in hardcover by the truckload, giving them to the new-diagnosis families who call her weekly from around the county.

The book features an eighteen-month-old child with terrible bowel problems and ear infections who was fixated on milk. He had words but lost them as his autism set in. Through diet, ABA, and family stimulation, he recovered within two

years. I tell Jack all about it. "Jonah doesn't exactly fit the profile, because this kid had diarrhea, and Jonah's had the opposite, constipation, although mostly when he was a baby. But
the kid *recovered*. You have to take away gluten and casein, the
basic ingredients of most baked goods and dairy products. It's
hard, but I might try it."

"It probably can't hurt. The doctor said to watch his diet
anyway."

"This goes far beyond that."

Jonah's in the kitchen, under the warm glow of the recessed
lights. Watching him, I realize he's walking in circles, his small
tennis shoes tracing a tightening O on the marble tiles. His
arms are bent at the elbow and his hands are flapping slightly
near his shoulders, like broken wings. I stretch my hand out to
him but he doesn't want to stop.

———

Another afflicted parent calls me. I run over and meet her, and
her nanny Julia, who's become an extraordinary baker for the
autistic child. They look at me as if I have been chosen for a
test they fully expect me to fail, but hope I don't.

"Baking with these flours is . . . different," says the mom
dryly.

"It takes a few tries," says Julia. "Have your housekeeper
come over and I'll train her."

"I don't have a nanny anymore."

Julia shakes her head. "You going to have to get one," she
says. "Why you not have one? I can find a good one for you."

"Well, not now," I say. "Maybe sometime."

They give me copies of exotic recipes, show me cupboards
full of pure honey, molasses, and nuts, freezers full of game

meats and bizarre flours. By nightfall, Jonah is off all milk, butter, cheese, bread, crackers, pasta, and cookies. Five days after our talk with Jane, we have begun the gluten-free/casein-free diet with sheer desperation as the catalyst. The next day, I take the diet book to a natural grocery store, and roam the aisles for three hours. I buy rice cereal, amaranth flour, gluten-free vanilla, peanuts, almond butter, pear juice, rice milk. I seek out fruit-sweetened ketchup, canola-oil margarine, xantham gum to bind flours in baking. At home, I order water chestnut flour (twenty-seven dollars per pound), stevia (which is a natural sweetener many times stronger than sugar), and several gluten-free/casein-free cookie mixes. Deciphering the labels of these unfamiliar commodities feels strange. And I'm not a baker—never have been. What I am going to do with all of these ingredients is still a mystery.

---

Over several days I break the terrible news to my family.

My grandmother Audrey—with a twist of the Appalachian mountains in her speech—says, "So what if he's artistic? You'll just love him all the more." Her sister, my ninety-year-old great-aunt Thelma, says, "He might grow out of it. Some kids are just funny when they're little." I don't have the heart to disagree with her, plus the faint hope in her old voice reaches the back of my mind. My mother is crushed. Both of my sisters tell me to take care of my marriage, and to take time for myself. It's apparent they all care for me, but as I listen to their loving voices, I'm thinking, *Nobody can help me now.* I try to be cheery, but really I am waiting for something else to come along and kill what's left of me. I cling to hope and action each day, and read dour, horrific autism books at night.

I also beg my husband to talk to me about his feelings. But the harder I try the more it backfires.

"I told you how I felt the first night, and now I'm the bad guy because I mentioned the pitocin. I was honest about my feelings and I just got shot down for it."

"But that was *blaming* me," I say.

"That was what I was *feeling*."

"So when will you talk to me about it?"

"I'll do it in my own time, and my own way. If you back off me, I'll try."

He's nice when we talk about the autism books we're reading, the research we're both doing. He comes home early, spends tender time with his son, and leaves me to sit in the kitchen thinking about autism diet recipes, and the disaster that has become our life. He goes through the motions of good-bye hugs and lip-brushing kisses when he leaves for work, but I can't stand how he won't grieve with me, and I feel stabs of rage when I think of the pitocin—not only that he blames me for taking it, but that I asked for it and that the doctor obliged with no word of possible risk.

———

Ross and Jane fly from their Maryland home for a visit. Jane enters the house with a black doctor's bag full of small toys. She takes out a tiny helicopter, shoots it into the air for Jonah. "Say UP!" she says.

He watches silently but with interest. Rubber snakes, frogs, a toy watch, all trickle out in a stream. Ross and Jack sit on the sofa and watch. I stand behind them, unable to sit; I am making cookies from ground-up macadamia nuts, DariFree powdered potato milk, sugar, and some other ingredients.

Jane takes Jonah onto her lap in the big chair, and they play with a green snake. Jonah fingers it, a look of wonder spreading across his face. Jane lifts him up and carries him on her back as I roll out cookie dough in the kitchen. I take up the first baked row of pale white cookies and flatten the second row, listening as she jogs him around the house to the soundtrack of her playful words: "Yes, this is UP! And down, then all around!" Then she sits down with him again.

He begins to squirm, trying to get off her lap. "Say, I want down," says Jane briskly. He squirms harder. "Say I want down. Say down."

I peek around the kitchen corner. He stares at her, then looks away and arches his body. Ross and Jack watch from the couch. "He definitely wants down," says Jack.

"No doubt about that," says Ross.

Jonah begins to twist his body around.

"I know you can say *down*," says Jane. "Just say, *down*."

Jonah looks away from her, crying, "Mommy, Mommy!" I know Jane is not going to let him down. I go back and beat the cookie dough in the bowl. Jane cajoles him: "Look at this. See this? A little airplane."

I come out of the kitchen to watch, because I know he likes airplanes, at least I think he does. She dangles the tiny airplane before his red face. "Say *down* and I'll give it to you." He looks sideways at her and reaches for it. She moves it away from his hand. "Say *down*."

He quits reaching for it and strains away, looking for me. "Mommy!" he cries. He struggles toward me, but Jane holds him fast.

"This is part of it," explains Ross. "You can't give in. I know it looks harsh. But Jane knows what she's doing."

I walk over to stroke his hair and face, and he brightens. "Jonah, honey, tell Jane you want down," I say. "Say, *down*. I know you can say that! Then I'll give you a fresh, warm cookie." I'm hoping they'll taste good, since I forgot to try one yet. He starts crying and splays his arms out for me. Jane offers more toys, and he takes them, still crying, but the airplane remains out of reach.

"I think you're making it worse," Ross said to me kindly, apologetically. "No offense, but he might do better if he can't see you."

From the kitchen, I can hear Ross's low voice and Jack's softer one as Ross tries to explain Jane's techniques. I've read some autism therapy books, and I am prepared, even hopeful, for a fight, since they say recovered kids often fight in the beginning. So I stay in the kitchen and make row after row of cookies, grim and hopeful, as the cries come from the living room.

———————

Forty-five minutes go by. Jonah is still on Jane's hip. She walks him around, showing him the pool, the bedrooms, and giving him rides between his tears.

Ross enters the kitchen. "How are you doing?" he says. "This can't be easy, hearing your child crying out for you, and all." He looks worried, avuncular, his black glasses framing his kind brown eyes.

"I guess I'm fine," I say. "I mean, I want him to learn how to do this, and that's all there is to it."

What, really, is there to say? Is it hard to listen to your help-less child, love of your life, scream in the arms of your expert niece? Is it bearable to know he's getting some kind of help as his face turns crimson and his eyes puff with tears? Do I realize that this is a warm-up for what will happen in the future and I had better get used to it?

Ross goes into the living room and tells Jack, "She's doing great. It can't be easy for a mother to listen to this." Jack murmurs assent. I stack the cookies in a new Tupperware container, and wrap the rest in organic waxed paper for freezing, as Julia had instructed.

I go to the bathroom and pat water on my face, wondering if I should be crying, but the pain is crystallized inside me.

After another hour has passed, I'm concerned.

Jonah has not given in, will not satisfy Jane, despite her sweet, friendly insistence on hearing the word *down*. The afternoon light is growing fainter, and all of us are wondering where to go from here. Suddenly Jonah looks at Jane and says, "Want down." She lets him down from her lap, and he reaches for the airplane and runs to me, crying. We all stand and cheer, the men clapping with relief. I hold him tight, his feet dangling against the half-apron my great-grandmother once wore.

"An hour and forty-five minutes," says Jane. "That's my longest one yet. Wait, there was one boy who took two hours."

"Were you trying to get him to say he wanted down, too?" I ask.

"No, that child was nonverbal. That was to make him sit in a chair. But Jonah is quite a fighter. I really didn't mean to get into all that, but once I asked him to comply, I had to follow through." She shrugged.

"How did you know he could do it? And he didn't just say *down*, either," I say. "He said, want down."

"I just knew he could. But he didn't want to do it!" She laughs. "He's very strong-willed."

"Yes, he's stubborn. But he did it!" I hug him again and put a cookie in his hand, sweet and good with the taste of macadamia and vanilla. Jane sits down to rest, and Jonah looks at her again, even veers her way one or twice, but stays carefully out of her grasp. Ross and Jane leave after darkness falls, and I put Jonah to bed and hold him as he falls asleep.

# 9

# Desperate Measures

*Center for Autism and Related Disorders*

*Gluten,* the Latin word for glue, is a grain-based protein found in almost every food. Casein is a milk product used as a binder in cheese and other items. Together, these ingredients infiltrate entire categories of food. Baked goods. Dairy products. Processed meat. Subtract these, and there is precious little else to eat in the confines of a suburban supermarket.

To rid his diet of gluten and casein, we take away Jonah's favorite foods. His penne pasta. His strawberry ice cream. His chocolate milk. The salty parmeggiano reggiano, aged Italian cheese he shared with Jack. We replace them with gluten-free, casein-free substitutes. His milk is wrung from potatoes; rice takes the place of almost everything else, with soy thrown in as filler. His meat is organically pure, his butter false. His ketchup is sweetened with fruit. Ice cream becomes Rice Dream. Artificial colors can foster bad behavior; they must be banished. Sugar, even natural sugar, creates yeast, it must be cut—yeast is the devil, it penetrates the brain, say the mothers I'm meeting, who point to emerging medical theories on autism spectrum biology. Fiber will fill him up and stop his constipation; it's the elusive friend. I constantly read labels, my eyes searching to find something for him to eat. *Malt, whey, sorbitol, barley malt, dyes by the numbers* . . . I begin to wonder about the things *I* consume.

I take Jonah to a kid's birthday party a couple of weeks after the diet starts. He wants everything—the gluten-stuffed hot dogs with rich, sweet ketchup, the soft white buns, the purple, sugar-laden Juicy Juice boxes—and I don't blame him. I offer him carrot-juice drink boxes, and stack brown rice cookies in his hand, hoping to keep his eyes off the pizza. Jonah isn't fooled. He doesn't grab at the hot dogs or pizza, but the Juicy Juices really get to him. He finds a neglected one, half-full, taken for granted by its owner. When I turn and see him, his mouth is fastened to the straw and his round cheeks are sucking furiously. He sees me and sucks faster; by the time I cross the wide toy-cluttered lawn and pull the box from his hand, it is drained.

But there's no doubt the diet is one of the reasons he turns his first corner so quickly. It's a warm summer night, and Jack is working late. Jonah can have McDonald's fries, according to the diet. So I bring him to McDonald's and get us a large order of fries. We sit in a cozy booth for two, its window fronting the darkened parking lot, the large red carton of fries spilling its golden contents out on the paper tray liner before us. Jonah picks through them, choosing an extra-long one, and blows on it at my urging. He's hungry, and he begins to grab handfuls and shove them in his mouth. "Slow down," I tell him. "Wait for them to cool."

I am focused on him, his solitary intensity, the colors of the tray, the arrangement of the food. I watch him, imagining what the hot fries feel like to him, wonder what he is thinking. Then he points out the window to the dark parking lot.

"What's that?" he asks, his small finger crooked, but unmistakably extended.

I look; there is a large gray minivan outside, bigger than the surrounding cars. Long and solid, it stands like a silver charger under a glowing light pole. "What did you say?" I ask carefully.

"What's that?" he asks again, gesturing to the van.

"It's a car," I say.

It is his first question.

He peers through the glass again, and adds, "There's cars in there."

---

Greta tells me, "Don't waste time like we did. We let the school district do what they wanted and it didn't work. Don't send him to PIP, their preschool intervention program. Get CARD to run your program. And don't think you can represent yourselves legally either. My husband and I are both lawyers and we couldn't do it. Hire the attorney we used, and get CARD."

"What's CARD?" I ask her.

"The Center for Autism and Related Disorders. Get an appointment and get on the wait list now. It used to take a year to get services."

I learn that CARD offers a program that sends therapists to your home, like Mark's program. I also learn there is a private, self-employed therapist available in our neighborhood, a college student with a will of iron named Anh. Jack and I hire her right away. Greta also tells us of an in-home speech pathologist,

Melanie, who is fully trained in ABA methods. She is leaving a private speech agency to start her own practice, and she has room for one more child in her total caseload of four. I call her up, my heart beating wildly, and she comes over and agrees to take us on. Neither she nor Anh can start until September.

Until then, Jonah will remain at Kid's House. I haven't told them anything yet; Jack didn't want me to, until we made our arrangements. Having heard Greta's stories about school district tactics, the lawyer in Jack worried that Kid's House might report us to the school district. I'm learning that early intervention and special education politics are wickedly complex. School districts and local early-intervention authorities are mandated to find and evaluate at-risk kids at no cost to the parents, but they nearly always recommend the least expensive therapies, usually those they offer in-house, from providers who may be poorly trained or non-credentialed in the disability. Autism is a complex disorder that often requires speech therapy, occupational or physical therapy for muscle control, and behavioral intervention, plus possible vision therapy and augmentative communication devices (to help a child communicate via visual or mechanical means). It's like a tidal wave washing over panicked authorities. In the case of schools, their position is shaped by IDEA, the Individuals with Disabilities Education Act, which legislates that schools give children a "free, appropriate public education" but has yet to be federally funded at the 40 percent authorized by Congress. "Appropriate" services are often expensive, although schools obtain partial funding from states and other places. Parents are reluctant to start the schooling process by hiring an attorney, but as the child's lack of progress becomes apparent, and the school's expectations for the child become increasingly negative, they take schools to court. It's a quiet war that boils down to desperation and money. So I've been getting all my ducks in a row quietly.

Then Sally, the owner, comes after me as I am leaving after dropping him off. "I need to talk to you," she says. "Can you come inside the office?"

We sit down and she leans forward. "Your little guy has been having a hard time here," she says gently. "Have you thought about having him tested?"

"Yes, we have." I remind myself to say nothing more.

"Well, the problem is," she sighs, "he can't stay here."

I look at her, my eyes fill with tears, and I crumble under her gaze. "We know he has a problem," I choke out. "We just found out. I was going to tell you, but I'm trying to arrange treatment for him. There's a lot to do."

"Do you know what it is?" she asks.

"We think it's autism."

"That's what we suspected. But we couldn't tell you that, or we could get sued." She laughs ruefully. "I'm so sorry to hear this. He's such a sweet little guy. We just love him. Are you going to put him in PIP?"

"No. We're going to get him an at-home program, forty hours a week. They say it can recover some kids. But the school doesn't know that yet. So please, *please,* don't say anything to them. I just need time to get this going."

"How much time do you need?"

"About three more weeks."

"He can stay here until then. If only all our parents could help their kids like you are."

"I don't know if we'll get the program, or what will happen with the school."

"You'll get it," says Sally. "There's no way you'll let them say no."

We've been booted out, but this time it was done gracefully, with love, and I am grateful.

---

Jane had told us to make Jonah ask for everything he wants.

Before, he'd never asked a question or answered one. I had thought he was just too young, that it would come in time. And even though he never pointed at anything, Jonah was able to communicate what he wanted—he took my hand in his and pushed it near the object he wanted, like the Band-Aids kept in a high cabinet, or toward the refrigerator door when he was hungry. I now understand that this was autistic behavior, called "using your hand as a tool." The autism books I'd been reading, very scholarly, clinical works, listed all kinds of behaviors that I—a first-time parent—would never have thought strange, like lining up toys in a row, looking at shiny objects, watching lots of videos, and repeating phrases. These are stims, short for self-stimulatory behaviors, actions that fascinate or calm people on the autism spectrum. They're more extreme versions of the nail-biting, toe-tapping, chain-smoking nervous habits of the "normal" world. Some kids have very subtle ones, like a pronounced interest in trains, letters, or asking repetitive questions; in other kids, nearly everything becomes a stim or a ritual. I'm relieved that we don't have some of them, like body-rocking, lining things up, licking or sniffing things, extreme preference for sameness, or major visual stims like flapping papers near the face or fixating on tiny pieces of carpet lint; despite the incidents of the butter knife and cookie-sheet gazing, his stims don't seem particularly visual (although eye contact, once normal, now seems impossibly difficult for him). But we have plenty of others, like his fascination with water, a growing interest in vacuum cleaners, his running all over the house, and occasional hand-flapping. I find it frustrating that the experts do not suggest what to *do*—their books read like tragic tourist guides, pointing out autistic behaviors and speculating on them, as if written by rare-bird watchers clustered in a remote forest. They offer no hope.

"Do you want juice?" I ask. We are in the kitchen. Jonah flings my hand to the refrigerator door handle.

"No, point at the door," I tell him. I pick up his hand and model it into a point. I get a cup and fill it with pear juice and water, adding a teaspoon of a sticky yellow vitamin B-6 supplement. "Say, I want juice," I cajole, holding the cup within tantalizing reach.

"Say I," he says, twisting in frustration.

"Say *I want juice.* Do you want juice?"

"Want juice."

He jumps with impatience on the kitchen floor, trying to throw out the answer that will win him the drink. It hurts to watch, but I know I'm helping him. Before Jane's visit, I didn't realize Jonah couldn't say "I." This pronoun is missing from the language of autism, say researchers, some of whom speculate this means an autistic child doesn't know he's a person, a hideous thought. I feel guilty that I never noticed his language, as facile as it sometimes sounded, was not often original. The phrases he used were nearly all copies of mine.

When we'd been in France for a week, at bedtime one night, Jonah had wrestled around the bed for a half hour, crying, then had gotten up and said, twice, "Want go home. Own bed." Now I know how much those words had cost him. Even then he hadn't said "I."

"I want juice," says Jonah, holding out his hands. He looks at my eyes for a second.

"Great asking, Jonah! You did it!" I hand him the juice.

# 10

## Pictures of Us

### *September*

It is the beginning of September. The three of us are in the car, headed for Official Diagnosis Day. The CARD clinic is a pastoral saltbox, set in a leafy glen under a freeway. The waiting room is filled with colorful numbered blocks. Jonah crawls around looking for one that's missing. "Where number eight?" he says. In the wake of the diet and our therapeutic cajoling, surprising pieces of his own language have begun to emerge. Hope has started to chip at my despair.

We are shown into a room where Doreen Granpeesheh, a famous psychologist who worked for Dr. Lovaas, and who, according to Greta, "can predict Jonah's future," joins us. She has long black hair and looks younger than I'd expected. After a lengthy history of my pregnancy and Jonah's development, Jack and I numbly recite the things he can and can't do. Good sense of humor when he can be engaged, very high energy, likes people

although has become very isolated, is interested in new sur-
roundings, very attached to his parents, enjoys books and mechanical items, repeats many phrases, observant. Lack of focus
or attention except to his interests, excessive activity, no pretend
play or dialogue with toys, very little cooperative play with
friends (he's lost interest). Won't go to sleep on his own, doesn't
respond to instructions. Hitting, biting, seems impervious to
cold, toe-walking. As we talk, he's been playing so well with the
pile of toys in her office that I can't help but hope that we'll
avoid the blow, that she'll say he's just fine. He comes to Doreen
and plays with her hands, smiling into her eyes.

"Well, he is definitely autistic," Doreen says. I hear her speaking as my mind struggles to absorb the blow. "He can certainly
benefit from the forty hours per week program. In the first two
months, his language will shoot up and the behaviors will lessen.
First year, maybe nine months to a year and a half, depending
on how fast he learns, language will be on track and we'll address
the social and emotional deficits."

"What kind of deficits?" I ask, bending forward to check
his diaper, remembering sixth grade, a daily detour from my
advanced classes for the riotous circus of slow-learner math.

"Mainly, theory of mind."

"What's that?"

"Can he tell what another person thinks or feels, for
example."

*Who can,* I wonder?

"He'll be in regular kindergarten by the age of five, with a
shadow, of course." After that, first grade by the age of six.

"And if he doesn't pass theory of mind?" I ask.

She shrugs. "Well, he'll just be odd."

*Odd.* It sounds aristocratic, slightly pedigreed. *My odd, wonderful son.*

"And if he does?"

"By the age of six, you may never know he had anything."

"Never know he had anything?" I ask quickly.

"Yes."

I would know.

"When do we start?"

She turns to Jack. "You're hiring an attorney, right?"

"Yes, and as we said, we'll self-fund until then," he replies.

"Then I think we can start fairly soon, maybe a few hours a week, until you have your IEP meeting with the school. You have a date for that yet?" By IEP she means our individualized education program, an agreement outlining what kind of services the child will get in order to meet the educational goals of his program. Parents usually attend IEP meetings annually to hear the school's recommendations, contribute their own opinions, and introduce any outside experts' assessments. Everything, including school placement, in-class or home assistance, special tutors, or educational devices, is determined by the contents of the IEP.

"No. We're waiting to hear from the attorney about what to do next."

"Good. The local CARD office will call you to set up services. You are aware of the costs?"

We are. Junior therapists are $46 per hour, seniors, $48. The clinical supervisor who will manage our case is $120 per hour.

"Yes," says Jack.

"Fine. It was nice to meet you."

She disappears upstairs. I can only imagine how busy she is, but our appointment was generous, unrushed. Of course, it cost a few hundred dollars per hour, and lasted over two hours. The fees are only partly reimbursable by insurance, but when we walk out, her staff tells us she's not charging us for the last half hour. The bill is still staggering, but the possibilities are priceless.

---

"This disease is economically unfair," I say to Jack. The long waiting period it takes for many people to get the school to authorize and pay for the treatment won't apply to us, since we can pay the costs to start. "I feel terrible. What about people who *can't* pay to start? They have to wait for months for their school district to approve the program. They still have to hire lawyers, and even then they may not get what they need. All the while, precious early intervention time is wasting away."

"Don't feel too guilty," he says wryly. "I'm not sure how long we can pay either."

"What if the school won't pay?" I ask with a sickening feeling. "I guess we can always sell our house." Selling the house isn't really an answer, though. Local housing prices have skyrocketed; if we were to sell now, we'd barely manage to stay in our school district, which offers us the best chance of getting the program, according to Greta. And moving to a new house would be extremely upsetting for Jonah. Changes in familiar environment are not advisable for kids like him, Dr. Kliman had said. He even suggested we rehire our nanny, as the change had probably impacted Jonah badly, but we really couldn't afford to now.

Another thought occurs to me. "I can't go get a job to help

out. The CARD rule is, someone has to be home during therapy at all times."

"We need to get them to pay. And we will," Jack says quietly. "It's the law. We just need our attorney to do her job."

———————

Weeks go by. Mentally I am still falling down a long tunnel of loss and confusion. I spend hours on the phone learning about autism and school systems from families I don't know and will never meet. We take Jonah to be tested by our school district's staff. I receive lots of forms in the mail from the Regional Center, a local agency in charge of helping people with autism, developmental delay, cerebral palsy, and other disabilities considered permanent. There are neurologists' appointments to schedule, vitamin supplements to order, bags of rice to boil, delicate cookies with the texture of foam to bake, spice labels to visually dissect for hidden words meaning *gluten,* and recipes that are gf/cf friendly and relatively easy to attempt. I walk around my house and get lost between rooms.

I buy ABA supplies. A set of picture cards, $159. Laminating the picture cards with plastic so they won't get worn out costs nearly $200. A Loving Family dollhouse with a mom, a dad, kids, neighbors, and toy furniture, over $200. Pretend food for the family, $40. Stiff putty for Jonah to squeeze to help his fine motor problems. A soccer ball, a large therapy ball, a small basketball and hoop. Crayons, paper, erasable markers, a chalkboard, a drawing board. Paints, a smock, dress-up costumes, child-sized cookware, musical instruments. Toy cars, toy animals, toy tools. Binders with dividers so the therapists can keep track of his progress. Photos of neighborhood places. A video camera for taping therapy. Pictures of him, pictures of us.

One day near the end of the week, I go to Kid's House to pick up Jonah. The tall blond teacher tells me, "You know you told me to tell you anything he said? He said something today."

"What?"

"We were playing in the front yard, in the sprinklers, and I could tell he didn't like it when the water hit him. He said, 'I not spray.'"

"He said that? *I* not spray?"

"Yes. So I turned it off."

"That's great!"

Original language, with the "I" in front, right where it belongs.

# 11

# Breaking the Spell

*Our New Reality*

Seven weeks into our new reality, instead of playing in the sink for an hour, Jonah's learning to use toys.

If I prompt him, he can place a toy tin pot on his new plastic stove. He still wants to play with the vacuum cleaners, but he's using new language to narrate their actions. "Vacuum go here, vacuum go in wall," he says happily as he sets them out, two upright soldiers under his command by the patio door. Jack and I "reinforce" his speech by commenting. *"Good talking, Jonah, I like how you make the vacuum cleaners play. What are they doing?"* He doesn't answer, but that's okay—our goal is to encourage him to use words. We've also been singing some sentences to him, in funny, meandering tunes, using old pop, rock, or kids' songs as partial templates. I sing of juice and doggies, I even call out an old cheer, *firecracker, firecracker, boom-boom-boom.* Like actors in a bad musical, I nudge Jack to narrate our actions with show-tune gallantry. This method, done strenuously, actually works—the worse we sing, the more he looks at us.

---

September thirteenth arrives and CARD is ready to begin our ABA program.

At nine in the morning, Jack and I climb the steps of a nearby office building, urging Jonah not to lag, entranced as he is with the railing, the stairs, the new place-ness of it all. We meet Hank, a spiky-haired young guy wearing tennis shoes and a Hawaiian shirt, who has a master's degree in clinical psychology. He's our case supervisor. Hank leads us into a small toy-filled room. Two young women sit there chatting. One is curvaceous, with bright blond hair, the other is tall and fair-skinned, with light brown hair. Fran, the blond, is to be our lead therapist. The other girl is a brand-new junior therapist.

"Jonah, hi!" says Fran. The other girl greets him softly. He looks at them, then drops to play with the toys.

"He's not one to waste words," says Jack, smiling.

Hank is very serious under his pop demeanor. He works with Jonah, points out some of his observations to the girls, and asks us a few questions about his behavior at home. Anh, the private therapist we've hired, can't attend today but she'll get Hank's instructions, as all Jonah's therapists will now work under his supervision.

As Hank talks, Jonah puts a toy hot dog and a plastic banana into a basket. He picks up the banana, looks it over, and announces, "It's a yellow hot dog."

"It's a metaphor," I say. No one hears me.

Hank sets up Jonah's drill book. We are told it contains the lessons he needs to become a well-rounded human being. The therapists will carry out each lesson, and keep track of Jonah's responses. He will learn to sit in a chair on request, stack blocks, stand up, point to his nose. This will set the stage for greater skills such as identifying, or labeling, objects and colors. Stacks and stacks of such drills will be learned, mastered, and "put on maintenance" until they are removed from the book, and replaced with higher-order skills like identifying emotions, listening to a story, asking and answering questions, and learning letters and phonics. Eventually, Hank informs us, social stories, short narratives on how to behave or make good choices in a given situation, will appear. Later, therapist-run play dates with "neurotypical" kids will teach him how to interact appropriately with peers.

By then, he's supposed to be nearing normal.

Hank asks if I have any questions. I peer at a drill sheet and see symbols that look like the ninth-grade algebra I nearly failed. Letters, prompts, check marks, rows of tiny boxes filled with minuses and pluses. Another language to master, perhaps one worse than gluten-free baking. I study the sheets, and although my mind bounces right off the markings, I shake my head *no*.

———————

Melanie, our elegant, red-haired speech therapist, recommended three hours per week of speech therapy, so on September the nineteenth, the day after Jack's birthday, she comes to the house armed with a box of toys and bubble-blowers. She wants me to overlap, or sit in, for part of every session, so I can learn to elicit attention and language in Jonah.

I lead her down the hall to his room, and sit on the carpet watching her work.

His first task is verbal imitation, repeating one- to three-word sentences *in context*—he must repeat the words she says in real time, not in an autistic echo later in the session. Melanie pulls out a paper box decorated with puppies, and holds up a cardboard bone. She lets Jonah puzzle over the box, to increase his attention to and desire for it, then uses the bone as a lure. "Look, I'm putting the bone in the box," she says, holding the bone up by her face, then watching his eyes follow it to the open-slot mouth of the dog on the box. "Can you put the bone in the box? The puppy wants to eat. Give him the bone."

He does it.

"I want bone," says Melanie, in a very large, exaggerated manner that he is meant to copy. She holds the bone out to him.

He struggles. "Want bone. Bone."

"I want bone," repeats Melanie.

"Want bone. Want bone please."

"Nice saying please," she says. She holds the piece to her face again. "I want bone."

"I want bone."

"Nice work, Jonah! Good job!" She gives him the bone. As he puts it into the grinning puppy's mouth, she tells me, "I was holding the bone up because I want him to begin looking at our faces, to read our mouths and faces for visual cues. Reinforce this when you work with him."

By now I've learned that reading people's expressions doesn't come naturally for people on the spectrum. Coupled with the avoidance of eye contact (some adults on the autism spectrum say eye contact feels too invasive and painful), it leads to missed social messages and hence, misunderstandings.

This minuet of clear-cut cues goes on the entire session. Melanie demonstrates a principle or technique that sounds easy, then she executes it and he responds. Her simple, clever techniques seem like ideas I should have had. I watch and berate myself, *Why didn't I think of that?* She blows bubbles for him when he does something right, her red hair flowing down her back as the bubbles stream skyward in an opalescent rush, breaking on the ceiling.

After the session, she and I walk to the kitchen. I'm in my house-mom clothes, and I sit opposite her, feeling plain, at the kitchen table. She begins to write in the blank notebook I provided. "His two main goals," she says, looking up, "are verbal imitation, and increased attention to task."

Two days later she's back. Jonah meets her at the door with a confused smile of recognition. By the end of session two, his goals have zoomed to five in number: the previous verbal imitation and attention goals, plus three others. One new goal is getting him to answer simple questions with visuals in play. To achieve this, Melanie takes a Loving Family daddy doll, and asks what the doll is doing, then gives the answer. This is intended to get Jonah to repeat "Daddy eats pizza" as he feeds the doll a slice of plastic pizza. Another new goal is turn-taking, having him say "Jonah's turn" and "Melanie's turn" while carrying out simple games together. The last new goal is to reduce the tag-on of "say" that he picked up from the amateur speech therapy efforts Jack and I made, because now he says "Say I want juice" when he asks for juice.

After Melanie leaves, Anh, the ABA therapist we hired first, arrives for her initial session with Jonah. She is a beautiful, serious young woman in a soft cotton blouse. I escort her in as if she's a midwife, come to redeliver a child whose original birth wasn't quite successful. She approaches Jonah, who looks confused again, but not displeased. "I'm just going to probe today," she whispers to me. "Do you have any food, like candy or something, I can use as a reinforcer?"

"Yes." I run to the kitchen and come back with some gluten-free, dairy-free cookies in a bowl. Jonah reaches for them.

"Not yet," she says sternly, smiling. "You have to work to get these. Wanna play at the table for a little while?" I show her the blocks in his nightstand's drawer. "I hope this doesn't bother you," she says to me apologetically, "but it will go better if you aren't here. They always want mom too much if she's around."

I've read the ABA books, I've watched Jane, and I'm ready for this. The little blue table with its twin chairs will be the setting for his most basic and important lessons—looking, listening, imitating, obeying. *Learning.* It's the foundation of what I hope will be Annie Sullivan-style teaching—firmness, enlightenment, and love in equal measure. So I kiss him, and leave, and she begins.

———————

Later, she tells me it went fine for a first time, and that I can read her notes in the drill book. Anh smiles and says good-bye to Jonah as he clings to me. She makes him say it back to her, prompting him until he says *good-bye*. After we're alone, I read through the drill book, walking behind him as he roams the house. "SD," I read, is shorthand for "discriminative stimulus," which is the instruction or question Jonah was presented with.

Drill: Block Imitation.

SD: *Do this.*

Response: *Jonah imitates.*

Notes: *Jonah has the ability to imitate for more than one block, but his attention is not there, so he just plays with the blocks. I ended up using just the one yellow block.* 60 percent successful.

Drill: Compliance (getting a child to comply with a request).

SD: *Come here.*

Response: *Jonah comes to chair.*

Notes: *Used cookie reinforcer. He started to pick it up toward the end without any prompting.* 60 percent successful.

Drill: Eye Contact.

SD: *Look at me.*

Response: *J. looks.*

Notes: *Had to use cookie in front of my eyes to get him to look. Otherwise, he would just ignore me.* Partial response.

Drill: Fine Motor (to help with manual dexterity problems).

SD: *Do puzzle.*

Response: *J. does puzzle.*

*Did the numbers puzzle all on his own without any help. He needs more help with the letters puzzle and loses interest in it more easily. Good job overall though.* Success rate: check-plus.

Drill: Play Skills (creative play usually needs to be taught).

SD: *none.*

Response: *none.*

Notes: *Looking through books and making statements about what he sees. Took baby doll in stroller for a walk around the house. Gave it a kiss good-bye and put it on the couch to sleep.* Success rate: undetermined.

The following day, the brown-haired junior therapist from CARD comes and does the same drills. Anh also comes, so Jonah has two sessions. Both offer highs and lows. For the junior therapist, who comes in the morning, he comes easily to the chair and sits down, winning a pistachio nut as a reward. For Anh, who gets the post-nap cranky shift, he won't come to the chair even for a cookie. He made eye contact with the junior therapist only when she drank from her water bottle, but did very well in lacing beads on strings and doing puzzles. He looked through a book on his own, and made toy French fries and pretended to eat them (Jack and I taught him this skill after Dr. Kliman's visit). They both worked with him on pedaling a tricycle, pushing his feet with their hands, and he learned it well. But, noted Anh in the drill book, *he doesn't really steer—will usually just run into things.*

Speech therapy—which offers Jonah the thrill of Melanie's wheeled backpack, disgorging new toys each visit—is having a great effect. By the third session, Jonah's verbal imitation is up, and she introduces the concept of negation, shaking her head and pronouncing emphatically, "That's not a girl doll, that's a boy doll!" And wonderfully, she reports, he's adding –ing endings to verbs on his own. Then at the fourth session, the novelty seems to wear off for him and he starts a "humming behavior," humming when he isn't supposed to, and it interferes with his verbal imitation. At the following session, Melanie does baseline testing, which reveals extremely low scores overall; one skill is so low it isn't even testable. But one is up in the thirty-seventh percentile and that gives me heart.

And new things *are* happening. The Loving Family dolls are walking up stairs under Jonah's hand, per Melanie's prompts. They eat lots of pizza and tiny cupcakes, then lie in bed and talk about how they feel (not hungry) or what else they want (milk, to be poured from a little pitcher). They take turns drinking from a cup, lying down, eating more food. They are a lazy pampered bunch, this loving family. They are multicultural, too, with dark- and white-skinned members. I debated this, standing alone with my thoughts in the Toys "R" Us aisle, an African American mom and a Caucasian dad dangling from my fingers. I knew my mission was to distill concepts like *family* down to their uncomplicated essence for easiest absorption, but I refused to let go of the discretionary part of child rearing left to me. I had always intended to present difference as part of normality, so I went ahead and bought both families. Now the unorthodox group, with its multiple parents, double sets of twins and assorted big kids, is turning out to be just a typically overfed, activity-oriented American family.

Just a week into speech therapy, Jonah starts trying to make Melanie's puppets talk. The puppets' heads face outward, oblivious to each other, while Melanie gives him verbal prompts, providing him with the puppets' words. He has yet to make a doll or a puppet talk to another of its kind. It is hard for him, very hard, Melanie notes. "A major area for him to work on," she cautions.

A couple of weeks pass, and Melanie asks me, "Can you tell me something he doesn't like, a food item?"

"Sardines, or vinegar, or olives. Maybe pickles or broccoli."

"I'll choose one, if we get to this exercise today," she says.

"We have most of them in the pantry," I say. All the therapists have visited the pantry, and know what he is and is not allowed to eat, as Jack has carefully labeled certain shelves with tags reading *Jonah's food, Jonah's juice,* and *Jonah's reinforcers.*

I leave the room and move around the house, organizing drifts of autism paperwork, sweeping gf/cf crumbs from the kitchen floor, calling people and leaving messages. But eventually I feel the need to see Jonah, so I go into his bedroom and sit down behind him. Melanie whispers, "Oh, I was going to tell you about this, but now you can observe." She holds out a paper plate with a glob of yellow mustard on it.

"Jonah, do you want this?" she asks.

"No?" he says, pushing the plate away.

"Do you want this?" she says again, holding out the mustard.

"No," he says again.

It is the first time he has ever said the word. He has never said "yes" or "no," he has never even nodded his head, and suddenly, in this small bedroom, he is answering, *No.* I stare at her as tears fall from my shocked, grateful eyes. It's the best moment I've had in a long time.

---

In October, Fran, our lead therapist, rings the doorbell at eight in the morning. She'll be the hands-on leader at home, providing guidance to the rest of the team between twice-a-month clinic meetings, where our family, Hank, and the therapists will meet to go over Jonah's progress. She enters, and I take her to Jonah's bathroom, where he is playing with water and cups, wetting his fresh clothes.

"Hi, Jonah! Remember me?" she says with a big smile.

He steps slowly down from the stool. I turn off the water.

Fran leads him out of the bathroom and over to the blue table for two in the corner.

"Blocks?" she whispers.

"Here," I say, pointing to his nightstand's drawer.

"Picture cards?"

"Here," I say, gesturing to the bookshelf.

"I'll need some reinforcers. A plate with little bits of cookies, or something."

"Rice cookies and rice sticks, coming up."

"Good," she murmurs. "Hey, let's play!" she says to Jonah. She opens the drill book to the first page and makes a note. "Would you like an airplane ride?" She gently gathers him to her, and bounces him on her knees, narrating, then swoops him up for a quick turn through the air.

He smiles. I go get the reinforcers.

Two and half hours later, she briefs me. "He did great," she says. "He came to the table. And I got him to stand up and sit down in the chair. We did block imitation. He was able to make a tower of four blocks, just like I modeled for him."

"Okay." *Four!*

"He liked the cookies, but he didn't want to work for the rice sticks." She points to the broken crackers on the plate. "So you'll need to give us other treats he'll work for. And I'll need some more things by the next session."

I scribble what she lists—binders, dividers, erasers, paints, and thick crayons—in my red datebook.

Jonah goes back to play in his sink, his lower lip slightly pushed out beneath his blond bangs. As he relaxes with the running water, I walk Fran to the door. I watch her stride to her shiny Jeep and drive away. Looking out over the chilly, fog-thicked morning, I remember how Jonah could place only a single block during his first drill with Anh. The thought of today's four-block tower glows in me like a magic castle.

I go back to his room and watch him play, knowing the water's bewitchment can be broken.

# 12

## Professional Boxing

*October and November*

It's time to get Jonah evaluated at Dr. Kliman's therapeutic preschool.

I take him to San Francisco along with Marie, a neighbor's young sitter I've hired for two afternoons a week. I spend a sleepless night in a hotel with them near Fisherman's Wharf. In the morning we line up for the streetcars before Marie leaves to enjoy the city. Jonah has a good time examining the bright orange traffic cones and fire hydrants until he inexplicably walks up to a lovely little girl and slaps her right in the face. Her parents and I are horrified, and I try to tell them I'm sorry, but they speak no English. There is no international sign for *autistic,* and I won't make a circle-the-head sign for *crazy,* which he isn't, so I grip him tightly and carry my fear to Dr. Kliman's.

At the school, a doctor I haven't met before has me fill out an enormous packet of birth records and developmental questionnaires. I warn her about Jonah's special diet and leave. I walk the neighborhood, visiting antique stores listlessly and looking for food for his lunch. After two hours, I return with rice and some chicken. The woman in charge informs me that he isn't hungry, since he had several Ritz crackers. She looks at me with dismay when she sees the shock on my face. My instructions weren't passed on to her. Jonah is filled with gluten now. "It can take eight months to leave his system," intones the reproving voice of Julia, the baking nanny, in my head. I can barely move as I think of all the work undone by the packet of crackers spilling across the classroom table.

Fortunately, before the crackers were eaten, our doctor was able to evaluate and videotape Jonah along with two other doctors. He is so excited by the changes he sees in Jonah since his visit to our home last July that his cheeks are actually pink. "It's quite a rapid bounce-back," he says carefully. "A remarkable turnaround." He writes me a prescription for the diet he had been doubtful about, in case I need it for the school district, and I am elated.

The three of us move into his private office. Jonah takes a toy from a basket and hits the windowsill with it, making a small divot in the wood. I jump up to grab him, but a slight hand movement from the doctor stops me. "Jonah, please don't hurt my house," he says. "I feel sad when you hurt my house. I'd like to share it with you nicely. Will you stop?"

Incredibly, Jonah stops. He looks at Dr. Kliman, and shame creeps across his stock-still face. He lifts the toy toward the window again, just for show, then stoops to play with it on the carpet.

"He actually listened to you and did what you said," I whisper. "He truly felt bad. I've never seen him show remorse that obviously before."

"He is doing remarkably well," he says.

"I've been reading about so many things," I start eagerly. We talk about pervasive developmental disorders (PDD), emotional development, what he's seen in forty years of child psychiatry.

"I hope someday we can get him to be considered Asperger's syndrome," I say. "That's the mildest form, and plenty of smart people have it. I would be happy with that."

"Well, hold on," he says quickly. "I wouldn't worry about that at this time."

I fly home armed with videotapes that show the doctor's play and debriefing methods, feeling encouraged.

---

Jack and I have already been doing the play portion of the doctor's method with Jonah; now I'm ready to teach Jack and the therapists the debriefing methods I learned in San Francisco.

After an ABA session or a play period, two of us are supposed to talk about Jonah in front of him, about his actions and thoughts. He's encouraged to listen and join in if he wishes. This triad sets the stage for theory-of-mind development, letting the child know he is a separate person with a distinct self, capable of making emotional and intellectual attachments with people who think differently than he does. Each therapist and I do the debriefing for about five minutes at each session's end. When Jack comes home at night, we also do one.

"Jonah went to the park today, Jack," I say, "and he met a

little girl, and they played in the sand. Jonah liked the girl and followed her up the slide. What do you think, Jack? Do you think Jonah had a good time?"

"Oh, yes, I think he did. Did he talk to the little girl?"

"Yes, he said hi, when I helped him. She liked it when he said hi. Jonah played and climbed, and ran and had fun." It continues in this vein, and sometimes focuses on current play as well. Each morning, I start with the first therapist, describing certain scenes from yesterday and the events of the previous evening.

As the weeks roll on, the sessions improve. As Jonah's words emerge, he can be prompted to join in, if only to supply two to three words in response to a question, such as answering "the park" when asked where he went. It becomes part of our regular good-bye with the therapists and part of the homecoming ritual for Jack.

We're creating an around-the-clock learning environment—the debrief is just one of the ways we supplement his overall CARD program. I also narrate the actions and scenery around us constantly, then give Jonah words and phrases to repeat to me appropriately. I tell short, dramatic stories, label objects, and insist on his participation for hours per day. This new mothering style is encompassing and automatic, sprung full-fledged like the goddess Athena from her father Zeus's head—the determined product of the biggest headache he'd ever had.

———————

Things are taking their toll on me, and just before Halloween I am feeling particularly angry and unhappy, tired and depressed. At a restaurant, I renew my questioning of Jack about his emotional reticence, and he's completely taken aback and hurt. He says he's been trying hard to be more open and emotional. "Christina," he says, using my name instead of a silly nickname, something he does only in grave moments, "what I can give you just isn't enough. Maybe you ought to just cut your losses."

He looks so handsome in his black leather jacket as the end of our marriage leaps up to settle greedily at the table. I'm suddenly very afraid of losing him, and I know right then that I have to stop pushing him. "I'll just have to accept it, I guess," I say.

"You mean you're just settling, resentfully? I don't want you to do that."

"No. I'll live with it. I didn't know you were trying so much, I appreciate it."

Later that week, I decide to visit a therapist. A friend of mine, a happily married mother of a grown child, recommends her own counselor and credits her with saving her marriage and her life. Although I feel strange seeing a therapist about something so concrete as a child's disability (after all, what can a therapist *do*?), it's a desperate clutch at knowledge. I feel I have nowhere else to turn.

I tell her our story, the litany of hopes and dreams, medical nightmares, and the wonder child who was lost. I talk about how I've awakened to the vast new universe of disability and difference, how much I think about autism and what it represents, how I try to join my own vision to Jonah's, how wonderful he is regardless of labels.

"You're moving very fast, you know," she says.

"Moving fast?"

"You've taken this in and synthesized it very, very rapidly. Most people take much longer. You're at least a year ahead of schedule."

"I am?"

"Yes," she says, and smiles. "Be kind to your husband. He needs your patience. It's going to take him about a year, maybe a year and a half. It's often worse for men."

"Oh."

We talk about antidepressants, which I don't want to try. She says to get regular exercise, and make something positive from my new worldview. She wants Jack to come in with me sometime. When I leave I feel better, more charitable toward my spouse.

At home, Jack asks, "So what'd she say?"

I tell him.

"A year or more, huh?" he says.

We go in together three weeks later. At first Jack is reserved and uncomfortable, but he relaxes by the end of the visit. She gives us some coping techniques: go out more without Jonah and do what we enjoy; try to say one nice thing per day to the other person; and especially for us, two critical, analytical Virgos, don't try to be right all the time! People feel things in different ways, so try to support the other person's feelings regardless of your own. Accept that the other person may have a different opinion and don't insist they agree with you. Jack says he's willing to adopt her approach, and even agrees to come back sometime.

We leave the office holding hands.

Since the day after Ross's phone call, when I choked out our news to the school district, we have been waiting for our first IEP, the individualized education program any special-needs student is guaranteed by law. The neighboring autism families warned us: go alone to your IEP meeting at your own peril. The things you agree to will legally affect decisions about your child for years to come. You may eventually realize what they offer isn't going to do the job, but this point can come years of precious time later, when fiery little neurons in the developing brain have slowed, more neural connections have been pruned, and the window of opportunity for improvement is narrowed.

Both neighboring families are IEP veterans. One sued the school twice and won twice, in order to get a home program for their son. The other family engaged in similar battles. The special ed attorney we hired is the mother of twins, one "neurotypical," the other severely autistic, and she doesn't miss a turn in the treacherous IEP road race.

Our IEP is set on a crisp late-fall afternoon in November, when Jonah is three.

I step inside the school building's lobby. Jack, his brown hair a bit grayer in the last few months, pats my hand, and I feel the tug of our bond. Hank, Jonah's home-program clinical supervisor, is there, with his spiky haircut, a Palm Pilot, and a deceptively quiet manner. Our attorney is there, with a wine-colored cardigan set and gold jewelry dignifying her jeans. We've spoken on the phone before, plotting strategy. She smiles and gives me a blunt look. "I'm wearing jeans," she says, "because I want to send the message that I will sit here all night long to get what I want." She pats her briefcase. "Got my granola bars, my bottle of water. I'm ready to be here until the lights go out." I like this strategy. Personally, I'm planning civil disobedience if we don't get help for Jonah. I look across the lobby, and consider where I will stretch my body in protest, should it come to that.

"I was thinking of civil disobedience if we don't get the program," I tell her.

"Can't," she says. "You'd be considered an unreasonable parent in the eyes of the law. Parents have to be seen as reasonable; you have to follow the steps or officially they can leave you out of the decision making."

"Reason? What does that have to do with autism?" I ask. She smiles.

Everything is at stake today. The only clinically proven program for autistic children is intensive behavioral therapy, the program Jane first told us about, created by Dr. Ivar Lovaas at UCLA. It involves forty hours a week of one-on-one instruction, designed to break learning down into manageable bits for autistic kids, who do not learn from their environment as other kids do. It has enabled kids to function in regular classrooms with typical peers. His studies show it only succeeds in an in-home setting. The original study's success rate is 47 percent. It is essential for Jonah's hoped-for recovery. In our area, it can cost from forty to one hundred thousand dollars a year.

Speech therapy will add another twelve thousand.

Occupational therapy another five thousand.

Health insurance partially pays for the neurologists, the genetic testing, the EEGs, MRIs, some of the allergy tests. We've already run up a pretty large bill, and we can't bear the costs much longer. Fortunately IDEA guarantees a free appropriate public education for kids with disabilities, so they aren't denied schooling as they once were. For us, this once-arcane law is a mighty sword, the slender protector of our household and health.

So today is an important day.

The four of us enter the conference room.

There are five people around the long table. I've met four of them before, twice, when they examined Jonah. They sat him at a table, asked him to draw a circle or a straight line. They encouraged him to stand on one wobbly foot, to throw a ball, to point to pictures on flashcards. They puzzled at his excellent enunciation, his refusal to give his name. I know they want to plop him in PIP, their special ed preschool, and we're here to refute that placement.

I am afraid of the director, an affable-looking man with dark hair. The warnings ring in my head: *Remember, they are not your friends. They will lie to you, trap you, and use anything you say against you.* This I've learned from other parents, specialists, and attorneys.

Introductions are made, and I bring out a large silver-framed 8x10 of Jonah. It's a vivid picture, his blue-eyed smile in a navy shirt on a deep blue background. I set the photo in the middle of the table, like an aggressive hostess determined to serve a beloved dish to skittish guests. Jonah faces the director, childhood happiness in his smile.

"There are some people in this room who haven't met the young man we're talking about," I say, "so here he is."

The psychologist, a tough woman who knows where her bread is buttered, speaks first. She brings out her report and a practiced smile. "Jonah is a handsome little boy who was examined for the characteristics of autism. We did find that he meets the criteria for autism on the examination that took place on two different occasions."

She doesn't mention that she wanted a third visit, which we refused. We had been warned that if she were able to make him demonstrate too much intelligence perhaps she could cut down on his services. She reads the goals she and the PIP team set for him. "By next January, one year from now, Jonah will be able to color within the perimeter of a drawing, with one verbal prompt as measured by therapist and parent data."

The items continue. They include hopping on one foot, holding scissors, and responding "yes" to a question. They think it will take a *year* for him learn these things. He'll be four by then. Hank and I exchange a quiet glance across the table. In the two months since the evaluations, Jonah has already started to color, cut, and hop. He's learned to say "no" and his yeses are beginning to flow. It is a minor miracle, one that never would have happened without the home program.

When they ask if we are impressed with their preschool class, our attorney replies, "The family finds it unsuitable for Jonah." The kids don't have autism, only speech disorders, and it's the highest-functioning classroom in special ed. Yet the teacher doesn't run the class with the quick, stringent approach Jonah needs. During our visit, children only responded to questions if they felt like it, so the more verbal boys dominated, and the others, including the lone girl, never said a word.

"The family feels that the home program is most suitable for Jonah at the present time," our attorney concludes. It is the line of demarcation. A collective tremble seems to travel through the room. "Is the district willing to offer the family the home program?" she asks.

The special ed director sighs and smiles wistfully. He leans forward as the others watch. "I won't fight a battle I know I will lose." He goes on to say that Jonah is obviously a great candidate to remain in his home program, and they currently have nothing to compete with its capabilities.

Jack and I are afraid to smile, but smiles are pulling at our faces anyway. Our lawyer's fingers are flying on her computer. She wants to get this in unmistakable language.

"Now this doesn't mean we won't have something in the future," cautions the director. "Two years from now, the annex next door will be offering a full range of programs for these kids."

Fine, fine, I nod, feigning interest. Two years is a lifetime for us. By then, we hope he'll be in a regular preschool with typical kids.

The director could argue about the forty hours of ABA, the three hours a week of speech therapy, or the hour per week of occupational therapy, but he doesn't. He gives them all to us. We're so grateful we insist on paying for the supplies, which right now are running two to three hundred dollars a month, and a weekly gym program.

Relief and happiness break out around the table, with the exception of the school's psychologist and speech therapist. They coldly excuse themselves and leave. The room lightens. The school nurse leaves, and only the director, his intake person, and our four-person team are left. I chat with the director, as Hank, Jack, and the attorney bend over the number sheet.

Our attorney reads the bottom line aloud. "One hundred and twelve thousand," she says. She's no longer impassive—this number has made even her a little nervous.

The director takes the paper. "Is there any way to get that number down?" he asks. "The board will have a hard time getting their arms around that."

"His board will give him hell," our attorney whispers to us.

Our pleasant agreement is at stake, and along with it, Jonah's future. We worry over the paper for fifteen minutes, then strike a deal. We settle for thirty hours a week of CARD therapists, and supplement it with ten hours of independent therapists like Anh, who are cheaper to pay but harder to find. The director smiles again. The intake professional isn't happy, but the rest of us are. I mention the expenses of the at-home program and how hard it is for families without supportive school districts, and he nods. He knows more than the rest of them; he did the right thing. We are also damned lucky that he didn't have a therapy program we couldn't legally find unsuitable for Jonah.

Jack, Hank, the attorney, and I walk outside. The late afternoon feels like a cool embrace, and the sidewalks sparkle lightly in the sun. The attorney looks at me in amazement. "Do you realize," she says, "what just happened?"

I do, but I look innocent. I know she wants to say it.

"You dictated your own IEP," she says. "I've never seen that happen. Never." She holds up a finger. "I take it back. I only had that happen once. And it was me." She stares at me, her china blue eyes round yet stern. "Do you know how lucky you are?"

"Yes," I say. "Yes, I really do."

"You have a better program than anybody now. And I got a stay-put, which means they can't take your program away without offering something better. You're set. Don't go off and mess with it."

"You're great," I tell her. "We know what a miracle this is."

"It is," she says. "If only you *really* knew."

Hank is happy. He's gotten a thirty-hour program for CARD, and he calls Doreen Granpeesheh, his boss, to tell her the good news. Jack smiles, and I see the lines in his forehead lift and crinkle his gray blue eyes. I see genuine relief and happiness in his face and I feel love for him.

"Great, huh?" I ask him.

"One less thing to worry about. One *big* thing less," he says.

———————

The next day, I send the director a note. On silver-edged marine blue stationary I take a silver-inked pen and write:

Sometimes, life can feel like a job,
But sometimes, if we're lucky, our job can feel like life.
Thank you for helping Jonah.

# 13

# Small Angel

My boy is fair, so fair, of face and eyes and blond hair.

I used to find it saccharine when people called children little angels, a term I associated with big-eyed porcelain collectibles. But as I watch him tonight at the table eating a watermelon Popsicle, his skin bare and creamy pale above the white paper fabric of his diaper, it's true. He looks like an angel. Not the chubby-cheeked cherub variety, but the classical, caught-between-baby-and-boy kind, with bones and muscles and smooth white skin, his small valiant shoulder blades emerging like wings from his narrow back.

He climbs down from his chair and clings to me, saying, "Wanna kiss, Mommy," then clambers into my lap, all knees and elbows and feet. The knobs of his limbs remind me of how those same parts roamed my restless pregnant belly, raising lumps as hard as coal under my skin or pushing steadily against my rib cage until I caught my breath. He jumps down just as I try to cozy up with him. A ninety-minute nap has fueled him like a rocket. "Wanna hide!" he says. "Wanna hide, Mommy!"

I raise my tired mother-bones from the chair and chase him down the hall. We play hide and seek for nearly an hour. When I leap from hiding, he shrieks with laughter and fear. His little nervous system, so hesitant at the sound of a blow-dryer, a drill, or lately a flushing toilet, relishes the jolt that shakes his body. I grab him up after each scare, but he's too excited for cuddling.

"Mommy, go away again," he says. Thrilled to hear him issue such deliberate instructions, I watch him run away, then I sink behind a door.

I hear his breath coming down the hall, then his anticipatory giggle. I watch as he runs into a room where he expects me to be and, uncertain, turns in puzzlement. I burst from behind the door and he jerks with surprise and screams with laughter. He runs to me with his arms out, my angel, a bird in the pose of flight, and offers me his universal embrace.

# 14

# Flying

*December*

We veer into true winter, by time frame if not by visible season. Christmas rises like a foreshortened road. I get a small potted Christmas tree with tiny birds, bells, and white lights to hold us until we go to my mother's house. Jonah and I spend an evening in a Christmas tree lot with his friend Jordan and his mom. The boys laugh and chase a pretend lion through the dark wet trees. Puddles of hours-old rain stand in for icy forest ponds. Cut boughs lie in piles, and Jonah and Jordan drag them about the dark asphalt. They hold hands for a photo before a line of little cross-hatched Charlie Brown trees. "Cheese!" they chorus.

Jack has to stay home for the Christmas trip because an important trial starts the day after New Year's. We are sad but agree that Jonah needs to see my family. More importantly, they need to see him. We haven't visited since the diagnosis.

His great-grandmother, born forty years to the week before me, can't wait to hug him. Great-Aunt Thelma waits patiently for "the baby," as she calls him still.

Just days before Christmas, we're in our front yard, a patch of green on a wide street. "Mommy, see the airplane? Do you see the airplane?" Jonah asks. He doesn't look at me but he knows I'm there.

"Yes, I see the airplane," I tell him in a big, encouraging voice. We're near a flight path, and when the Santa Ana winds are strong, they divert the planes over our street.

"I see the airplane," he cries, as the jumbo jet lumbers overhead.

"Baby, do you want an airplane for Christmas?" I ask him.

"Yes," he says.

"Okay, you got it."

"I want to go on the airplane," he says. "I want to go up in the sky, on top of the clouds."

"And you shall."

"I want to walk on the wall." He walks carefully around the edge of the brick planters, balancing, his hands stiff flanges from his hips. "Want to jump to Mommy!" he calls.

"Okay, ready," I say.

He backs up, putting one worn white leather tennis shoe awkwardly behind the other. "Gonna jump to Mommy!" he shouts. With a dash of fear on his face and a mischievous grin, he takes three steps forward and jumps wholly into my arms. I twirl his long lean heft around, three feet and thirty-five pounds of boy, and smack a kiss on his chilly red cheek.

---

Jack and I have dutifully started going out, something we used to do every Saturday night, to have a drink and talk. In the murmur of a restaurant, my questions seem to reach him better, and he talks about his childhood, times with old friends, and things we want to do in the future. Our conversations, less strained and more natural than the things we must discuss at home, make me feel like we're connecting again. Overall we've reached a situation much better than the uneasy détente of the first three months. I always loved him; now I find myself liking him again.

----

I call a neurologist we saw in November. He says Jonah has Asperger's syndrome. I realize that Jonah's progress has been so good that the doctor never truly saw the isolation that had fallen upon him. When I tell the doctor that Jonah displayed past traits more appropriate to an autism diagnosis, he says there are no criteria distinguishing high-functioning autism from Asperger's. I bring up language delay, and he gets annoyed. He insists Jonah has Asperger's, and the call is over.

In a strange way, it's something to celebrate.

----

My mother's house is warm against the cold mountain night. Jonah, a little confused at first, steps gingerly up the stone path to the door, then strides into the house, my father close behind. The last time he came here was a year ago. We watch him look for things he'd seen on that visit. The thirty-year-old faded turquoise vacuum cleaner that still runs. The hidden closet under the staircase. The antique medical equipment on a glass-topped table holding arrowheads and fossils. With unerring memory, he finds them all, kneeling to greet them like old friends. Yet he easily breaks with the vacuum cleaner to entertain his grandfather's attempt at a hug.

Jonah approaches the Christmas tree and looks back at me for permission. My parents and I stand smiling, so he gently fingers the decorations. We watch him gaze at the tree, and we point so he will look above his head at the cobalt blue ornament bearing my childish crayoned reindeer. Here he is himself, not a statistic with autism but a cherished child by a Christmas tree, part of an old and wonderful story. He is the perfect face of our family.

Christmas passes in a familiar way, but with new meaning. We go home with the memory of being welcomed in a traditional, loving way, despite all our new complexities.

———

Jack's January trial starts, a big one, in which he's representing a twelve-year-old boy who was molested by a nonfamily caretaker. The boy, who was already damaged from family strife, was making good progress, but his mind was so impacted by the sexual and emotional abuse he's in a lockdown psychiatric ward and will need expensive care for the rest of his life. In his closing argument, Jack talks about how this child has become a special-needs child, how he has lost his future (the child psychiatrist says it is among the bleakest) unless he can obtain intensive hospitalization and therapy. Jack says we shouldn't make the boy a throwaway child, that every child deserves a chance to recover from his injuries, that he knows this because his own son is autistic—and then he begins to choke up.

Right in court, this capable litigator who has never lost a trial breaks into tears. I am horrified in my seat in the front row, because I have never seen my husband cry. All my desire to unearth his pain so I won't feel so alone evaporates right there. It's obvious to me at last that he's as badly hurt as I am. He wins the trial; the boy will get the help he needs, just like our son will.

---

I'm getting tired of vacuum cleaners, Jonah's first true love besides water.

His obsession with drains makes me a little uncomfortable (although, I reason with myself, maybe it'll lead to a water-systems job), plus they're boring. I decide it's time to further groom his interest in airplanes. So I drop him off at the gym with a helper. I have one hour.

There is a pilot supply store nearby, with an open door beneath a welcoming red windsock. I step inside, but I'm nervous. I have never asked for anything connected to Jonah's disability other than the home program. I don't know what's going to happen.

The sunlit shop is large and crammed with accessories. Looking at the banners spanning the shop, I start to feel positive. I picture a small Disneyland of friendly pilots, a flying corps of do-gooders on standby to help my child. A slender woman with tart brown eyes steps in front of me. "Can I help you?" she asks. There is a tightness in her face that gives me pause.

"Is the owner around?" I ask.

"I can help you."

I tell myself I am here for Jonah. "I have a son, he's three. He loves airplanes and—"

The phone rings. She holds a nail up to me, steps to the counter, and takes the call. Her impassive face becomes pleased, lively, and I think, *Yes, this might work.* She hangs up. "Yes, you were saying?"

"Do you know pilots?" I asked.

"Yes, why?"

"I know it's a strange question, but my son is handicapped. He has a form of autism. He is so interested in airplanes and they make him talk more. Would it be possible—"

"I'll be with you in a minute," she calls out to an older gentleman looking around the store. "And?" she says, looking back at me. Her mascara-heavy lashes are very black in the sunlight, like spiders.

"Well, if he could just sit inside a plane. It would be so good for him. Just once, to sit inside of one."

Her face freezes. "No way could I do that. I can't put myself in a position like that."

"Oh," I say.

"That's just too much."

"But you know pilots, right?" I ask. I'm aware I am begging.

"Yes, I know pilots. We have hundreds of pilots. Jet pilots, commercial, airlines," she says with pride, looking over my shoulder.

"Well, I want to find a pilot who would let him sit in a plane."

"No," she says. "I'm far too busy for that. You can't ask me to put myself in that position."

My face crumples, then hardens. I had called Jonah handicapped before her, given her our greatest need and confidence, and I'm angry. She keeps talking after me as I head toward the

door, and I think, *Maybe she misunderstood?* "I'm not asking for
a *flight*," I say. "Just for him to sit in a plane."

"I'm way too busy for that. You can't ask me to do that."

"Yes," I say loudly. "Too busy."

*Too busy to help a disabled child,* I want to yell as I'm shaking
on the sunny street outside. But I can't let myself give up. I
remember my childhood riding lessons and think, "This is just
a horse who's bucked you off. Ride this horse again." I drive
through the surrounding streets to the small airport. A young
man and woman in uniform sit behind the desk. "May I help
you?" asks the girl.

I go into a scant explanatory sentence about Jonah, telling
her he is a special-needs kid who talks about planes and needs
to step inside of one. I say I live close, that I can drive over at
any pilot's convenience. The girl nods; the boy listens. "We
don't know of anyone like that offhand, but there are some
really sweet pilots that come in," she says. "I'll keep your number and ask around."

I return to the gym for Jonah and his helper. I sweep
him up and tell him, "Mommy's going to get you on a plane
someday."

"See the airplane?" he calls in a high excited note, pointing
to a helicopter over our heads.

"Yes, baby, I see the airplane!"

I feel sick the rest of the day about the woman at the supply
store. I wonder if she feels guilty, if she repeated the conversation to a boyfriend, or maybe a pilot. I wonder if she defended
herself, and if her listener looked sideways at her with doubt in
his heart. Then I realize this is a fantasy, and that I'll be happier
if I can think charitably of her somehow.

Before noon the next day, a young male pilot calls. He got our number from the flight school. Would we like to come do a check-out on a Cessna right now?

My eyes dart to the clock. We have an hour before nap time. "Give me ten minutes," I tell him. "Jonah will be thrilled."

It's a wild, bright blue day. Paul, the young pilot, hops in our car and directs me to drive along the wide windy runway. Planes bump through the air overhead as they approach for landing. Out Jonah's open window, smaller craft are parked wingtip-to-wingtip, their blue, red, and green markings like the flags of small nations.

Paul leads us to his plane, a white one with green paint. Jonah's eyes are transfixed. "Here's the oil," says Paul. "Look, I'll let you test it." Jonah plunges the dipstick fearlessly in the open hole, then watches as Paul declares it clean.

Paul deposits Jonah in the plane, in the copilot's seat. He puts Jonah's hands on the yoke. "This is the yoke. It steers the plane," he says.

"This is the yoke, it steers the plane," repeats Jonah, his echo planting the information in his mind.

"This is the throttle. It helps put fuel in the engine."

"Put fuel in the engine."

Their hands on the matching controls look remarkably similar, both wide and strong for their ages. Pilot, twenty-three, copilot, three.

They go over the radios, the principal of lift. Jonah is seriously absorbed. He catches sight of the backseat, and demands, "I got to sit back there." He examines the seat, handles, and view.

Forty minutes have passed. "Jonah, time to go," I tell him.

"Bye, Paul," he says, easily surrendering. His rapt attention has tired him.

I have no commonality with this man of tender age, with no kids, no wife, no inkling of my pain. But he called a perfect stranger, and altered his schedule for a child he will never see again. I smile, thank him again, and wish him the best in life.

Before I reach the first stoplight, Jonah's asleep. I wonder if this small imprinting will stay with him, make him gravitate toward airplanes instead of vacuum cleaners. But it's not about that anymore. Paul responded to a need, without calculations and wariness. He helped me leave the woman in the store behind. I hope Paul will remember us, as we will him. A blue day, a blue-eyed boy, and a mother with a face full of gratitude.

# 15

## Kiltered Vision

### *Six Months In*

Jonah and I are headed to a neighboring town for an autism support meeting. This one is based on the gf/cf diet. Although kids aren't usually allowed, the founder, a dedicated autism mom, has a soft spot for my boy and enlisted her husband and nanny to help watch Jonah and her son, Jake. I told Jonah he was going to meet a boy named Jake on our first visit three months ago, and he has called him "Boy Named Jake" ever since. Green-eyed Jake doesn't talk very much. He has oral dyspraxia, an inability to use the muscles of the mouth to create speech, a malady common among autistic kids. But he is alert and appealing, and uses PECS (Picture Exchange Communication System). These are symbols that denote whatever it is he wants or thinks. He points at pictures of books, food, drinks, the words *I Love You*.

He and Jonah play well. That is, they're easy together in the same room. Jonah says a few words to Jake, like "Hi, Boy Named Jake." Jake can say "Hi" back and wave his hand vaguely. That's good enough for them. They explore the wide backyard on their own terms, Jake placing tiny gifts of a rock or a miniscule dirt clod in a visitor's hand as Jonah walks around saying, "I'll get the ball for you," and "I want to go in the swing" to anyone within earshot. They fall into an exploratory heap occasionally, but other than that, it's a breeze.

The living room is full of parents, angular, friendly folks with an air of strain, people not unlike me. There are more on the e-mail list who aren't present, bringing the group's membership up from forty-five to ninety-some families within the last three months. We form a straggling oval in our host's chair-filled room as she relays the latest news from the autism front line: gene-banks, heavy-metals toxicity, rumors of cross-contamination in supposedly wheat-free products. Blood transfusions, anti-yeast medications, cod liver oil. Flaxseed, secretin, vitamins. Chelation, a process that strips the metal from a child's brain and bones via medication. EEGs, MRIs, psychotropic drugs, ABA, the troubles with school districts.

It's only been six months since we began, but I feel like a veteran. When I mention I found a pediatrician who gives antibiotics via a one-time shot (instead of a ten-day course of liquid that ends up killing the good bacteria of the gut and exacerbating yeast overgrowth) many parents clamor for his name. But the mother of an eleven-year-old next to me says, "We did that too. Until he ended up allergic to it." She asks me what kind of antibiotic we use. I've never asked the doctor for the name of it. I feel small and on the edge of making a big, unwitting mistake.

I ask the woman about her child. He's on Klonopin to make him sleep, one of those class of drugs I'd previously thought only went with asylums. Until he was ten, she says, the lines in her young face moving as she talks, he rarely slept. He roamed the house at all hours, banging cabinet doors, running out into the street, and raising general hell.

So many things raise no eyebrows until placed in the context of autism. "My four-year-old is a picky eater" takes on new meaning when a mother reports that *all* her child will eat is peanut butter, from a certain bowl with a certain spoon. And "we're making progress" in some homes can mean that one year, in a single drill, a child can stack three blocks in a row as prompted by a therapist, and that the following year, he can stack seven blocks in the same row. A block per quarter, in business terms.

Jonah already has thirty-plus drills, in only six months. More than forty if you count those he's mastered, including counting to thirty and identifying shapes like sexagon, diamond, and pentagon. I decide to keep quiet. I remember at Christmas, when my sister Dana heard me explain how I feel separate and lonely around typical families, yet embarrassed for our success in the autism world. "Well," she said, with her good-natured shotgun delivery, "you guys just stand out in any crowd."

This particular crowd thins into the kitchen, where a big pot of gf/cf soup I made awaits. It's turkey meatballs and rice in organic vegetable broth. A nice guy from the San Fernando Valley, two hours away, tells me, "This is my birthday dinner."

I meet a thin intelligent woman, with glasses and a bobbed haircut. She whispers that they were hit with the news only two weeks ago. Their darling dark-eyed baby son, twenty-two months old, has the secret signs of this disorder. She knew, she said, six months prior, but her husband disagreed until two weeks ago. Something resolved the issue with ugly clarity, but I don't ask what. I promise her a list. Doctors, therapists, clinics, books. Families, groups, schools, attorneys. Her eyes fill with grateful tears and so do mine.

The meeting closes. Mothers stream into cars with hugs for one another, exchanging e-mail addresses. Dads carry thick copies of papers with one hand, patting their wives' shoulders as farewells are said. I check in on Jonah and Jake. Jake is standing before a video on the television, jumping and flapping his hands with excitement. Jonah pretends to watch, but he's really circling the room, looking for novelty.

"Do you have to go to the potty?" I ask.

"No?" he says, in the queried way he has of delivering that new word.

"Yes, I think you do," I say. When he produces a *no,* we're supposed to honor it, but we've been here for hours, so I prod him to the bathroom.

He narrates, saying, "I'm a big boy. I don't pee-pee in my underwear." He looks with fascination at the pipes in the unfamiliar bathroom and says, "Water going down the drain, down the pipes, and into the ocean." He's enthralled with a jumble of square soaps. "These soaps are square shapes," he says. "I want to wash my hands with square soaps."

He washes, looking at himself with those big blue eyes. We used to stare into the mirror together next to his crib, when he was a year old, but later, I never saw him do it alone. Did my subconscious make a note of it, like so many tiny flakes of puzzlement that blew away unexamined? He walks to the front door alone, confidently for such a small boy. Or is it the normal thing for small boys to do? I really don't know, but it fits his style. We hug the hosting mom good-bye, and go home.

———

It's a Saturday night and I'm alone at the movies. Normally Jack and I go out, but tonight he's in Utah, at a school for way-ward teens, where one of his clients resides. The movie is about the painter Jackson Pollock, the tortured "drip-painter" of the 1950s. In one scene, the surly, mentally unstable painter enters a small store on Long Island, New York. The Norman Rockwell-type proprietor greets him, but Pollock doesn't respond. Wood-enly, he branches off into the different aisles of the store, as if occupying a borrowed body. As the proprietor watches, Pollock mutely drops his groceries one by one on the counter. I imagine Jonah as a grown man, blond and weathered like the movie Pollock. Suddenly I am shivering, waiting to see our future come alive on screen as the painter is driven from the store.

But that doesn't happen. The amiable proprietor honors Pollock as a member, albeit a strange one, of his small commu-nity. He gives Pollock a charge account.

The film spools out, revealing Pollock's madness, his extreme sensitivity. He's fragile, yet a circle of people forms around him. They envy and feed off his genius. He's broken, blessed, and finally he "makes it" in the art world. Still, the pressures get him in the end. But his life awoke an entire sleep-ing century.

Leaving the lobby, I'm reminded that all art is off-kilter. Art is the vision of those who see without the filters of regular peo-ple. It is what the soul fuels, the brain directs, and the body radiates. Just this morning my son declared he saw "a rainbow" in the curved trim of his breakfast ham, and he called a swinging hammock "a nest." He has a complete world inside his head. I always wanted a child who was different, who would envision things in an original way. What I got, I now realize, was a small unruly prophet with the gift of kiltered vision.

---

After a series of allergy tests, blood panels, and lab tests, we start Jonah on Nystatin, a mild yeast-killing medicine prescribed by Los Angeles neurologist Dr. Nancy Niparko. He loves the medicine.

"Can I have medicine? Want the yellow medicine," he says. I pour the liquid Nystatin into his cup. Regular pharmacies use sugar-based preparations, so I found a compounding pharmacy that uses stevia, the natural white powder many times sweeter than sugar I've been using when I bake his special cookies. It's derived from a South American plant, and I imagine a woman paddling a canoe, a toddler in the bow, searching for plants to sweeten her son's meal.

As the days progress, we float into his best month yet. Week after week, he does amazingly well. Tantrums are down, say the teachers. Language is fantastic. Eye contact is better. Compliance—is he willing to sit in his chair, use a crayon, answer a question—is excellent.

I'm feeling so proud. We're on our way now. I've allowed myself to dream of his getting better, to hesitantly nod when others have said it will happen, but only now do I let myself feel it. Then one Sunday comes something new. "Come and get the paper with me, Jonah," I say.

"There it is," he says, dragging the heavy Sunday newspaper

up the driveway and into the hall. *There it ith,* he said. It's a lisp, kind of cute. We go inside and read, play horsey on the carpet.

Jack readies him for a Sunday train ride. Jonah puts his railroad engineers' cap on. Jack says, "Wait, you need a bandanna."

"Where'th my bandanna?" Jonah calls.

"Go find it in your bedroom," I tell him. This ability to search and retrieve is a new skill. His eager bare feet pound down the beige carpet toward his room. Jack and I smile at each other in the silence, wondering what he'll come back with. He returns with the navy bandanna around his neck, but he's holding it strangle-tight like a noose.

"Honey, don't choke yourself!" I say, laughing.

"Wanna choke mythelf," he says.

"No, that's silly," I tell him.

"Wanna be thilly," he says. They leave for the train.

Tuesday morning, Melanie comes down the hall looking serious. "Something's going on with him," she says. "Have you noticed this lisp?"

"I thought it was kind of cute," I say.

She is too reserved to reproach me, but I can see that I've said something boneheaded. To a speech therapist, a lisp is not cute. It is cancerous and must be cut out.

"A lisp just doesn't happen like this. He had no signs of it before."

"No, he didn't," I say. "One thing about him, he's always had perfect diction."

"I'm alarmed by this," she says. "With no previous signs, I think it might be something physical."

"Like a speech impediment?" I ask. Visions of a tied tongue

float to mind. A bit of red tissue beneath the tongue like in old-time stories my relatives told. In the kitchen, we'll cut the binding thread with Jack's pocketknife.

"No, like something in his body. His head or his throat, like tonsils. Or maybe side effects of medication."

"I can look into that," I say. *He's fine,* I think. "Can you call any speech pathologists you know? Ask them if they've heard of this before?"

She nods her head. "I can think of one person," she says. "She was a nurse, before she did speech. But I think you should call your neurologist immediately."

"It could be something neurological?"

"Yes, maybe," she says. "A lisp, especially a full-blown one like this, just doesn't happen. All the letters. *T's, V's, S's, F's . . .* he's got it all."

"So, like what kind of neurological?" I demand, becoming concerned.

"I'm not saying it's this," she cautions, "but there's the possibility of a stroke."

*A stroke.* "I'll call right now."

She leaves, promising to call me. I fly into my office, stepping on piles of papers devoted to autism. I call the neurologist, but she's not available. I leave a message. Absently I stare sideways into the antique mirror beside my desk. I look frightened.

I call Greta. Mark not only has autism, he also endured the removal of a rare baseball-sized brain tumor at eighteen months. At six, he's lucky to be alive. I leave a message asking if she's ever heard of a lisp coming from Nystatin. Jonah is coming down with a cold anyway, so at his pediatrician's appointment this afternoon, I will pose the horrible question of stroke.

I go to Jonah's room. All the therapists are gone until after the doctor's appointment, and there's just the two of us. I pick him up in a full body hug, then feel his limbs. No quivering, or crookedness. I set him down on the flowered blue carpet and stare at his face. It's as angelic as ever. His ocean blue eyes, the long black lashes like flower petals. The small, patrician turned-up nose I saw in his ultrasound photo at eight months of pregnancy. "Perfect," the nurse had said.

At three o'clock, Jonah and I enter the new pediatrician's office (we left the first after she missed his diagnosis). Jonah immediately climbs the carpeted half wall that hides a pen of toys. My cell phone rings. It's Greta. The nurse tries to wave us back to the examining room. I hold up my hand, drag Jonah back over the wall, and ask Greta, "Have you ever heard of a lisp just happening out of nowhere?"

"No, never," she says. "I can call some friends and ask." She thinks for a moment. "Hey, has he played with any kids with a lisp lately?"

"No . . . wait!" I say. "Last Thursday. For an hour and a half. Kid was five, has a lisp."

"That's it," she says. "I bet that's it."

"You're a genius!" I tell her. It has to be true. It's so Jonah. His ear for prosody and pitch, his incredible aural memory. He often says phrases that are months or years old, that he only heard once. My heart laughs with delight.

"How smart is that?" she asks. "He's so aware, he picked it up just like that!"

"You're right, I just know it. But I'll ask the doctor anyway."

"Now keep him away from that kid!" she warns, laughing.

The pediatrician, a veteran doctor with a teen son, has seen a lot. He knows very little about autism, like nearly all

pediatricians, and raises his eyebrows at my bulldozer treatment strategies, but he always says, "Whatever you're doing,
it's working, so keep it up." I mention the lisp, and Greta's suggestion that Jonah's copying it. He smiles in spite of a long day
of sick children. "Of course," he said. "That's it."

"Aren't you surprised?" I ask him.

"No. Because, you see, he is smart," he says.

I am thrilled. Finally, a problem tied to his intelligence, not
his disability.

---

We are told to stop the Nystatin. He's been taking it, along
with "good bacteria" supplements to keep his gut healthy, for
four weeks and thriving. Now the neurologist wants us to go
without it for at least a month. She says half her families see
gains and keep them after only one month of usage. Jack is
nervous. I also don't think it will work, but I do as she wishes
and stop the treatment.

Within three days, he starts to regress.

First, it is incidental. Jonah gets a slight fever, and lolls
around listlessly. I chalk it up to his being tired because he had
a short nap. The next day, he walks a thin emotional edge, crying and getting worked up at the drop of a hat, and by the end
of the first week, we're worried. I don't want to be one of those
hysterical give-me-medicine moms, not if the medicine isn't
needed. But Jonah just isn't himself.

Jack tells me he thinks it's the lack of Nystatin.

I say let's document it and then we'll know.

The second week starts badly. Jonah, who wears big-boy
*Blue's Clues* underwear and has been dry for months at night,
wets the bed. Twice. The wet sheets disturb me. It's not like him.

Neither is the head-rolling he's starting to do, eyes flung toward space as he "stims" on the sensations. Nor is the faltering language, the groping for phrases that don't come, the slow movement of his body as he pulls himself on the couch to lie down.

That Saturday evening, Jonah climbs up on our bed and stays there. The minutes pass. Jack and I look at one another. What is this, to have a child remain in one place for longer than a minute? We lock eyes over his head. He's never been like this.

"Mommy, can you . . . can I . . . Mommy, come on the bed!" calls Jonah.

I climb up and hug him, to stop the bad feeling in the pit of my stomach. Usually, he says, "Mommy, come and get in the bed with me," then says, "You go over there," pointing to my side.

"I think he's regressed. He needs to go on the Nystatin again," says Jack.

"I think you're right," I tell him. "We gave staying off it a good try, but this is too much."

"Can you call the neurologist?" he asks.

"Jack, it's Saturday. Let's wait till Monday."

"See if she can call it in to the Sav-On pharmacy right away, and I can get it on the way home."

"We don't go to Sav-On for this," I remind him. "We have to go to the pharmacy down south, or order it from a lab someplace, because the stevia base is a compound, and only certain pharmacies can make it like that." I realize I'm talking with an alchemist's range of phrase. I never intended to become my child's doctor but slowly that is what's happening. Now I know why all those moms I spoke to in the early days, with their rapid talk of medical interventions and mail-order

pharmacies, intimidated and overwhelmed me. I didn't realize
how quickly I'd become one.

Jonah's still lying on the bed. I stroke his lovely pale forehead, so warm and round. "Mommy, take your shirt off," he
says. "I wanna see your tickle-tickle."

This is another new fixation. Telling people to lift up their
shirts or take off their jackets so he can see their navels. I look
sternly at him. "No, Jonah. I don't want you to see my tickle-
tickle right now."

"Do you see it? See grandmother's tickle-tickle?" He is
referring to Christmas, when he convinced my mother to lift
up her shirt and spotted a mole on her stomach, which she
called her "tickle." Only grandmother isn't in our bedroom,
and the tickle incident happened three months ago.

I sigh. "Grandmother isn't here right now."

Over these past two weeks, I've noticed that our conversations aren't linear or even spiked, like the lines on a medical
monitor. It's more that we talk on a sliding time–space contin-
uum. He throws out a phrase, I recognize it from past or present, and together we project it into the future.

"Grandmother went on the airplane. She went on the green
bus," he says. This one bugs me. It's from our trip to France,
pre-diagnosis. Gamely I tackle it.

"Grandmother is at home now. She's in her house in Ten-
nessee. That trip was a long time ago."

"That was a long time ago!" he says happily. He likes the
concept. "That was a long time ago."

Whatever fragment or sentence springs to his lips, I
instantly recognize it. I pick it up and speak the context back
to him. We converse in shifting worlds that come together in
our conjoined lives. He stands up and starts to jump on the bed.

"Stop it," I tell him. "That's dangerous."

"I jumped on the bed, then I fell and break my nose!" This happened to another boy we know, but he's adopted it into his own mythology.

I sigh again, and say, "You didn't break your nose. But if you jump on the bed, you could fall, and it would hurt and you would cry."

"I would cry, if I fall off and break my nose," he says. The tale of the broken nose fascinates him. He stands stock-still on the bed, thinking about it. He sits down and lays his hard round head on my chest.

"I want to touch Mommy's nose. Can I touch your nose?"

"Okay," I say. His finger reaches out in its childlike moistness and touches my nose. He looks into my eyes, leans forward, and kisses me on the mouth. I melt. Then he grabs my hair. I whipsaw from delight to irritation, and take his hand from my hair.

"Baby, how do you feel?" I ask.

"I feel fine," he says, drooping over the side of the bed.

"Do you want me to tell you a story?"

"Yeth," he says, lisping.

"Okay. Once upon a time—"

"Wonth upon a time," he recites.

"There was a boy and a Mommy."

"There was a boy and a Mommy."

"They had to go for a long car trip and they got lost."

"Dey got lost."

"But then they looked up and saw a sign and they went the right way."

"They went the right way. I wanna go the wrong way!"

"No. Then they went back home and lived happily ever after."

He is silent. He lays his solid blond head on my bone-thin upper chest again, and rests his hand on the slope of my breast.

"Okay?" I ask.

He thinks. "An audience is when people clap," he says.

"Okay. Are you my audience?"

"Yeth."

"So clap for me, clap for my story."

"Okay." He claps his hands over my chest. "Want another story."

Jack watches us on the bed. "I'll leave you two to your love-fest," he says, smiling, and heads to the kitchen.

"One more story," I tell Jonah. "How does a story start?"

"Once upon a time," he says without the lisp.

"Yes, that's right. Once upon a time."

And I spin out another story, about little boys and Moms and animals and mountains. He listens, lying with unusual ease and drape on my chest, as I spin and he interjects. Tamed by stories, we lie on my bed, held by the poetry of our odd, comfortable communion, and I wonder what will happen if he keeps slipping away.

# 16

# A Fine Patchwork

*Back to Preschool*

We go back on the Nystatin. It kicks in within four days, and a week later it's clear: Jonah is coming back.

He is two weeks away from being three and a half. It's easy to overlook personality quirks in a three-year-old, and part of me doesn't want him to turn four. I want to hold back time—and hurt. But this week there is much to celebrate. Jonah, on the way to the mall, said, "Mommy goes to the circle bathroom. Daddy goes to the triangle bathroom." I assumed he was referring to the shape of some plumbing-endowed toilet. But when he points (now a frequent gesture) to the bathrooms, it hit me. The circle is the symbol for women, the triangle the symbol for men. He figured it out himself!

And then in the dressing area of our bedroom, he said, "Mommies have breasts. Daddies have nipples."

"Oh?" I said. "And what do you have?"

"I'm a boy. I'm not a girl. I go pee-pee in the potty."

A fine answer, function following form—he will be an engineer or architect.

And then, as we drove down the freeway: Jonah cried, "I want to see the culvert!" The day before, he'd dragged me away from the park playground to see both sides of a nearby culvert—concrete ditches filled with water being his latest obsession. The freeway was lined with bushes that resembled the park's culvert area. "Baby," I told him, "there's no culvert there." He looked out the car window, disappointed. A few minutes passed. He kicked his feet half-heartedly against the seat. "Look, Mommy, see the culvert?" he asked.

I sighed, feeling irritation. "Where, baby, where is the culvert?" I asked.

"Here it is," he said, looking down.

I looked at his hands. They were bent together at the knuckles and joined at the thumbs, making an oblong tunnel. "What is that, Jonah?"

"It's a culvert. I made a culvert," he said.

Damned if he didn't. Visions of trickling culverts sang like waterfalls in my ears.

———————

I just can't bake anymore.

I put up a flyer, advertising for help, but no one responded. I tried to master the sticky, expensive flours, the odd ingredients, the wrapping and freezing. But slowly I baked less and shopped more. I've mastered labels, haunting three, four, six grocery stores a week in search of commercially prepared gf/cf products. I turn up all kinds of things: a brown rice pizza crust we all like, that I spread with ground turkey and tomato sauce;

Asian rice noodles; pastas made from various grains. The bean pasta stunk unbearably when it cooked, but corn pasta is okay. I find rice cookies, nut crusts, stiff breads, uncured meats. For snacks, it's popcorn, cookies, cucumbers, and nuts, plus corn chips, rice chips, potato chips, veggie chips, and soy chips.

Other people I know order delicious gf/cf donuts and hamburger buns, but they're nearly two dollars *apiece*. I've cobbled together a fine patchwork of grocery-store foods, including tofu-based cheese. I've got Rice Dream ice cream for milkshakes and birthday parties, and my neighbors baked a great gf/cf cake for Jonah's third birthday party that I froze in pieces and will defrost when needed.

We still eat out, but in restaurants I must ask about cooking oils (do they fry wheat-coated onion rings with the fries?) and butter. For Jonah I order a turkey or beef patty plain, no bread, with a baked potato and corn on the cob, no butter, or rice with no soy sauce. We decline the free kids' chocolate milk or sundae, and whisk breadbaskets under the table. I frown at Jack when he orders pasta, because Jonah wants it, and he frowns at me for letting Jonah gorge on rice, and slowly, we adjust.

---

On the advice of Dr. Kliman, we've tried to keep Jonah attached to familiar places and people, so after being absent for around six months, we pay a visit to Kid's House. Marci, the director, and Jonah's former teacher Shari greet him. He replies, then starts playing with two kids. The women stare at him with tears in their eyes.

"He's better. He's better, isn't he? Look at him," says Marci.

"He's better," says Shari. "It's a miracle."

"When can he come back?" asks Marci.

"You want him back?" I can't believe it.

"Sure. It's obvious he can come back. Just let us know when you're ready."

I fumble for words. "Yeah, okay, we'll let you know." In the car, I call Jack. "You'll never guess."

"What?" he says.

"We're going back to Kid's House. They want us, Jack. They want us back!"

"That's incredible."

"They could see the difference in him right away! I didn't even *say* anything!"

"That's amazing." He laughs. "Are they sure they want to take him on again?"

"They really do. We'll send a CARD shadow too, though, so he can learn the right way to socialize and behave. It's just like Doreen Granpeesheh said."

"That's great news. We'll have to celebrate," Jack says. "See you two tonight."

When Jack walks in, it's a good party. Quiet music, soft lighting, and a waiting guest of honor, wearing size-three overalls he buttoned up himself.

# 17

# Blink of an Eye

Another good week goes by, one filled with new words and capabilities.

In the kitchen one night: "I will do it," Jonah tells me, taking the milk pitcher from my hand and setting it on the counter. "Let me pour the milk." He attempts to make coffee in the coffeemaker, and a dark torrent of ground beans cascades to the counter. In the shower, he turns the water on, adjusts it, steps in, shampoos, soaps, and rinses.

Then one day at breakfast I notice Jonah blinking.

At first I think there's something in his eyes. I look into them and see nothing amiss. He keeps blinking as he eats his gluten-free waffles and nitrate-free bacon. He blinks steadily as he drinks his Nystatin-spiked milk, as if seeing invisible pulses of light. At eight, the first therapist arrives, and I point to my eyes, silently mimicking his blinking.

At ten thirty, we leave for the occupational therapy gym, and his lids flutter consistently during the half hour drive. He doesn't look surprised or concerned, just caught up in a new mechanism, like he's matching his blinks to the ticking of a clock.

I watch him in the mirror as the low bushes and brown hills beside the freeway stream by. I know he's looking for a culvert.

In the car seat he blinks in small uneven patterns as he turns his head to me. "Mommy, I want music!" he says, and I turn it to a classical station. The music's demanding structure supposedly stimulates brain development. I hear the strings leap gloriously and I think, Aaron Copland. Jonah keeps time with his shoes against the seat's back, and asks, "Do you hear the horn?" when the brasses add their voices to the instrumental chorus.

At the gym, I do the pointing-and-blinking routine behind his back for the OT (occupational therapist). This pantomiming, including shaped silent words and raised eyebrows, is shorthand communication between me and all his therapists. I've learned that we can't say the words that describe his behaviors in front of him or, like a listening sponge, he'll exaggerate the behavior for his and others' amusement.

"Is there any chance he could have gotten the blinking from a kid here?" I ask the OT, remembering how the lisp struck without warning too. She doesn't know but agrees to look into it. I feel better as I sit in the waiting room and read old magazines.

"No, there's no kid with a blink here," she reports at the session's end. Jonah blinks off and on all day and the next.

On Wednesday, we gather in the small CARD office where we meet every two weeks for clinic. Two parents, five therapists, Hank, and our three-year-old enigma are present. He blinks quickly, keeping time to an invisible marching band.

Possible seizures. That's what Hank says. "Either that or he got it from another kid. Anyone at preschool?" I don't know, but I'll ask. Jonah blinks in the corner, where he is playing with a dollhouse. He makes the daddy climb up the stairs and sit down in a chair, but I'm too nervous to savor his play.

The Los Angeles neurologist has us on a wait list for an overnight EEG. She has hinted that his leg muscles might be a little tight, and in case he has a condition called clonus, we must rule out a seizure disorder. This thought petrifies the dark space at the back of my mind. *Please,* I beg Jonah silently, *please stop blinking.* The clinic passes with the usual laughs and tension. A therapist asks Jonah, "What is Hank?"

Jonah looks around at us. "Hank is a person," he replies. Everyone cheers.

"Hank is a pee-pee," he adds. He laughs, looking at us to join in.

We aren't supposed to reinforce potty-talk, so we keep straight faces as we begin to discuss Jonah's recent progress. Without our attention, Jonah is bored and tries to leave. Hank blocks the door with his chair.

Jonah says, "I want to go out."

Hank says, "Then what do you have to do?"

The logical step is to ask the person to move. Jonah is learning how to do that, but says, "I want out," instead.

"When you ask me nicely, you can get out," Hank says.

Jonah thrusts and parries around the offending chair, ignoring Hank, trying to get at the door. We watch the drama, and our senior therapist asks, "What's Hank doing?"

Jonah studies Hank, then says, "Hank is Hanking."

We burst into giggles, which we smother in our hands.

"I want out!" Jonah says.

"What do you need to ask me?" asks Hank, like a policeman.

Jonah is silent. Stubborn. He goes behind Hank and grabs the doorknob with his strong hands. Hank tips his chair back to secure the door. Our discussion resumes.

"Trips?" calls out Hank. "Trips" is a drill—for example, going into the kitchen and then describing what's there. "Trips have been good," says the lead therapist. "Okay, put it on maintenance," says Hank. That means Jonah's learned it and needs only to practice occasionally, like people who remember how to ride a bike when they're seventy. "Okay, maintenance," says Fran.

Jonah has learned so well that over ten of his dozens of drills are put on maintenance. He is the PF Flyer of autism!

If only there are no seizures. No God could do that to us, could he?

The meeting marches on. Jonah will not ask Hank to move. He attacks the closed door again like a scientist, figuring out how to blow apart the atom without its cooperation. We snicker as he circles his target.

Hank looks at him. A brief staring match ensues. Jonah looks away. He goes to the blinds, pulls them back, and opens the window. "I will get out the window," he says.

"No," I tell him, making sure I am firm while on display in clinic.

"I want to go to the bathroom!" he says.

"Ask me," says Hank.

Jonah goes to Jack. "Daddy, will you take me to the bathroom?" he asks with perfect eye contact, and in keeping with his potty schedule.

Like a game of chess, he's checkmated us. Hank moves his chair silently. Jonah, blinking, leads Jack triumphantly out the door.

Hank sighs and smiles. "He's a good-looking kid, and very smart," he tells everyone. "He can and will manipulate anyone to get his way. With his cuteness, one smile from him and the teachers in his future will let him slide. Our goal is to see that he earns whatever he gets."

---

Saturday comes, and the blinking is still on my mind as I go to a support group meeting. I'm telling my friend in charge about the blinking, but I stop short. He hasn't blinked so far today. "He just stopped," I say. "This morning, now that I think about it."

He doesn't blink Sunday either. The experimental little rat. The blinking issue rests.

# 18

## Fragmented Hours

### *Spring*

One March morning, my breathing becomes short and shallow.
   As the day wears on—let therapist in, set therapist up with
food, toys, and directions, show therapist out the door, make
Jonah lunch, make him sleep, make him get up, open door for
another therapist—I still can't breathe well. A strong, invisible
band is tightly constricting my chest. My heart starts pounding
and skipping beats in a roguish way, complete with chest pains.
The problem continues for weeks. Jack and some friends insist
I get a cardiac checkup, and truthfully, I'm worried I'm having
one long heart attack, but when I complete the treadmill test,
the cardiologist says I'm fine. But I must, he insists, restructure
my life to reduce stress. I don't try to explain it can't be done,
just nod my head. But I make myself sit down quietly for a few
minutes every day, and slowly my regular breathing returns.
Eventually the heart pains diminish.

I want to choke every last one of the people who invade my house with demands that never end. It is twelve thirty, half past lunch. I haven't yet showered or eaten.

This morning was supposed to be my "day to relax." But counting the two carpenters, who are building Jonah a schoolroom in the garage, and the roof-repair man, and the babysitter who came in to help out, there are nine people due at my house today. That's a bit much even for me—usually only five people ring our doorbell per day, from eight A.M. until six thirty P.M.

The sitter takes Jonah to the park, and I clean myself up and put on an AC/DC T-shirt. My damp hair hangs limply and I can't be bothered with makeup. I go to the grocery store, and fill my cart with nearly $200 worth of food and cleaning supplies, like a mother preparing for the Exodus. I find myself staring defensively at career women swinging in on their lunch breaks. Then I rush home for the sitter's departure, and the next therapist reports for duty.

My autism to-do list, like the Aegean stables, replenishes itself every time it's cleaned out. IVIG was the latest addition, and now our long-booked appointment with well-known immunologist Dr. Sudhir Gupta has arrived. IVIG (intravenous immunoglobulin) is a blood transfusion process for kids with immune system problems. Dr. Gupta is studying an off-label use for kids with autism. In his study, this procedure seems to help three out of four kids with autism improve language and social skills, and reduce hyperactivity.

In the exam room, Jonah plows through a bag of wheat-free

pretzels. He washes his hands pleasurably in the sink until I stop him, dumps my bottle of water down the drain, climbs on the examining table, reaches for the blood pressure cuff, then selects ear-examining cones from the wall dispenser. "I'm a doctor!" he says. I start feeding him cookies, which I had hoped to keep for the doctor's appearance, but it's been thirty minutes now and equipment is at risk. "I want to go to the circle bathroom," he says.

"No, you just went to the bathroom."

"Daddy, can I go to the triangle bathroom?" Jack takes him to the triangle bathroom. Sometimes it's better to give in.

They return. I point to the red sharps container on the wall and explain to Jonah, "This is where the needles go after you get a shot. The doctor puts the needle in the red box so no one will get hurt." He looks at the box with careful astonishment, and I can tell that the information is sinking in deeply.

Finally Dr. Gupta enters. Gently he greets Jonah, waiting for his return greeting. He lifts him onto the examining table, and asks him if he wants to go to the university's medical school while listening to Jonah's chest. We discuss the IVIG procedure. The only significant risk is the yet-unknown specters that might haunt the blood products. "They are the safest blood products available," he says. "But . . ." his hands lift and he smiles. "If you decide to do it, you should know if it helps after four treatments. If there is no improvement, then stop," he says.

Our neighbors and several other families I know are doing it. One child had a shocking overall improvement. I questioned a doctor who saw him before the treatments. "He was like a wild animal," said the doctor, shaking his head. "He crouched in the corner, couldn't even be examined." Now, after

IVIG, and an additional forty-hour home program, diet, and medicines, he's one of the few who's totally fine. He's even *off* the diet and meds.

Mark, Greta's boy, wasn't cured from IVIG. But he's using two-word sentences now instead of one. He asked his sister and brother to play for the first time and Greta almost fell over in her living room. Some autistic kids who can't speak actually hold out their arms after six weeks, asking silently for another infusion. Yet Jonah is already high-functioning, and I am wondering, *is this procedure worth the potential risk?*

As Dr. Gupta completes the physical exam, I indicate Jonah's legs, where our regular neurologist noted possible muscle tightness. "She wants to do an overnight EEG next week, to rule out seizure disorders. Something about his toes too."

"Let me see them," Dr. Gupta says. "Jonah, will you take off your shoes, let me see your handsome feet?"

Jonah peels off his white cotton socks, then beautifully undoes his Stride Rite navy tennis shoes. His cream and pink feet are revealed, small and graceful. The doctor takes Jonah's feet in his hands.

"See the toes?" I say. "I guess that might mean something."

"Yes, LKS."

The ease with which it rolls off his tongue. Landau-Kleffner syndrome. A rare seizure disorder that can create global brain damage. I'd heard the words before, months ago.

"The two middle toes here are slightly crooked," he says.

"Is that a hallmark of LKS?" I ask.

He assumes the slightly nervous doctor-face I'm starting to recognize. "Ah, well, I wouldn't say hallmark. It sometimes . . . well, it is there, but there are other conditions in which it can appear."

I'm no longer thinking about blood products.

"Are you saying that his muscle condition means he might have LKS?"

"Well, the muscle condition can be attached to it, but you are having the EEG next week. I would say the chances are against it being LKS. But it is good that you are having the test."

A nurse knocks at the door. It's obvious that nothing more can be said, in this small university-funded room, that will make anyone more comfortable.

The doctor looks at us sheepishly. "I am far behind, and it is almost noon," he says. "The nurses will have my head if I don't hurry along."

We thank him for his time. Jonah's playing with the pedal-operated trash can.

"Good-bye," says Dr. Gupta, his words floating back to us.

"Good-bye, doctor," said Jonah.

---

Outside in the hilly parking lot the wind is blowing. I look at Jack, then away. "We should look into the IVIG," he says. "But I don't think I want to do it."

"I agree. Or at least not now."

"As far as the Landau-Kleffner, I'll e-mail Dr. Kliman," he says. "Maybe he knows something."

"Yes, maybe a list of questions," I say.

"Okay. That's a good idea. I'll go straight to the office and do that."

"Okay," I say, still standing there. He looks at me hard. He's seen some of these states of mine by now. He takes a deep breath and says, "We can talk more about this tonight."

On this Sunday morning my first printed piece about Jonah's autism has been published. It's for a major newspaper's opinion page; I wrote about our home therapy program, reproaching school districts and the county's Regional Center for not telling parents that home programs—the only *proven* method to help the skyrocketing number of children with autism— exist. I'd worked on the article for weeks, interviewing a special-ed director, and a high-level director at the Regional Center, who both carefully admitted they hadn't done enough for autism. Both of them also swore there would be no retribution. I'm not sure I believe it.

Jonah is on fire this morning, running bare-naked through the house after his shower, singing with delight. I help him get his clothes on, giving him verbal prompts only, and he dances into the kitchen.

"Jonah, sit down and eat your waffle."

"Poke it, dip it, and put it in your mouth," Jonah says, gleaming with joy in the morning sun. He forks a huge bite of waffle into his mouth and mumbles something, then laughs through the crumbs. Jack smiles at me.

"Mommy's quite the celebrity today," he says.

I frown modestly but laugh too.

After kisses, they vanish by inches, stopping to gather jackets, keys, and sunscreen on the way out. I can see them walk down the hall by the pool, framed in the glass windows. Their voices float from the garage, then I am alone. But right now thousands of people are thinking about my life. The thought makes me uncomfortable, because I never wanted to write about autism. But how many of them share our circumstances? How many more will?

---

The day for the EEG comes, and we check into the sleep lab.

I sit Jonah in their bed at lunchtime, and we wait. We wait for technicians to affix the twenty-odd wires to his head, for a doctor to explain what will happen, for a nighttime bed in the main hospital. At six, we're still waiting for the hospital bed. Jonah, his head adorned with bristling wires like a war god's helmet, has read books, played board games, eaten several plastic baggies of cookies, and repeatedly adjusted the motorized bed. The therapists, who've come to make this day productive, and I have sung and talked until our mouths are tired. Jack left his office early to join us, and he has fetched drinks, snacks, and read books too. Finally, the three of us move to the children's wing for the night.

Although it's a "sleep test" we're running, catching Jonah's deep night sleep in electrical waves and videotape, they've put us in a room with a seven-year-old recovering from a vicious dog attack. He's fresh from a week of intensive care, whimpering and crying with pain when they clean his wounds. Amazingly Jonah and I fall asleep at ten P.M., but I wake an hour later to visitors streaming in for the dog-bitten child. Jack lies down with Jonah, and I retreat to another bed. After the visitors leave, three nurses enter and chat loudly, flipping on banks of fluorescent lights and decrying the orderlies. I ask, "Do you mind lowering your voices? We're trying to do a sleep test here." At four A.M., a cleaning woman comes to wash the bed next to me. I'm nearly awake, as shrieks and the loud thumping of kids' feet on walls had kept me on the edge of a dream. "Is it always like this in here?" I ask.

"Yes, well, not always. It's pretty busy tonight, I'll grant you." She snaps out a thin sail-like sheet. "I'll be done in three–four minutes."

Finally, the thick hot plastic of the mattress cover puts me to sleep. At seven, the phone rings, and a man asks for Jonah's breakfast order. At eight, a pretty brunette nurse in her forties enters. "We'll get those wires off you in no time," she tells Jonah, who's awake and beauty-flushed with sleep.

"How are you?" she asks him.

"I'm fine," he says.

"Do you want to go home?"

"Yes," he says.

She takes his vitals. Jonah watches her with familiarity. "There's a stethoscope . . . it's for listening to my heart," he says.

"So," she says to me, as Jack takes him to the bathroom, his wires still trailing. "How come he has this other diagnosis?"

"Oh, for good reasons," I tell her.

"He doesn't seem autistic to me," she says. "He talks so much, he seems fine."

"We've done a lot to help him. Plus, it's a broad spectrum, this disorder," I say. "It doesn't always fit the stereotype."

"Well, I've seen a lot of them. He's nothing like that," she says thoughtfully.

---

Outside, the gray dawn feels cool and clean. The father of the dog-bite victim is standing on the hospital steps. He's been here for five days, he says. His cigarette smoke blends and rises into the gray morning air.

"So your son, is he okay now?" he asks.

"It's a test," I tell him. "We'll know next week."

He nods, tired.

The trade-offs always lurking in my mind pop up. Would I put Jonah through a dog attack, a tearing bleeding confusion of pain and danger, if it would cure his autism? Would I put him through cancer, a quick curable one, if it would take away the autism? Would I give him a car accident at age forty-five in exchange for a full American life without autism?

Stupid questions.

Today the answer is no. Today I am grateful for the autism.

# 19

# Semiotics of the Heart

*No Significant Event*

The dog-bitten child's family has called Jack for legal help, so he leaves to inspect the attack site. All afternoon I struggle to keep Jonah out of the cabinets, away from the water faucets, off the ladders, out of the refrigerator. He's at full capacity, talking, asking, observing. "I will help clean up the mess," he says after spilling a picnic-sized bag of potato chips on the floor. "Okay, get the paper towel! We need some water." He starts to run the sodden paper towel through a mountain of Lays.

"See? I helpted Mommy to clean up. 'Cause we don't want crumbs on the floor!"

It's either get us out of the house or shoot myself with a tranquilizer gun.

We're going to Borders.

We enter the large bookstore, and I hear, "I need to go to the circle bathroom. Then I will see where they cook." He wants to go to the bathroom, then the cafe's kitchen, where appliances emit clouds of steam. I want to look at books, maybe get him something with Pokémon characters. "No, you don't need to go to the bathroom now. You pee-peed before you left the house."

"I need to make poop." He's got me over a barrel again.

"Okay," I say. We slowly cross the vast Borders floor, as he scrutinizes every book, rack, and light along the way.

"We're going to the circle bathroom," he says with an air of calm satisfaction.

Inside, he picks the largest stall. "Close the door," he says. "Hold me, Mommy. Hold me." He carefully arranges a paper cover and sits on the end of the seat. I hold his thighs. "Lift up my shirt," he says. He's right. His shirt is a bit long, so I hold it up. He's fully happy now, and squeezes out one little brown dot.

Moving leisurely, he says, "I can do the soap myself."

Finally, we exit and look for Pokémon books. I prefer classic children's literature, but we must also have modern-day symbols, the semiotics of shared childhood experience. They don't have Pokémon books, only videos. I buy the most human-looking one, featuring multiple yellow Pikachus at a birthday party.

Jonah's been having a great time circling the stacks, reading books, trundling up and down the children's steps.

"Okay, now it's time for you to come with Mommy so I can buy my magazines. Walk nicely beside me," I tell him, like the therapists do. "I'm in a hurry and I need to you move along with me."

He stops and takes tiny controlled baby steps. "I'm walking nicely," he says.

"Sheer meanness," my mother used to say to me. "You'd get that look in your eye like you were looking for something to get into, and it was sheer meanness."

I see that look right now, a glazed, self-pleased look of defiance in his eye.

I want to grab him by the wrist and pull in march-time, but I say, "Good walking, Jonah. Can you make that nice step beside me?"

"I want to go to the bathroom. I can make poop."

"No, you do not. We just went."

I set him on a step stool, where he can wear headphones and punch up trial CD samplers as I seek out the literary magazines. Every thirty seconds I look for the top of his head. I select *Boulevard* and *The Iowa Review.* I go to the stool and he's there, suspiciously content.

"I have to make poop."

"Oh, no!" I cup his sagging bottom, and there it is, a warm bundle of marbles.

"I want to take off my underwear," he says, shifting from foot to foot. There is a small brown oval flattened on the step stool.

"Don't move," I tell him. I look around like a shoplifter, then mash the pebble in a check I tear from my checkbook. Another one falls and bounces off my hand and I grab it too. "Walk straight to the bathroom," I tell him. "We'll take off the underwear there." He can tell by my voice that I am dead serious, and he moves. So far we're not leaving a trail.

I stand him up on the lidless rim of the seat and lower his underpants. A meteor shower of pebbles falls into a watery grave. A cold-water scrub with a paper towel cleans his bottom, and I wrap the telltale underpants in a paper towel and stuff them into my purse.

As we step into the parking lot, true evening is upon us. Jonah turns back to the stone building and says, "I see navy blue."

"Navy blue?" I scan the beige portico, the shirts of customers. "I don't see any navy blue, Jonah. What's navy blue?"

He points. "The drain." The rectangular hole under the sidewalk is filled with a darkness lighter than black. Navy blue.

"And there's royal blue," he says. I look down. Under his feet are the lines of a handicapped parking space, cobalt in the gloom.

"The colors of the evening are all around us," I say slowly.

After the fast-rising stress of this half hour, I see only a dark parking lot to cross. But to him, darkness isn't black or gray. It's visible, and in color.

---

On Monday, I shuttle him off to preschool. As I return for the halcyon period, two hours totally alone, my Landau-Kleffner worry rises. Should I call for the EEG test results or wait? But there's a message from the nurse-practitioner. His preliminary results are in, and she's faxed them to me.

I race to my office. The fax machine sits in the corner on an old table, but there's no paper protruding from its mouth. I scramble through my purse, looking for the nurse-practitioner's card. It's sideways in the zipper pocket, the only clean, crumb-free spot in the whole purse. I call her and miraculously, she answers.

"I didn't get the fax," I say breathlessly, my heart pounding. "Can you send it again?" Is it madness, I wonder, to have it sent to me while I'm alone, unprotected by Jack's presence or even a neighbor to hear my scream?

"Yes, I will," she says.

"Can you tell anything?" I ask. "I mean, will it make any sense to me?"

"Oh, yes," she says. "There was no significant event. That means, really, that it was normal. Nothing showed up."

*Normal.* "No seizure activity at all?"

"No," she says. "For his age, it's totally clear."

"Thank you," I tell her. "You've made my month, if not actually my life."

"That's good," she says. "I'll put it in the machine now."

We hang up. Hot tears of relief fill my eyes.

The day passes in a haze of delight.

———————

Child neurologists are busy people these days. Last week, our newspaper ran an article about California's "alarming" rise in autism. Our neurologist, Dr. Niparko, told me, "I don't know if you're a genius, but autism has some connection to genius that no one has figured out yet." Does this mean a lot of smart people are having children?

When I call her at six P.M., I am surprised that she answers.

"Hi, it's Christina. I want to talk to you about Jonah's EEG results."

She sighs. "I'm in the middle of three projects here, and I have to go to the hospital. Can you come in?"

"When?"

"What about tomorrow morning? Can you be here by nine?"

"Yes, I can." She's in Los Angeles, behind Cedars-Sinai,

choked in the tangle of roads around the Beverly Center, a giant fashion mall. It's hell to get to. "But, wait, just one question?"

"Yes?"

"The EEG was clean. No seizure activity. Did it rule out Landau-Kleffner?"

"Well, was it overnight?"

"Yes," I say, "from one P.M. until eight thirty the next morning."

"Yes, then it would rule out LKS."

"What about other things?"

"I . . . well, it's just a matter of prioritizing. Come in and we'll talk about it."

"Okay. Thanks." We hang up, her mind on the present, mine on the future. I find Jack in the bedroom, and tell him the neurologist has ruled out LKS. He smiles with relief, and pats me on the shoulder. Then I tell him we're taking off at six thirty in the morning to go see her. He frowns. "The report was clean. Why don't you wait until Monday when we're already going to LA anyway for the other doctor's appointment?"

"I can't wait that long."

"Well, I can't lose another day of work since I'm already going to lose Monday."

"But I can't handle him by myself and talk to her at the same time!"

"I don't see why you have to rush off tomorrow. That's fine if you do. But I don't see the need for me to go. I'll miss some legal filings I need to do."

He's right, but I'm angry.

"After a *month* of worry, don't you want to hear what she has to say?"

"Yes, I would, but we're going Monday to the other doctor! Let's wait and see if we can do both appointments in one trip."

"I can't wait that long," I say. I just need to settle the matter—now.

---

We leave so early the next morning that Jonah's sweet face is dazed. I drive through McDonald's for a sausage patty and hash browns, which I am not totally certain contains no gluten but have scrupulously avoided checking. Jonah eats the food hungrily in the back beside Mayra, our babysitter, who will help keep him occupied. We reach the doctor's office in an hour and a half. We're so early we can visit the enormous Beverly Center mall. A series of escalators rises higher and higher outside the building, so we rise in a dizzying ascent above the Hollywood Hills.

Later, in the waiting room, Jonah sings songs, jumps on the furniture, and throws a magazine over the receptionist's desk before we're called back. In the doctor's tiny office, she greets Jonah, and he says hello back. He takes the Rubik's cube off her desk and sits near Mayra.

"The EEG," she says, rustling for the thin piece of fax paper. "Any EEG has only a 50 percent chance of catching a seizure. But," she says, shrugging her shoulders, "this is okay. You can always do it again. It never hurts to do another EEG."

"But there's no reason to suspect anything, right?" I ask.

"Not unless any events happen."

"I've never seen any seizure-type things happen. What would that look like?"

"Behaviors," she says. "Say he suddenly breaks out into a

behavior for a few seconds, then stops. But there was no provocation. Like a temper tantrum for no reason that stops abruptly."

"Haven't seen that," I say, although I wonder if I have. I've seen sudden emotion crop up in him, a sadness derived from my tone of voice, or defiance when reprimanded. And the blinking has never returned.

"Jonah, come here," I say. He comes over.

"I want that," he says, grabbing for a white stack of round plastic blocks.

"Ask better," I say.

"Please, Mommy, can I have that?" His eyes flutter and avert under the pressure of my question. Round and direct for the first seconds, then away.

"Yes, you can."

He stands before her desk, pulling the round blocks apart one by slender one.

"I want to examine him," she says. "Have him sit on the chair over there."

"You can tell him," I say.

"Jonah," she calls. "Will you go over and sit on the chair so I can look at you?"

He looks up briefly, but is too intent on putting the rings back together to answer.

"Jonah, she's talking to you," I tell him sharply.

"What are you making?" she asks him. Again he doesn't answer. So much for showing off our four months of tremendous progress since our last visit.

"Sit over here," she tells him. He sets the tall white structure down on the flat wood seat, says something, and sits in the neighboring chair.

"Did you hear that?" I say.

"No," she says.

"It's a candle. He said, 'It's a candle.'"

We turn in unison and look at the white cylinder of blocks, reflecting off the dark polished wood like a taper on a Jeffersonian dining table. All it lacks is a flame. The doctor smiles. "The perception is so fascinating. The way his brain works." She shakes her head as she examines his two crooked toes, mallet-taps his sturdy, sensitive legs. "This guy is unique," she says. "He really is something. No longer fits the typical picture, you know."

"He doesn't?"

"Well, no," she says. "Even for an experienced professional, it would take them at least a half hour to pick him out of a crowd. Can I see him here every four months or so? I'd really like to follow him."

I update her on the diet. Months ago, she'd said it probably wouldn't work. Now she shakes her head. "Obviously he's made remarkable progress."

"Thanks," I say. "This was very good news today."

"Oh, yes," she says, shuffling her papers. "You're helping me," she says suddenly, surprising me.

"Glad to do it," I say. "Jonah, tell her good-bye."

"Good-bye, doctor," he says.

Happy and relaxed, I drive Mayra through Beverly Hills and up Rodeo Drive, although we must hurry home so Jonah can rest before his next therapist.

———————

At five, Jack walks in. "I've got a present for Jonah," he says peacefully. "And another one for you."

There's a beginner computer game for Jonah, chocolates for me.

I remember how my dad would storm out of the house after a rare argument with my mother. As kids, we three girls would sit in silence or cry, or, in our teen years, make scathing remarks. In fifteen minutes, he would return, a foolish grin on his face, with Planters Peanuts and a Pepsi to float them in for my mom, and Brown Mule ice cream bars for us.

I recognize this familiar dynamic, now modernized, me as the emotional one, Jack as the gift-giver. I knew this four years ago, before Jonah. But the backdrop of our new lives forces closer examination. I'm slowly realizing I married someone I needed, a man who can slow me down and take care of many details, while I tend to our family and home, along with my projects and responsibilities. It's a kind of caretaking, the sort I'd love to do for him, but often can't because Jonah's needs push me to my wits' end. So it's comforting to see his tentatively cheerful face, my familial pattern in our kitchen.

I accept the chocolate with a smile.

# 20

## Trickle-Down Theory

### *My Laugh Is White*

We were having a rare candlelit dinner. At the oval table, Jack and I ate takeout as Jonah devoured a homemade bowl of rice pasta and organic tomato sauce with ground-turkey meatballs. I gloried in the peace.

Then Jonah laughed. But it wasn't his laugh, it was Kim's laugh. Greta's five-year-old daughter Kim, a vivacious little slip with almond brown eyes, had a cackling girlish laugh. He'd been imitating it for weeks since they started playing together. Walking around the house, I'd hear Kim's laugh. It was a bit disconcerting.

"Jonah, I want to hear your laugh," I said. He laughed a perfect imitation of his own laugh, not real. I shuddered at his talent.

"Kim's laugh is red," he said. "My laugh is white."

"What did you say, Jonah? What color is Kim's laugh?"

"Her laugh is red," he said.

"Jack," I said quietly, "did you hear what he said?"

He looked at me mildly. "Yes. He calls music colors sometimes."

"He does?" I'd never heard him do that. But he and Jack played guitar and piano together. It was one of their special things to do. "He calls guitar music a color, like orange or something," Jack said. He turned to Jonah. "What color is guitar music?"

"Guitar music is yellow," Jonah answered, drinking his watery juice.

I asked him, "What color is Kim's laugh?"

"It's red."

What color is your laugh?"

"It's white."

"What color is my laugh?"

"Your laugh is white, too."

"What color is Daddy's laugh?"

"Daddy's laugh is blue."

Jonah got up, went to the sink, and stretched up on tiptoe. He turned to me. "I want the ladder. I gotta wash my hands." He'd been playing with the tomato sauce, delicately touching drops of it on the pads of his fingers.

"Jack, I read about this just a month ago," I whispered. "It's called synesthesia, where one kind of sensory input brings out another. Some people see colors when they hear music, or smell colors, or taste or feel different shapes in food or objects."

"Jonah, what color is guitar music?" asked Jack

"It's yellow."

"I'll get you the ladder, baby boy," I told him. I dragged the small stepladder from the pantry and he climbed atop it.

"I want to make a shower," he said. He turned the faucet on spray and began washing his hands.

"Jonah, what color is piano music?" asked Jack.

"Piano music is white."

"What color is violin music?"

"Violin music is purple."

"What color is my laugh?"

"Your laugh is blue."

"So I'm blue, huh?" Jack said. "What color is Mommy's laugh?"

"Mommy's laugh is white."

"He's your boy, alright," said Jack with a smile.

The colors of his earlier answers hadn't changed, which meant maybe they hadn't been thrown out at random by his imagination. So much for the theory that autistic kids can only answer questions with previously supplied answers! We had never taught him anything about sound having color.

"What do you think?" I asked Jack. "The book I read says it only occurs in one in 25,000 people. What he's doing seems pretty amazing."

"Well, I'll have to look at the book. What else does it say?"

"Do you want me to go get it?"

"No, not right now." He got up and went to Jonah. "What are you doing?"

"I'm pouring," Jonah said. He'd taken the dull pink plastic pitcher the nurse at the hospital had given him, and was pouring water into a small silver creamer.

"Give me a hug. Can I have a hug?" asked Jack.

"Yes," said Jonah. He didn't raise his eyes from the pitcher.

"Put down the pitcher and give me a big squeeze. A really hard squeeze. Okay?"

"Okay, Daddy. Here's a hug."

"Oh, that was such a good hug," said Jack.

They stood there wrapped head-to-head with the ladder between them, Jonah's glistening blond head next to Jack's dark brown. "I'm going into my office," I said. I left them under the soft glow of the kitchen lights and typed "synesthesia" into the search box in my computer, and up came an article by the author of the book. *Runs in families,* says the article. *Found in normal bright individuals of high intelligence. Most often in creative females, accompanying right–left confusion, difficulties with math, and splinter traits of memory, especially for passages of prose, lines from songs or movies, etc. Fifteen percent of cases have first-family histories of dyslexia, ADD or autism.*

The writer Vladimir Nabokov had it, as did various painters, composers, and other creatives, as well as individuals of all backgrounds. Many have thought themselves crazy, been given diagnoses of schizophrenia, when they talked about seeing a person "in color," such as, here comes the blue shape who is John, or hearing colors in a person's voice, or tasting circles and squares in their food. Many also perceive numbers and letters in color, or as having personality traits or other characteristics. Some are very sensitive to sounds, smell, or texture. Some people believe it's more common in children but diminishes with age.

I didn't expect to see myself in these pages—I don't hear colors—but as I read on, I remember.

When I was a child I thought numbers had distinct personalities. I still do, although they've faded with time. I memorized the first few pages of *Heidi* before I could read. I can remember the visual details of early childhood down to the pitted texture of the wood floor, the woven fabric of a dress, the translucent blue and copper flames of a fire the neighbor boy set when we "played house," the carapace of a dead brown bug in the sunshine. People often remark on my vast recall of song lyrics and prose. When I worked in the Pentagon, I had a handy gift for storing the middle initials, state of origin, and party affiliation of dozens of congressmen and senators. I couldn't tell left from right until high school and even then I had to work on it. When I write poetry, the sensation of the emerging words buzz in my chest.

My amazing, perplexing little boy. He is so very mine. The brain, the willfully dodging, unrecognized seat of the soul, reveals that I am his mother and he is my son.

# 21

# Broken Bits

*Eight Months In*

If only I hadn't eaten swordfish so often in midpregnancy.

Now they say swordfish has mercury in it.

If only I hadn't ridden the gondola on Aspen Mountain in my fifth month, even though my doctor said I could go on the trip—the air was so thin. If only I had picked a less-busy hospital to deliver, where a doctor could have been by my side sooner. If only I hadn't worked so hard on a pregnant friend's shower that I was placed on bed rest for a week. If only I hadn't taken antibiotics in my seventh month. And the difficult one: If only I hadn't asked for pitocin, that drug that moved my labor forward. *If only.*

If only Jonah wasn't autistic.

I had thought the terrible blaming of the first months was behind us. It turns out that most spouses go through some sort of blaming at first, either openly or not. Some point to the other's family or parenting style; often one parent refuses to accept the diagnosis and resents the parent who does. We'd largely escaped those pitfalls. But we went to a new pediatrician, Dr. Michael Goldberg, who specializes in autism, ADHD, and chronic fatigue. He believes autism is a wastebasket term for a collection of symptoms, and that the new types of autism—which differ from rare classic autism—are neuro-immune deficiencies. Among other observations, this doctor said Jonah's tight leg muscles might have been caused by a birth accident—the records show I might have been made to wait until the doctor got there to deliver. When he says this I remember how labor struck like lightning after I got the pitocin; Jonah began to descend so quickly the nurses had scrambled to call the doctor.

Blame resurfaced in the tight look of Jack's face on the way home. He couldn't look at me with that pinched, painful face.

"So here we are, back at the old blame again," I said. "I took pitocin."

"I didn't say it was blame."

"Sure you did. You've said it before. I thought this was behind us, Jack."

"I thought it was too. But you keep on saying it has nothing to do with it, and I think it does. I think it *does*." He looked me in the face stubbornly.

The awful feeling of a gulf rose between us again.

"How do you know? What research have you done? Who have you talked to?"

"That attorney I met in court. The one who'd defended eight negligence cases against pitocin," he said. "He says he knew it has harmful effects on the kids."

Thinking of some high-paid jerk in a suit affirming pitocin's dangers sickens me. So much for believing its common usage was an indicator of safety—as I'd said to Jack all along. "Someone who's defending negligence cases against the drug *would* say that. A real moral authority."

"So you're going to be sarcastic now. You always tell me I don't share my feelings and when I do you criticize me for it."

"Feelings are different than facts," I say. "You ought to know that."

———

"Here it is." Jack was carrying a large red book. "Information that pitocin can cause damage."

I stared at him. "What's that?"

"A *Physician's Desk Reference.*"

I pulled the book slowly on my lap. It was heavy, with thin printed pages like an old-style dictionary, printed 1994.

Pitocin: Indicated for the initiation or improvement of uterine contractions. Precautions: all patients should be under continuous observation by trained personnel who have a thorough knowledge of the drug; a physician qualified to manage any complications should be immediately available. Contraindicated for patients with hypersensitivity to the drug.

Among adverse serious reactions reported in the infant: permanent central nervous system damage; brain damage; fetal death.

"See what it says?" asked Jack. "It says that—"

"I saw what it says."

"Then you see that it may have been responsible for his condition."

"For all of his condition?" I ask bitterly. "Tight leg muscles or the autism?" From far away I hear Jonah in his room, talking to himself.

"No, not all of it. But I knew it might have made a difference."

The television was playing. The blanket over my legs felt like a stiff tent.

"So the pitocin probably caused *some* portion of the damage," he said.

I couldn't look at him. I felt awkward and acutely ugly, stranded in the middle of our large bed. I started crying, a slow, swelling, desperate crying that I hadn't done in months. "Well, you showed me," I said. "You had to prove that I was wrong. And you sure as hell did."

He approached the bed, concerned. "You just kept saying it couldn't have been the pitocin, and the truth is that it could have been. Do you want to talk?"

"What is there to say?" I said.

"We can talk about it. You didn't know."

"Just go away," I said. "Go out of here."

I stared at the television. I forced myself to make out the figures of the horses cavorting across the screen of the old movie western. The colorized blue of the sky and the powdery red of the desert bluffs faded like a watercolor through my tears.

I held very still and a half hour went by.

Jack returned from putting Jonah to bed. He looked alarmed. "I didn't mean to make you feel bad. You didn't know about the drug."

"So? What does that change?"

"It could have been me. It could have been me that could have done something to damage him," Jack said.

"Like what?" I asked.

"If he fell out of his stroller, or hit his head. It could just as easily have been me."

"But it wasn't, was it?"

"You're tired," he said. "You need to go to sleep."

I was afraid to sleep. It would be a black whirlpool, the worst sleep since the diagnosis. "I'm not sleeping in here tonight."

"Are you going to sleep with him?" he asked.

I took my pillow and went into the hall linen closet and gathered a sheet and blanket. I thought of Jonah in his crisp butter yellow sheets, his petal mouth breathing in the dark. I didn't deserve to sleep with him. In the living room, I dropped the linens on the sofa. Jack followed me. "You can't sleep out here. It's not comfortable. Come to bed."

"No."

"Don't you think this is setting a bad precedent?" he asked quietly.

"That's not my intention."

"How often are you going to sleep out here?"

"Only on nights when I find out I damaged my son."

He took a delicate step toward me. "I didn't mean to blame you for it."

"Well, you do, so why lie? You blurted it out right when we found out."

"I told you what I *felt*. I was angry, but you wouldn't leave me alone. So I told you."

"Yes, you certainly did and I've been paying for it ever since."

"I've been paying for it too," he said. "It would have been better if I had lied."

I hesitated. "Did it ever occur to you to protect me?"

"What do you mean, protect you?"

"Couldn't you have said, 'Honey, we'll never really know, so let's forget about it'?"

"I was trying to be honest, but you're right. I should have, and left it at that."

"Then I wouldn't have to live with this for the rest of my life."

He sat down next to me and extended his arm around the back of my shoulders. I leaned away from him. "I'm sorry," he said. "I don't think you should feel so bad about it. You didn't know. The doctor didn't tell you."

"That does me a lot of good now."

"Please come to bed."

"No."

"Okay. I'll turn out the light."

He went into the bedroom, and the lights went off. I was filled with panic, like a child in the dark after an angry parent departs. "Jack," I called.

"Yes?" The lights turned back on and he reentered the dark living room.

"I have a feeling of hate for you right now."

He sat down at the end of the couch. "I'm sorry you feel that way. I hope you can understand why I showed it to you and that you won't always hate me."

"I didn't say I hated you. I said I have feelings of hate for you right now."

"I've tried to tell you that I don't want to blame you and I really don't. Maybe you can think about it. Maybe someday you won't hate me."

"Maybe."

He pulled the covers over my legs and went back to the bedroom.

———————

The next day passed in a quiet chill. Then night fell again and Jack came home. I left Jonah with him and did paperwork I couldn't do during the day.

Later, he came into the bedroom. "Look, I know you aren't happy. You think I blame you but I really had let it . . . diminish. It seemed like it had faded over the past few months and I thought it was gone. I really don't blame you."

I looked at him with fury and hurt. "Think back, Jack. Do you remember how I quit caffeine, exercised three times a week, never drank alcohol? That I choked down those huge prenatal vitamins? That I tried to do everything right?"

"Yes," he said steadily.

"Remember how I read piles and piles of books and magazines on pregnancy and childbirth, and asked you to read them and you didn't?"

"I read some things."

"You read *one* book."

"True. I read one book."

"So knowing that, can you possibly think I would have done anything with the slightest risk of hurting him?"

"No," he said quietly. "I know you wouldn't have."

"That's why you left it up to me. You knew I would do a

good job, and that's the way it works in most pregnancies. Except it didn't turn out that way this time. But you still can't get over it."

"No, I think I did," he said. "I really did."

I stared at him.

"If I did something to hurt him, you would have blamed me too," he said.

"No, I wouldn't," I said automatically, but a memory came back to me. Jack had allowed one-year-old Jonah to wander around our fenced pool area; he tripped and gashed a deep cut in his chin. I was aghast that Jack had let him walk alone around the patio, instead of following him mother-duck fashion as I did, even though the fence was up, and there were no apparent hazards. My anger at the incident hadn't faded for nearly a year. And really, Jack hadn't done anything wrong.

"Yes, I might have blamed you some," I conceded.

That night we went to sleep quietly, in the same bed.

———————

Two days after our fight, we're seeing a new nurse-practitioner at CARD. She starts the appointment by remarking that she couldn't tell Jonah was autistic—he kept peeking into her meeting with a family with two boys, asking to play—and she's surprised he's her next client.

Her words make us feel good. She approves of the diet and Nystatin. She tells me to remove the ketchup (yeast) and bananas (phenol-like reactions and sugar) I'd allowed to creep back into his diet. I mourn these small bits of dietary fun but I agree. In answer to her questions, we speak of my pregnancy.

"The pitocin," I say. "I asked for it since I'd been in labor for two nights, and I'd stopped having contractions for the second time. Have you ever heard of pitocin causing nervous system problems?"

She pauses, then says, "Well, possibly. But the use of pitocin might not have been out of line since your labor had stopped a second time. Usually with that kind of indication they *would* do something."

"Why? What would that mean?"

"That something was keeping labor from progressing. Was the cord wrapped around his neck?"

Her words bring back a partial memory. In the slippery confused rush after birth, I think I heard a nurse murmur, "The cord was around his neck."

"I might have heard those words in the delivery room," I say, just as Jack answers, "No, it wasn't."

"At any rate," she says, "the fact that labor had started and stopped twice could have been significant and pitocin would often be used in these situations."

"Why would they use it if they knew it had possible side effects?"

"Well, the mother could become too tired from the labor to push. Then the baby could be in jeopardy."

I feel my self-hatred lift. *Maybe there had been something wrong with the labor's progress? Maybe I really wasn't bad, lazy, selfish—maybe I really had been tired!*

"There's no way to know what caused what at this point, unless you seek genetic testing and examine certain genes in the DNA to see if they are affected in any way," she says. "Then perhaps you'd be able to separate out some of the medical issues."

We talk about genes by number and how some of them

turn up with certain characteristics, as if discussing bowling balls. Although this kind of thing appeals to our analytic minds, I don't wish to narrow this inquiry down endlessly, like a sauce being reduced over and over to its edible essence. I'm glad we did the medically necessary tests, like fragile X and a few others, but they revealed nothing unusual. Witnessing his challenges and accomplishments over the past months, I've come to see perfection in him, purer and greater than I could have believed before. Although we're striving to make him as capable as he can be, he deserves the dignity of being himself. To check out his genes without a significant reason at this point feels like an invasion of his privacy.

"He is doing so well," says the nurse-practitioner. "I would say by the age of five, he may be pretty well normal."

There it is again, that tantalizing promise. And what is normal, anyway?

"What do you mean by that?" I ask. "Language, mannerisms, or what?"

She shrugs her slim shoulders. "Just, overall, you wouldn't be able to pick him out of a typical classroom. That he would possibly have some issues, maybe social situations, but that overall he would be . . . normal."

"It's so good to hear that," I say. "I mean, we were told that by Doreen Granpeesheh last September, but it's so hard to remember it in the middle of—this."

"There are some children who do outgrow this diagnosis. He is making such rapid progress, according to what his clinical supervisor told me, that he will . . ." She hesitates. "Probably continue to move toward that goal."

Someone was telling me that Jonah's life could bloom in full after all. Our future had contracted to a dark and chaotic place, like a crushed kaleidoscope, just over eight months ago. And now the sun was shining through the broken bits of glass like a stained glass window.

On the drive home, I have to say it. "Did you hear what she said, Jack?"

"About Jonah?"

"About the pitocin. You are going to have to let it go."

He hesitates, then shrugs his shoulders slightly.

"I think she made it clear that it wasn't out of the ordinary under those circumstances," I say. "That I did have a reason for asking for it. And we'll never know, anyway, until years from now, if more studies come out."

"I guess so," he says, and nods slowly.

As the sun slants warmly on my lap, I take Jack's hand and he squeezes mine. I feel the weight of a thousand black thoughts lift like a thundercloud.

# 22

## A New Mosaic

### *Yeast Bites Back*

"If he does well on Nystatin," Dr. Goldberg said cheerfully, "he'll do even better on something stronger." Nizerol, another yeast-killing drug, is powerful, and it's the first one he wants to try. I've talked to two mothers whose children improved with it, and I've spoken with their doctors too. One of the kids is the one who totally recovered through IVIG transfusions, drugs, behavioral therapy, and diet. "We had to do IVIG to get him up to where yours started," she told me. The other child is only nine months behind his developmental curve. With those twin inputs—motherhood and medicine—Jack and I agree to try it.

In the first few days of replacing Nystatin with Nizerol, tantrums appear.

Jonah's cranky, without his usual sweetness. He writhes with anger in my arms, and jumps and leaps with abandon, wearing me out like the bad old days. Greta cautions me that Nizerol can cause bad reactions for up to three weeks; the period when the internal yeast is dying and releasing toxins is called "die-off," and Nizerol's die-off is long. Dr. Goldberg's office confirms this. Each day is hard and getting harder. Hank is the only member of the CARD staff who knows about the medication change; we do not usually tell therapists about medication or diet changes so their feedback isn't biased. Hank says to keep therapy demands normal, but the rest of the day easy for Jonah.

By the end of the first week, I've had it, but Goldberg's office assures me it's too soon to quit. Grimly, I hang in there, but he's wild, in a bad mood, his aggression is returning. It feels disastrous. The second week is just as bad. But every time I call the doctor's office, they tell me to hold on until twenty-one days are over. One night, he seems better, so I take him to the Burger King Play Place to meet Jordan and his mom. The kids push each other in the small play area, but other small boys, including Jordan, instigate that. It's only when I hear a smaller child scream that I get worried.

"What happened?" I ask Jordan's mom.

"Jonah bit that little kid," she says.

*Oh, God.* I look at an older woman—probably the grandmother—holding a child in her arms. "Don't go. Let me," says my friend as I grab and hold a struggling Jonah on my hip. She comes back. "He bit her pretty hard."

I hand Jonah to Jordan's mom and approach the woman. "I am so sorry—is she okay?" She stares at me with extreme anger and disgust. "He's a special-needs child," I explain. "He didn't know what he was doing. He didn't mean it." She looks away, and it's clear our excuse is none at all.

The woman has picked up her bag and left with the crying

child, and I tell Jordan's mom, "I have to take him out right now." I tell Jonah to say good-bye to Jordan. He doesn't want to leave but I drag him out. I put him in the car seat and I start to cry. "Do you understand that you will have no friends left if you bite?" I say, inches away from his face. He looks at me but I'm not sure if he's listening, and he says nothing. "This kind of behavior is unacceptable. No, no, no!" I shout. "Do you want to stay home forever, and have no more friends? That's what's going to happen!" I want him to feel badly, to know he cannot bite people or we'll be quarantined like wild animals.

Darkness is falling, and now he's as upset as I am.

I get in the front seat and drive, but I can't stop crying. With the diet changes and his new language ability, his biting had largely diminished. *And now we're back to this?* I call Jack and beg him to come home early, I am going crazy with fear. He agrees to leave right away. Jonah's in a frenzy of crying, just like me. This is sick, we are in a sick disease with no way out.

I call Dr. Goldberg's office the next day.

"He bit a child in a play area," I tell his staff. "He wasn't doing that before. Please, *please* take us off the Nizerol."

I wait until afternoon, when they call and say, wait a few more days to see if it's just die-off or something more. And keep him out of overstimulating situations like Play Places during med changes!

After a few more days of bad behavior and tantrums, we remove him from Nizerol. He was possibly allergic to something in the pill, the doctor says, not the anti-fungal itself. I don't give a damn what it was, I never want to see it again.

Dr. Goldberg replaces the Nizerol with Diflucan, a drug often given to women for yeast infections. Jonah gets it in a white liquid form in his drink every night. Within days, he is calm again, and getting better. He's more verbal, more inventive with his language than ever before. "When I grow up, I will be a man," he says.

"That's right," I tell him.

"And then when I grow down, I'll be a boy." He looks pleased with himself, assured of his rightness.

"Honey, you won't be a boy again, you can only grow up, not down."

He thinks and rejects it. "No. I'll be a man, then when I grow down, I'll be a boy again."

———

The therapists report a new presence, a mastery of words and loss of stims (those self-stimulating behaviors every spectrum kid has, however small). He only hand-flaps maybe once a month, but he has other less-noticeable stims that pop up here and there, such as occasional toe-walking, or echoing a phrase or facial expression too many times, and they're all down. Melanie says his language has zoomed upward. On Diflucan, he's surpassed the Nystatin's good effects and he's still gaining. His skin is smoother too—the small white bumps on his cheeks are gone. His fiery cheeks faded with the diet, but now he isn't really red-cheeked at all.

———

We've come to realize how sharply his behavior deteriorates when he gets sugar. My support-group friend has us over and gives him a cup of rice milk and a gf/cf cookie. Within ten minutes he's a different child, hyper, defiant, not listening. He runs through the house with his head down, and can't be stopped. I grab him by the arm, and he writhes and pulls, resisting any direction.

"Wow, he changed within minutes," she says, her eyes wide. "I didn't think that stuff had much sugar in it."

"It doesn't take much," I tell her, hauling him off the floor and out the front door. He kicks the back of the seat on the way home, asking the same question over and over again. I know he can't stop himself. I keep my mouth shut so I don't speak harshly. I have tears in my eyes.

We attend a Saturday birthday party, featuring a fine, sweet gf/cf chocolate cake. Jonah helps himself to a second piece without our permission. He begins to fall apart when we get home. He's irritable and uncommunicative, roaming the house in search of satisfaction he can't find.

Later, he lies in bed, crying, "My tummy hurts. I ate too many sweets."

This is a first—he's never commented on how he feels, let alone assigned a cause to it. Jack draws Jonah close. "You'll feel better tomorrow. Go to sleep."

After Jonah's fallen asleep, puffy-cheeked and miserable, I tell Jack, "We've got to be more careful with sugar."

"I agree," he says.

The Monday after the party, I call a friend, and she says her severely autistic child giggled maniacally all night after eating that cake. She thinks it was the chocolate, not the sugar. We think it's probably both for us, and now Jonah's bottom is red, with some sort of infection. Although we cover it with antifungal cream, it takes a whole week for him to recover.

Jack's so paranoid about sugar now that he begins to read labels for it too.

---

Mother's Day. Jack takes us to our mountain cabin. We set out on a hike, chase lizards, stop for lunch, and go home. It's a nice day.

Jack hands me a card. He'd already given me one from Jonah, with two bears hugging, but this is from him. Another set of animals, this time two large furry woodchuck-creatures kissing. One is large and shaggy, the other small and delicate.

> *Dear Christina,*
>
> *I hope you enjoyed your Mother's Day. We didn't do anything very exciting, but we did get to spend a quiet Sunday together with Jonah.*
>
> *Jonah is really the reason we are celebrating Mother's Day and I do think he is reason to celebrate. He has been making tremendous strides, so much so that our goal of attending school with his peers seems achievable. Despite his limitations, I think Jonah is the best thing that ever happened for both of us, and he never would have happened if you had not agreed to become my wife.*
>
> *I hope we can celebrate many more Mother's Days together in the future, and that Jonah learns to love and appreciate you as much as I do.*
>
> *Love, Jack*

A declaration from the quiet heart of my husband. It touches me so much I can't respond, so I hug him tight and stroke his head. I feel the muscle and bone of his body silent and accepting against my chest. We are still together, still conjoined despite our increasing trials. Mother to his child, wife to his husband. I am still a fortunate one.

———————

It's six o'clock in the evening, and there have been four, five, six, seven tantrums so far today. Not normal for Jonah, who tantrums a bit, sure, but never to this degree.

First thing in the morning, he dawdled over his Velcro shoe buckles. I closed the Velcro straps myself. "I will do it!" he repeated, over and over, tears and anger rising. "No, I did it, because you didn't listen to me," I said. Tentatively but willfully, he hit me on the arms with his two fists, staring into my eyes the whole time. "Sit down!" I said, and put him firmly on the carpet. The doorbell rang, and thank God, it was Fran, our lead therapist. Jonah broke his time-out and followed me, startling her, a passing neighbor, and an arriving contractor with tear-stained shouts of "I wanna do it! I WANNA DO IT!"

Fran met my gaze with approval. "Remember, in clinic last month, when Hank told us not to let Jonah control everything?" she asked.

"That's what I'm doing right now," I said and grabbed his arm to keep him from running down the front steps.

"I wanna do my shoes!" he shouted. "I will do it, I WANNA DO IT!"

The contractor looked at me and shrugged his shoulders.

"Jonah, come in right now," Fran said. He threw himself on the cold hallway floor and hit the ground with his fist. I sighed. Hell, I hadn't even brushed my hair or teeth yet. It was going to be a long one.

The tears, touchiness, and emotion ran all day. Near therapy's end at five thirty, he'd thrown a major tantrum, a screaming, puffy-faced, gasping-for-breath tantrum that rose and fell like the tide on a beach. I stood outside the door of the schoolroom in the garage, clutching my stomach. I'd ignored the screams as long as I could, but the final scream, a high, angry, shrill sound, made my heart lurch. I knew he was okay with the late afternoon therapist on duty, but I couldn't stop listening outside.

Finally he was quiet, so I put my head through the open door. Jonah was sitting calmly in the little blue chair taking the deep breaths we'd taught him, but when his eyes met mine, he burst into tears again. "Mommy! I want my Mommy!" he cried.

The therapist looked tired. I knew if I went to soothe him, it would reward him for crying. I turned from his pleading face and hurried up the garage steps and into the house. It had to be the allergy meds. We'd given Jonah a half teaspoon according to Goldberg's latest order, to "get the light bulb burning in there," as he said. Instead, it had thrown him into a miserable frenzy of emotion.

Now, as the day moves to a close, I sit wondering what to do. I look out the window to the concrete breezeway, where the tomato plants Jack and Jonah tended last summer wilt over their stakes. The bright narrow space hurts my eyes.

*Why must a boy struggle like this? Why must we infuse him with medication, inundate him with teachers, overload his central nervous system with conflicting urges week after week, month after month?*

I'm tired of the pressure, tired of caring so desperately about his future, tired of trying to make him like everyone else.

Jonah appears at the door. His face is bright pink, his eyes amazingly round, like a doll's, lashes pointed and black with dried tears. "Mommy?"

"Yes, sweetheart?" I call out encouragingly.

"Look," he says, taking a step toward me.

Behind him, the therapist prompts, "I made . . ."

"Look, I made dis for you."

He holds up a green piece of construction paper. A kite, drawn from a homemade dot-to-dot outline, with a beribboned tail swirling in a paper breeze.

"Oh, sweetheart! Let me see it. Can you show it to me?"

"Yes, Mom. I will show it to you." He runs around the desk, his small feet avoiding the briefcase and document boxes beside the desk. "Here it is, Mommy!"

"Oh, thank you. You are a good artist!"

The young woman smiles patiently from the door as he nestles into my lap.

"Honey, I'll make you a nice dinner and then you can rest with me. Do you want that?"

"Yeth," he says, a remnant from the lisp. His head bends and he puts his nose too close to mine. His eyes dazzle me with their gray flecks in the ocean blue iris. Their blue is my own. Their flecks, like depth markers, are his. He has his father's lashes.

*No more meds,* I say to myself.

But I know I lie.

———

A day later, Jonah is hunched in my lap like a pet rabbit as I stroke his hair. Tonight has offered two tantrums. He played with his rice at dinner, so after a warning, I took it away, and he repeated "I want rice" over and over again, in a tremulous, angry voice, then hit the table. During cleanup, he sprayed the water faucet onto the floor. I used behavioral rules on him, like any well-run household, autistic or otherwise, but I knew it wasn't his fault. It was the long day of feeling poorly.

"How was he today?" Jack asks, our standard exchange after a hello kiss.

"We've had the worst tantruming ever. Let's cut the allergy medicine dose."

Jack likes to give the dosage as ordered. He frowns. "I gave him what the doctor ordered, a half teaspoon."

I prefer to seek the right medication level with a behavioral dousing rod. "I know, honey, but he's so sensitive," I say. "Let's cut it in half."

"I'll cut it by a third," Jack says. "I think that's a good first step."

We cut it and the next day he seems better. But the unreasonableness persists.

The next night, we cut it again. The next morning Jonah wakes up like an on-call fireman, calm, alert, and giving directions. "I want to wear my black shirt. Then I can have a waffle. I need to go to the bathroom. Don't make the water too hot." His calm, language-driven self is present all morning. In the afternoon, he's a bit absent, slightly tired, but clearly the lower dose worked.

Yet after all this trial and error on the allergy medication, he's only a tiny bit better than before. We'll keep the low dose until it's time to add something new to the daily Diflucan, another vitamin, medicine, or supplement to chop, grind, mix, and spoon up each day.

---

One night before bedtime I prompt a made-up story. "Once upon . . ."

"A time," Jonah says, "there was a big mountain."

"Yes," I say. "And a small tree stood outside the mountain in the surrounding wilderness."

Jonah says, "There was a . . ."

"Cocoon," I continue. "Clinging to a branch. It was small and quiet and nobody could see inside."

"Nobody could see inside . . ." Jonah whispers.

"Then one day the sun came up and the cocoon got very warm."

"The moon went to bed, the sun came up, and it was day-time!" adds Jonah.

"Yes. Then slowly, slowly the tiny cocoon began to writhe and squirm, and then it tore open. And guess what came out?"

"A bear!" he says.

"No, a butterfly! A beautiful, orange and black butterfly."

"And he had blue eyes," says Jonah.

"Okay, big brilliant blue eyes. Then what did he do?"

"He flew!" Jonah said with a long pure u-sound to "flew."

"He flew far up above the treetops, and went to see many lands."

Quiet.

"The end," I add.

"The end. Story's over," he says. He rolls over and puts his hand on my neck. "I am happy," he sighs.

"I'm happy too," I say.

———

Today Anh's on duty. She's capable of handling anything, her beautiful face a lovely mask for her strong will. She's caught Jonah's vomit neatly in a bowl, wiped and toilet-trained much older kids, and she rarely needs me. But she and Jonah knock at my bedroom door.

"Mommy!" sings out Jonah. "Come here!"

"I want . . ." prompts Anh's voice.

"I want to show you something!"

"Okay, guys, don't move. I'll be right there." I swing off the treadmill and around the four-poster bed. I open the door in my exercise clothes, my hair a mess.

"Mommy, look. I drew a happy face."

"Oh, that's good!" I look at Anh, puzzled. They draw happy faces all the time.

"He did this *all by himself*," she says. Her voice and eyes reveal excitement.

Jonah brandishes the magnetic sketch pad with pride and I see a perfectly round face with two round eyes, a nose, and an upturned single-line smile. The head is formed with one long stroke, perfectly attached from beginning to end. The eyes are slightly humorous looking.

"Anh, did he really do this by himself?"

"Yes!" she says, trying to keep her voice level but failing. "I told him to go sit in his chair and draw for a while so I could write some notes. Then he said, 'Look, Anh.' I couldn't believe it! I mean, we draw faces all the time together, but he's never done anything like this without my help. Developmentally, many regular kids his age can't do this."

It's a huge leap up from the slashes of crayon he makes over and over when left alone. I'd wondered if he would ever be able to draw, let alone write legibly, but this makes it clear his fine motor skills are improving, his fisted pencil-grasp yielding to the correct "triangle-grip" of thumb and first two fingers. Our program's overall formula of repetition, attention, and emotion is working, even on his physical capabilities and self-initiative. I hug Jonah hard.

"Jonah, this is so great! Wow, you are a great artist!"

He likes the hug, but he sees an opportunity to examine the treadmill. He pulls away and starts fooling with the bolts.

---

On Memorial Day weekend, we're nine months into this new universe, and Jack makes a trip to the hardware store. Now Jonah has a trampoline. Jumping calms his off-kilter vestibular system (which helps a body locate itself in space), cheers his equilibrium, and launches him into the heights he adores. He jumps and jumps, and I wash dishes, read *Vanity Fair* and *The New Yorker*, a miracle, then watch him in his safety net enclosure.

"Mommy, come inside wif me!" he says.

I crawl in and sit down on the springy surface. He's overjoyed. "Mommy, jump wif me! Hold my hand. I will help you."

I cautiously stand up.

"Okay, Mommy, I will bounce you," he says. He jumps industriously. His hair is soaked with perspiration.

"Come on, baby, let's go in. You can have a drink."

"I wanna stay."

"Nope. Let's go. Then you can come back."

He steps off the trampoline. "Pick me up."

"No, that's not necessary."

"It is too necessary," he says. "I'm necessary."

I pick him up. "Yes, you are," I say.

# 23

# The Wonder of It All

*Ten Months In*

A mild-mannered mother by day, I can leap picnic tables to grab forbidden foods in a single hysterical bound. I'm able to lift heavy medical terms like *benign Rolandic epilepsy, immune markers, opioid effect,* and *peptides.* I can diagnose a possible autism spectrum disorder over the phone by asking a few simple questions. When the need strikes, I become . . . Autism Mommy!

The other Autism Mommies told me this would happen. "Just wait," they said. "You'll know all of this stuff," referring to the medical and diet information that hung like an avalanche above my head. Or they'd say, "You'll get so good, you'll be able to look at a kid and know right away if he's on the spectrum." I listened to them with a numb sense of incompetence. *No way,* I would tell myself as I hung up the phone, or left the meeting, or the house. *No way.*

There are several levels of Autism Mommies (and daddies). First, we start out as Special-Needs Parents, a wide umbrella group, just by getting the news. The majority remain at this level. They accept the school districts' programs unquestioningly, as they have no reason not to. Their autistic kids get the typical three hours a day in the special ed classroom, and maybe a half hour a week of speech therapy. No diet, no medications, no behavioral therapy, no family guidance. Just the school's scant resources.

Next comes the Upgrade Crowd, the parents who enhance the basic school package with other attempts to help their child. They try a few vitamins or mood-altering drugs, cut down on dairy products, and push to get the child more speech or occupational therapy. These parents often come to the table late, after they see the school districts' promises dry up and blow away, or their child remains in diapers, or hasn't learned to speak by age five. Or when symptoms worsen and tantrums or other debilitating behaviors intensify. They hang at the edges of support group meetings, asking quiet, tentative questions, and I brace myself as they inevitably say, "But the school district *said* this would *help* . . ."

Then there are the Autism Mommies. This is a slender tier of women who do everything that sounds remotely reasonable. They do the diet. They draw vials of blood from their children and test it for signs and deficits, like oracles looking to foretell the future. They run twenty-five- or thirty-hour-a-week home programs, and send their kids to the special ed classroom twice a week to keep the school district happy. They make the immediate round of specialists, trudge to occupational and speech therapy twice a week. They share gf/cf recipes, educate relatives, and generally walk the intervention treadmill for years.

Then, the highest category: Autism Super Mommies.

This is a hair-thin category, for it takes a watchdog-fierce personality, advanced domestic science skills, a river of money and time, and a formidable brain. To become an Autism Super Mommy, you must have the bleeding heart of a philanthropist, the skills of a champion telemarketer, and the patience of a saint. These mothers cook with the purest, rarest, most clean ingredients. They devote their days and weekends to cooking and activism, their nights to their child, their sleeping time to counseling others. They run forty-hour-plus home programs. They use speech pathologists, occupational therapists, nutritionists, homeopaths, neuro-feedback providers, auditory trainers, and the latest therapies from around the world. They visit or fly in renowned autism pediatricians.

Those with exceptional means go to amazing lengths. One local mother I know, an executive, built an entertainment clubhouse in her backyard. Their son, a beautiful speechless boy of ten, would otherwise never socialize with "normal" kids, so she staffs it with therapists and stocks it with food six days a week. Any child can play on the giant trampoline, ride the assembled bikes, and snack to his or her stomach's content. She flew in a New York lawyer to fight her school district and established a legal precedent that ensured other kids would be helped, then went on to found a special school. She also raises money for autism research.

My local Autism Super Mommies are beacons of help. They are never too busy to counsel a newly grieving parent, send recipes, hold wonderful fund-raisers, and provide medical tips. Because of them, I put Jonah on his diet five days after diagnosis. They told me what lawyer to hire, what therapy providers to go with, which foods to buy, what depression they have survived so far.

So where do I fall on the spectrum?

I am not an Autism Super Mommy. No, my craving for solitude, my desire to keep a small portion of my own life, precludes that. I am only an Autism Mommy. But I do have some Super-leaning traits: I run a forty-hour program, I write editorials, I counsel people, I help with fund-raisers and political action. I incorporate music lessons, seek out specialists, perform therapy on my darling tired son every minute of the day. I go to meetings and end up speaking quite a bit, maybe too much. And always, two or three mothers seek me out afterward and ask, "What doctor did you mention? Who was the lawyer? How did you manage the twenty-four-hour EEG?"

If I have Super Mommy traits, they reflect the best of autism. The drive, the compulsion to problem solve, the ability to latch onto a topic and find out everything there is to know about it. I have the single-minded, perhaps discomfiting focus on saving my child and helping other families to do the same. Whatever causes Jonah to talk over and over again of drains, of red and green traffic lights, of power poles, of the latest emotional incident in his dramatic young life, is similar to the thing that drives me.

If I have become an Autism Mommy, it's because Jonah is a shining example of what life with autism can be. If I can become attached to what moves him, share in his understanding of the world, and make it better with every filament of my being, I will find a new life along with him.

Our latest allergy blood panel revealed Jonah—who has been eating so many products made of rice—has a new rice allergy. Cow's milk and buttermilk are also highly allergic to him. But now his gluten and wheat sensitivity isn't significant. Dr. Gold-berg said to take a "baby step" and try introducing a very processed wheat bread, like Wonder Bread, into his diet. My mother considered Wonder Bread junk food when I was a child; now I'm in the grocery store, getting ready to buy it to feed to her grandchild.

I'm also shopping for low-sugar products. Since he reacts poorly to even fairly small amounts of sugar with bad behavior and defiance, plus a red ring around a certain location, we've created a new epigram, *When behavior is heinous, check the anus.* It's shocking how much sugar is in food. Pancakes, cereals, breads, and granola bars contain double-digit grams, and juice boxes are worse than cookies and cakes. We've experimented with sugar-free candies, cookies, and lemonade to bury medi-cine in, and they work, but too many of these and it's just as if he's eaten sugar. I search mightily for low-sugar products, use stevia sometimes, and allow certain artificial sweeteners for spe-cial occasions, and finally I've gotten him down to about two to four grams of sugar per serving of any food.

But with gluten's possible return, I must find wheat prod-ucts that are totally dairy-free, low/no sugar, and very processed. I search the bread shelves for something other than Wonder Bread, but even the thicker, cleaner breads contain ammonia, plus sugar, yeast, and milk. I move slowly, like a snail on a brick wall, reading label after label. After two hours of grocery store research, I buy the Wonder Bread.

---

The antiviral drug seems to be helping Jonah. He's been full of conversation the last few days, inventive, pointed, demanding. We're eating at Ruby's, a 1940s-style diner. Jonah is having a turkey burger sans bread, but his fries arrive first.

"I want some ketchup," he says. "I want that ketchup on this table."

He's pointing to ketchup bottles over on a service counter. Jack and I are talking, but he won't wait.

"Mommy, get that ketchup."

"Jonah, you have to wait. The fries are hot. When they cool, you can have it." Jack is saying something and I try to listen. The waitress spins by and Jonah points at her.

"Mommy, I want that dinner-woman to bring me ketchup."

I am amazed. "Jonah, a woman who brings you food in a restaurant is called a *waitress*. A man who brings it is called a waiter."

He lights up. "I want the waitress to get me the ketchup."

"Boy, do you deserve it," I tell him. "Asking for your food so nicely."

We've been stinting on the ketchup (sugar and vinegar, yeast-making elements), but today we give in. He squirts it with abandon and chews through his fries. "Mommy, here's an onion ring," he says, tendering it from Jack's plate. "Do you want ketchup?"

"Yes, thank you, but I'll get it."

"Here, Daddy, here's your onion ring." He proffers one to Jack.

"Thank you, Jonah. That's very nice manners."

We smile at our dinner companion, the delightful child sharing our table.

Later that night he gets hungry again, so I make him a turkey burger, with a Wonder Bread bun as an experiment.

Sitting at the table, he bites the edges of it, then squeezes it. The fat homemade burger slips from the side.

"Mom?"

"Yes, Jonah?"

"This round bread isn't working right. I want my square bread."

"The round bread will work okay too. Don't you want it?"

"No, I don't. Get me my square bread. It will work right."

I fetch him a single piece of regular Wonder bread. He puts the meat on the bread. "There, now it's better." He chews the bread and meat with his sharp little teeth, perfect squares echoing the shape of the bread. "I'm done," he says.

With words, he's arranging things his way.

He's fit a round burger into a square piece of bread.

# 24

# Riches

*The Difference between January and July*

Today is a testing day, Melanie, our speech therapist, announces when she arrives. Jonah follows Melanie into the schoolroom. I close the door but leave a crack so I can watch. Sitting at the blue table, she props a paper booklet sideways between them, showing elephants, lions, monkeys, and tigers. "Show me the cat," she says. His finger reaches out and hovers above the cat, then descends. "Show me the monkey," she says. His index finger settles on the monkey.

I head for my office, to make autism phone calls and shuffle autism paperwork.

Soon Melanie comes to the door. Before I can steel myself, she says, "He did very well today."

"Good," I say.

"Let's go over it. This is a retest of the CELF Preschool test. It tests language in terms of where he is in comparison to all preschoolers his age. Overall, he did very well. There are some weak spots, but he can work on those." She pulls out her papers, standing in my small cluttered office. "We first did this test in January. Today is July fifth. This is a grammar and language test, not pragmatics, like in conversation. His conversation is still weak, as we know, but we can work on it."

"Okay."

"In linguistic concepts, he went from being in the first percentile in January, the lowest"—here she looks at me—"to the eighty-fourth percentile. That's quite a jump, very good progress. He needs to learn the concepts of first/last and before/after. He missed those a couple of times, so we can teach him those separately."

"Okay. How?"

"CARD has a drill." She traces down the paper with a thin perfect nail. "In basic concepts, he went from fiftieth percentile to sixty-third. He's right in the middle of the pack, so there's nothing to worry about there."

I don't know what basic concepts are, but it sounds good to me.

"Sentence structure. He went up, from ninth to twenty-fifth, although this is still a weak area. He needs to improve his interrogatives and create more complex sentences."

"I've been trying to get him to ask more questions. He certainly has no problem doing it when he wants," I tell her.

Recalling sentences in context is next. "What's that?" I ask.

"That's where he can select the right sentences to give back to you. If I read him a story, then ask, 'What did the mother say?' he can tell me without narrating the entire story back to me, as he used to do."

"So how did he do in January?"

"I couldn't even test him. He probably knew the answers, of course, but he couldn't do it. He would just repeat the whole thing back to me."

"Oh. So he was at zero," I say.

"Well, he couldn't be tested. Now he's at something high"— she looks down the paper again—"the seventy-fifth percentile."

Formulating labels, a vocabulary activity, was a troublesome spot. He was at the sixty-third percentile in January, but he fell down to the thirty-seventh.

"Why is that?" I wonder. "He seems to have a great memory for words."

"Well, he needs more vocabulary in his drills. We'll add the CARD drill for vocabulary and that will take care of that. Also, the test might have covered some subjects he hasn't been exposed to yet. Plus, they assume that kids between the ages of three and three and a half get a large number of new words in that time. He did get more, but not as many as he might have."

With his love of words, his excellent aural memory, I thought he would have done better in that area. I'd have to step up the field trips, expose him to more things.

"But in word structure, he went from the ninth percentile in January to the ninety-fifth."

"Ninety-five?" I asked. "Of all kids? Regular kids?"

"Yes," she says, nodding with a smile. "Quite a leap. He did very well."

Hearing these numbers is as unexpected as a butterfly coming through the window and alighting on my head. It is a birthday present, Christmas Eve, and last night's fireworks all rolled up in one.

"On the whole," Melanie is saying, "everything we've done has worked very well. Now we need to address the areas of weakness and just keep him moving."

"Okay," I say. "Will you let Hank know, or shall I?"

"I'll call him. He can have the new drills in by next clinic."

As Melanie leaves the house, the phone rings. On the line is another autism mother. I tell her the test results, and she says the R-word (recovery) and sounds very excited. I've been given a basketful of riches by my son, who has worked so hard for his words, who must plumb unimagined depths for his questions. Nearly a year ago, dreams like this went away. Now, I hardly know what to do.

I call Jack and he's thrilled. He asks for the test scores, so he can write a letter to his brothers, their usual method for sharing important news.

I go out to the schoolroom and peek at Jonah, who's playing on the computer with our babysitter, Mayra. When he smiles at me, I pick up his boyish body, his long legs dangling, and squeeze him tight against my chest. "You did so well on the test, my boy!" I say. "I'm so proud of you. You sat still, you did good listening, and you did great!"

"I did good listening with Melanie," he says, looking a bit bewildered but proud.

"Yes, you did! Now you get to have a snack and play! Come in the kitchen with me."

He puts his hands on my hips and says, "Mommy, do the conga line."

We form a parade. "Boom-boom, boom-boom, boom-HEY! Boom-boom, boom-boom, boom-HEY!" I sing, swaying my hips from side to side on each boom, thrusting them on "HEY!" Jonah laughs and steps along, tripping on my heels and shouting "HEY!" on the high notes.

---

Jonah races into the kitchen, followed by Serena, his preschool "shadow."

"He really didn't want to work today. He resisted me quite a bit," she says. "Temper, and he threw a toy once. The usual tricks, but it was really noticeable today. He isn't often like that with me."

"I am afraid it's the resistance to therapy I've been anticipating," I say. "I'll bring it up with Hank. I worried about it before, but he told me it was too soon in the program. But now . . ."

"Yep. Mr. Smart-Pants here is starting to figure us out," she says.

"I want some juice and water, Mommy. Can I get it?"

I look at Jonah. He has opened the refrigerator, gotten out some sliced cucumbers, and a heavy glass bottle of juice. He set the plate of cucumbers on the floor, and is filling his cup to overflowing. I jump for the bottle and set it on the counter. "I'll get it for you, just a minute."

Serena winks. "I'll see you Monday," she says. "Bye, Jonah."

"Bye, Serena," he says, hovering over the juice. I sit with Jonah, nibbling some pita bread as I try to converse with him and make eye contact.

"What are you eating, Jonah?" I watch his cheeks expand and listen to the cucumbers crumble under his teeth.

"I'm eating cucumbers," he says. It's a food he discovered himself, and it's gf/cf.

"How do they taste?"

"They taste . . . cold," he says thoughtfully.

"Okay. What meal are we eating?"

"We're eating lunch," he says.

"That's right. Lunch is the meal we eat in the middle of the day. Breakfast is what we eat when we get up in the morning."

"We eat dinner at the nighttime," he says.

"Yes, we do."

"I want to light a candle. Mommy, can you light that candle?" he asks, pointing to the candlesticks.

"How about we save it for dinner."

"Okay." He crunches his cucumbers masterfully and looks at me. "That made a funny noise!" he says, laughing. I admire the way his blue eyes stay on mine.

---

The jewel of summer, the county fair, is here. My fair was the Prince William County Fair, in the heart of Northern Virginia countryside, past the battlefields, near farms and rural houses. My sisters won several awards in cookie baking and crafts; I won honorable mention in flower arranging. Twice before I'd taken Jonah to our local county fair. The first time, when he was not yet two, the jerky child's train seemed to unnerve him. Our last visit was barely two weeks before the diagnosis.

Today is a perfect opening day, breezy, sunny. We eat brisket at the chuck wagon station, but Jonah tires of Jack and me and slides cozily up the picnic table bench to a girl around his age, smiling at her mother's surprised face.

"How old are you?" the woman asks. An Asian inflection blurs her English words. "Fine," he replies.

"How old are you?" she asks, trying again.

"I'm fine," he says.

"He thinks you're asking how he is. Jonah, tell her how *old* you are," I tell him.

"I'm three years old," he says after a long pause. I wonder if she catches his delay, but I know I'm on guard for a less-than-perfect response. I need to relax.

"I want to ride the Ferris wheel. Mommy, can I ride the Ferris wheel?"

"If Daddy says so. Ask him."

"Daddy, can I ride the Ferris wheel?"

"Okay, Jonah. You can ride the Ferris wheel."

We thread through the crowded midway. The carneys, dressed in new uniforms but with too many cigarettes and towns in their voices, call to us. "Hey, Mommy, guarantee you a prize! Hey, there, family, get lucky, lucky, lucky!"

The sign says it's the largest transportable Ferris wheel in the United States. I'm okay when flying on commercial airlines and helicopters, but I hate open-cockpit planes, hang gliders, and parasails. There's something unnerving about being suspended in open air. I decide to let the boys go on alone.

As I wait, I watch the human carnival too, all the social strata on public display. Women of every age squeezed into tube tops and shorts, men breezing by with beer guts flying from opened shirts like the expansive prows of ships, teens with glittery faces and shaved heads. Children of all shapes, sizes, and colors display typical fair behaviors: running away, whining, tantruming, pulling their parents' hands to distraction. All things that Jonah does at home on a regular basis. I've seen two children with Down syndrome. A boy in a very complex wheelchair passes me, pushed by his sister. Earlier, I'd spotted a repaired cleft palate on a brown-eyed girl of six. Any autism-spectrum kids are either invisible or not here. It's a very stimulating environment. Many parents would risk disaster by bringing their autistic children here.

Back over at the Ferris wheel, I can see my guys briefly in the window of car number twenty-three, slowly rising high above the fair. They can't see me, but they can see the tiny crawling threads of humanity below, the juncture of heaven and sky above.

It must be a very good view.

# 25

## Wine for Breakfast

*Creating More Days Like Today*

After three weeks on the antiviral drug, Jonah's gaining ground. His language and interaction are at full throttle.

"Hi, Mommy. I am drinking dark wine."

It is breakfast time, and he is standing in the corner by the kitchen table drinking imaginary wine. "Oh, what does it taste like?" I ask him. He thinks. "It tastes dark. Sour." He drinks again. "Mommy, do you want some white wine?"

"Okay."

"Here is your white wine." He pours it into my hand. I raise it to my lips and make sipping noises.

"Do you like it?" he asks.

"Yes, it's very good. Thank you for offering it to me. Honey, it's time for breakfast." I get out some corn-bran cereal and pour some watered-down rice milk on it. We're out of

DariFree, the potato milk. I set it before him at the table. He begins eating his cereal, brown squares drenched in the thin rice milk. I feel so proud and sad for him, eating all these things without a big fight. Yesterday, I'd made him quinoa pasta for lunch, with turkey meatballs. At first he wouldn't eat the pasta, a rough yellow grain fashioned into spaghetti. But after he'd eaten the meatballs and stirred the pasta, narrating how he was stirring it the whole time, he ate the entire tomato-sauced pile.

He dances from his chair at the table. "I want to get dressed. I want to wear my black shirt! Mommy, where's my black shirt?" He'd been requesting black shirts for a month so Jack had gotten him two. "Black is my favorite color," he'd been telling us. Serena is subbing for another therapist today and she's due for the morning shift in five minutes. "Run and brush your teeth and hair, and I'll get the black shirt for you," I tell him.

He runs off to his bedroom.

I put away the food and follow. At the sink, he's dangling a large clot of shimmery blue toothpaste over his toothbrush. Water runs in a seductive stream, pink under the red overhead warming lights. He's naked and happy.

"Okay, I have to brush your teeth, since you didn't do it by yourself."

"I want my chance back," he says.

"No."

I assault Jonah's perfect little child-star teeth with the brush, trying to be tender in the hollows of his mouth. He's surprisingly tolerant.

"Go and take your old clothes off, put on clean underwear and shorts. Then—you can wear this!" I open a drawer.

"My black shirt!" he says.

He does it with unusual focus and speed, eyeing the black shirt to make sure it doesn't go away. His narrow little body stands knees-together as he puts on new dinosaur underwear. He pulls his gray shorts over his belly, their elastic waistband half-rolled.

"Now I can have my shirt!" he says. He wrestles it eagerly over his head.

"Good job," I say, although I hate saying this, since the therapists, Melanie, Hank, preschool teachers, Jack, and I all say it. Sometimes it's said in practiced professional tones, usually with real enthusiasm, but there's no way around it, it's the number one phrase you'll hear in a house with an ABA program.

"Now, I need . . . a hat," he says. He rejects the pile of hats I point to. "Where's that hat?" he murmurs, then finds his favorite blue one in the corner.

"I can wear these sandals. They won't hurt my feet." He pulls out a pair of size-seven Nike black sandals, although he wears nearly an eleven, because he loves the damn things. He manages to fit his feet into them, his toes edging over the sole.

"Now, I'm ready," he says.

Serena rings the bell. They greet each other with hand slaps, a joyful shorthand.

"Mom, come in with me. Stay here. Play this game with me," he begs, pulling me into the schoolroom.

"Baby, I have to go get ready. Today is a big day. After Serena, we're going to the gym, then to Hank's office. So I'll see you in a minute."

"Tell Mom, 'See ya later!'" says Serena.

"Okay, Mom, see ya later." He turns to the Don't Break the Ice game, willingly trading me for the opportunity to assemble plastic cubes tightly within a frame—and to beat Serena.

I've got an hour and a half before our road trip to occupational therapy. After OT, we'll eat lunch together, then I'll get him to nap. I'll get him up, drive to clinic, spend two hours with the team, then take him home for dinner. All with the goal of creating more days like today, when we had pretend wine at breakfast.

# 26

## Movie of the Week

### *Missing*

Greta and I spend an August afternoon standing respectfully by a pool at the house of local Republicans, listening to our congressman. We want to lobby him for autism causes, tell him how many families there are in his district now. After delivering his speech, he moves into the packed living room. When we finally reach him, I tell him I once did congressional liaison work with the Hill (something I mention for credibility) then give him my quick briefing. Greta also presents her statistically razor-sharp statement. We talk to him for about two minutes each, after which he says a colleague has two kids recently diagnosed as autistic, and that he's "been going through it with him."

His staffer takes our materials, and they promise to get back to me. I head for home, my mission accomplished.

When I pull in the driveway wearing my cocktail dress and heels, Jack's standing out front. "He's gone," he says. "Jonah's gone."

"What do you mean, he's gone?"

"I was inside and he was jumping on the trampoline, then I looked away from him for just a minute or two, and then he was gone. I was sitting on a chair in the living room watching him. I could see him through the glass doors."

"I'll go search inside. You go look for him in your car. And call the police!"

Inside, the house is cool and quiet. Jonah is not inside the house.

I am out on the sidewalk again when Jack drives up. A neighbor I don't know is behind him in a red Jeep. "I didn't find anything," Jack calls. "I'll keep looking."

"Did you call the police?"

"No."

"How long has he been gone?" I ask.

"Twenty minutes."

"Twenty minutes!" I exclaim angrily. "Call the police! Wait, *I'll* do it." I reach for his cell phone.

He hands it to me and drives off. I call 911 and report Jonah missing.

"Here," the neighbor says, "take my car and drive around, while I get some other people to help."

In a borrowed vehicle, I drive down the hill and make the gentle right turn below our yard, beneath Jonah's trampoline and plastic cabin. Sharp images of swimming pools and cars whizzing by faster than legal speed crowd into my mind. My foot eases up and the Jeep stops in the street. I have no idea where to look. My small child is lost with heavy cars careening around like tanks, dangerous pools calling to him with a gentle shimmer. *Where do I look?*

I turn the vehicle around and go back to my house, to wait.

Two men come to the door in camouflage uniforms, carrying assault rifles. "How old is the child, ma'am? His approximate weight and height? What type and color of clothing was he wearing? Do you have a recent photo?"

I run to my office for a preschool photo. Their radios crackle, and they leave. I'm alone in the backyard, scanning the yards beside me, in case he decides to reappear. Then a large black helicopter comes into view in the air above my roof. It hovers, then circles, and I know it's looking for Jonah.

I clutch my bare arms even though it's hot, and with full clarity I know this is really happening, the thing all mothers dread. I thought waiting for a missing child to be located would be like the suspended reality of a film, a bad dream, or a mental breakdown. But it isn't. It is totally clear, as measured as breathing, as washing dishes, and terribly non-negotiable.

It's a movie of the week, only it's not a movie.

One policeman returns to ask more questions, then Jack comes back without our son, and as he talks to the cop I step outside. The streets are filled with kids and parents, all searching for Jonah. More time goes by, and I watch the helicopter buzzing over the neighborhood. I think, *If a man in a car took him, maybe the chopper could catch him? If we knew what vehicle it was, before the car sped away on the freeway . . .* Could he have gotten into the nearby bay? He could easily have done so. And swimming pools and cars really worry me. Could this last all night? A month? Forever?

The preciseness of minutes is extreme. It's been three-quarters of an hour.

The policeman is preparing to leave when Max, a white-haired retiree from up the street, leads Jonah into the living room. I snatch up Jonah and hold him tight to my body. He is unconcerned, happy to get hugged.

"He was walking along the sidewalk, happy as you please," says Max in a husky, worried voice. "I couldn't believe it. I knew where you guys live, so I brought the little fella home."

Jack strokes Jonah's head, his own silently bent over it, his eyes closed. I can't let Jonah go, and I question him, for the sake of the policeman and to engrave this learning experience, because it's clear he has no idea what he did.

"Why did you go off like that, leave the house? You can't do that. No leaving the house without Mom or Dad! Ever!" I turn to the policeman. "Tell him," I say. "Sometimes it sinks in better coming from someone else."

He tells Jonah, do not leave the house, it's not okay, and adds some other safety rules.

"Okay," says Jonah. The policeman gives him a gold badge sticker.

We're all too alarmed to be relieved yet. Jack and I say our thanks, and the policeman and Max leave. After a few minutes, we settle Jonah in his bedroom and talk it out.

"I told you to call 911, and you didn't," I said. "Why not? It had already been twenty minutes."

"I didn't think I should call right away!"

"You can't sit inside, you have to be out there with him! Or by the kitchen window, so you can see the whole backyard. That's what I always do." I pause. "But I know you thought it was okay, so I don't want to rub it in."

Jack shakes his head. "He moves so fast. I only looked away for a minute."

We don't say much more; we both realize the symmetry of the incident. It's true that I'm more attuned to the tempo of Jonah's movements and attention span, the length of time he can play before creating mischief, but Jack is a loving, capable father. And I am not immune—it could have happened to me too.

My support-group friend is alarmed; "auttie-parents" have heard that autistic kids are far more prone to elope, as it's called, than NT, or neurotypical, kids. She urges me to poll friends and neighbors, to see what they would do. One neighbor's son, a regular kid of four, was missing for twenty-five minutes, but she never called police, just found him at a neighboring house. Some people say they would wait, while some would call 911 right away. It's a matter of great variability, which makes me realize Jack's delay was in fact the norm. My friend asks me to speak about child safety at her autism meeting. I do, and the autism parents take the incident seriously; many make safety plans for their own children.

I get an estimate on building a higher fence, and it's ten thousand dollars.

I never hear back from the congressman.

# 27

# In the Woods

*Anxiety*

We had a long clinic meeting with all the therapists today, followed by a special meeting with Hank. He's concerned that Jonah is now fighting for control at every turn.

I'd noticed he seemed to deliberately ignore or delay any requests I gave him lately. "Put on your shoes" would be met with a turned-up head, a saunter to another part of the room, or a dragging slowness in putting them on. "Get in the car" meant he would trail me slowly or run into another room. If I got mad at him, he'd shrug it off and find another piece of mischief, or get angry and hit his hand against a table.

And we've noticed his anxiety's up too. In the bad old days, he didn't seem to understand talk about his biting, like "You hurt Mommy." Now his empathy has emerged terrifically, but when I bang my knee, or look perturbed, Jonah says, "Mommy's sad. I don't want Mommy to be sad. I want Mommy to be happy." Then he starts crying, and it can spiral from there.

Hank reports that Jonah simply doesn't want to work the way he used to; the obliging, excited little boy of the first six months is gone. Now he tunes out, rolls on the floor, blows spit bubbles, talks silly, or simply refuses to look at the therapists. They're getting discouraged and we're losing therapeutic ground.

Hank goes over the language results from Melanie's recent test. "He's moving through the program so fast, and he could go even faster if we could get rid of these behaviors. I showed his language results to another clinical supervisor. He was impressed—you just don't often see this kind of thing. In linguistic concepts, he went from the first percentile to the eighty-fourth, and in word structure, the eighth to the ninety-fifth? Whew."

I smile a bit but I'm in no mood for rejoicing.

"So, he is extremely bright," says Hank. "And my goal is, I want to work myself out of a job. I can do that and I won't settle for anything less. And I don't want the therapists to either."

"So, despite any neurological damage or whatever there is, you think this shows he still has the framework for complete intellectual functioning?" Jack asks.

"Oh, yeah," Hank says.

"Do you *really* think he is extremely bright, or are you just saying that? I want the truth, not a sop to our feelings," I say.

"There's no question about it. The problem is he wants to stay ahead of everybody. Doesn't want to go along with what we want. He has to have things his way all the time and he's darn good at gettin' it."

We sigh.

"His anxiety and compulsiveness are up," Hank says. "He gets so anxious about maintaining control, or what's going to happen, he can't relax and focus. I remember you said there was some of that in your family."

"A bit here and there. I know it's partly hereditary," I say.

"There isn't a branch of the family tree she can't point at for something that might be hereditary," Jack says.

I look at him. "Well, your mother is gone, so all your history remains a secret."

Both of our families contain enough material to go around, but in truth there's really nothing remarkable at all. No history of disorders, no mental illness. This diagnosis is like a metal detector, beeping on harmless bits of trash that appear more tantalizing when underground.

"I would like you to consider putting him on Luvox," Hank says decisively. "It's a medicine approved for use in children by the FDA. I think it could take the edge off his anxiety, calm him down, and let him get to his thought processes. It could really open him up to learning."

"Isn't it better to hold off on medicines so he can learn to get his behaviors under control himself, without drugs?" I ask. "Then use them later if we have to?"

"Many parents prefer to do that. But if you wait until he's six, say, and he's standing in line at school, and he's anxious about getting to the head of the line, and he gets nervous, he could start hitting kids around him. I have a kid like that. They waited to do the medication, and now he's got those behaviors ingrained. So it's a lot tougher."

I imagine a larger Jonah standing in a cafeteria line, hitting kids, getting expelled, the subject of chilly phone calls from school.

"We'll look into it," Jack says.

Hank lists more things for me to do. Be available at the beginning of every session to inform the therapist how Jonah is doing, what his mood is, how he slept, and what the previous therapist encountered. Wrap up with her at the end of the session, going over each problem and behavior. At four sessions a day, this makes eight meetings at probably fifteen minutes apiece.

This doesn't include "generalizing," the twenty minutes I spend each session exchanging talk, play, and drills with Jonah and the therapist.

It doesn't count the fifteen to twenty minutes I work with him twice a week at the beginning of Melanie's sessions, so she and Fran can confer. Or the half hour once a week Melanie and I work together, or the fifteen minutes I spend every session so I can learn the latest techniques and teach them to Jack at night.

It certainly doesn't count occupational therapy, which involves a half-hour drive each way once a week to a specialized gym. It doesn't count the shopping for food, the reading of autism books, the hours on the phone exchanging information, the Internet searches, the sorting of bills from the therapists, the Regional Center paperwork.

I'm going to go crazy.

"I already do what you're suggesting, about two-thirds to three-fourths of the time," I tell Hank. "Jack has to work six days a week. I hired a part-time sitter so I could go to the grocery store, to the doctor, to get a haircut. I won't miss anything within reason when I'm home, but I must be able to leave the house sometimes!"

"It's mainly Fran, the lead therapist, I want you to be available for," Hank says, backing off.

"What time does she leave?" asks Jack. "Maybe I could come home early?"

"At five fifteen on Tuesdays. You can't be home that early, honey," I say.

"Maybe I can."

*Ten months* of ringing doorbells, hour after hour, day after day. I can't let them dictate my life more than they already have. "If I need to be gone on a Tuesday for some reason, I'm going to do it," I say defiantly. Then I feel guilty and add, "Of course, I'll try not to."

With this schedule, I'll rarely have more than an hour free at a time. Not enough time to go to the grocery store and post office without running back home. Not enough time to work out, straighten our bedroom, take a shower. Not enough time to have a train of thought.

"I'm sorry," says Hank. "But this is what has to happen right now."

"I will do everything I can to support this program," I reply. "Our whole lives revolve around it."

Hank nods.

"But I have to maintain some kind of life for myself."

I don't care how I sound. Sometimes I need to go to the bathroom without a knock on the door, chew my food without a therapist in my face, take a shower without pulling my clothes on as the clock runs out. But I am nothing and everything in this process. As mother to a child who assumes primacy, as he must, I'm the crucial wheel in a giant set of cogs.

The meeting continues—about our upcoming IEP in the fall, school district contracts, and more. Hank has an answer for everything. If you are a highly skilled human behavioral professional, with thousands of people besieging your door, you usually know what to say.

We step out of Hank's office, his words swirling about our heads. It's already six P.M., two hours after clinic's typical end. But there's still a therapist on the clock. "Can you take the therapist across the street with you to the mall?" I ask Jack. "So she can do some generalization with Jonah for the last half hour?"

Jack looks as if he doesn't understand. I realize he doesn't.

"Generalization, Jack. Like when I take him around other people so he can apply what he's learned to the larger world."

"Okay. See ya later." He kisses me.

I walk down the stairs, to drive home. I watch Jonah leap into Jack's arms. I blow him a kiss. "Bye, beautiful. I'll see you tonight!"

"And it will be your turn to put me to bed," he says.

The evening sun is bright and heavy with warmth, but I can only think of the long road ahead for my family. *He's going to make it,* I tell myself. His shining personality, the will and curiosity that have dragged him from autism's worst thickets, sustain me. I think of the autism autobiographies I've read. Their authors hit, kicked, and screamed, they bit or flapped, they spit or avoided their way through years of school. They were oppositional too, often defying people who made them do things they found inexplicable or unacceptable. They had curiosity, will, intelligence, original thought. And they made it.

*If they can make it,* I tell myself for the hundredth time, *Jonah will too.*

---

At the end of the week, we go to our small mountain cabin. After we arrive, I open the refrigerator door. A foul smell rushes out and I see a mold Garden of Eden.

A can of cookie dough has exploded and ribbons of green droop through the grates of the shelves. Breads, cheeses, and juices are fecund with mold in the sealed heat. Snakes of mold writhe up the refrigerator walls. Even the mustard and pickle containers are coated with black and green. The smell is unbelievable.

I shut the door. "Jack, you won't believe this," I say.

"What?" He comes over.

"Stand back before you open it."

He pulls open the door and his face contorts. "I guess the electricity went off." He prepares to open the freezer.

"Wait, let me get Jonah out of the way." I set him up with a book on the couch.

When I come back, Jack swings the freezer door open. It's even worse than the lower half. The vanilla and chocolate ripple ice cream has outgrown its container, and a spore-filled river flows from it. The frozen waffles have sprouted bushes. Mold whips its long hair across the freezer with wild, lush abandon.

My heart sinks. "Do you think we had a power shortage?" I ask. I turn on the lights. Everything works except the refrigerator.

"Either that, or the thing quit working. I'll take a look at it."

The room is becoming unbearable, probably what a dead body would smell like.

"You'd better get Jonah out of here," Jack says. "This can't be good for him."

We agree that Jonah and I will head into town and get new groceries, and Jack will begin the cleanup. I don't want him to have to do it alone, but I can't let this murk penetrate into Jonah's tender little body. "Let me put this fan on you," I say, and set the portable fan toward Jack. Then Jonah and I head out.

In the town's grocery store, I shop in the bread aisle. After a distracted second I look up and see a toddler go by, clinging to the front of a woman's cart. It is Jonah. "I guess I've seen it all now," I say.

The woman smiles at me. "He moves really fast, doesn't he?" she says. "That's okay. He's having a good time."

In the checkout aisle, he twists away from me, crouching under people to get to the candy display. "I got a lizard!" he shouts.

Heads turn in line.

"Here lizard, eat the candy." He holds a candy bar up and makes eating noises at the plastic lizard's mouth. His eyes catch mine. I know he's feeding the lizard candy so he can consume it vicariously.

I sign the credit card slip, then look back to see him prone on the grocery store floor. "Here is the lizard," he narrates. "He is swimming across the ocean."

"Jonah, come here," I command. He eyes me, puts the lizard back, and comes toward me. "Put your hands right here on the counter and wait for me."

As we exit the store, he enters a revolving turnstile the wrong way, meeting a swinging bar that traps him. He keeps pushing, but remains stuck.

"Go under," I tell him.

He looks at me with big concentrated eyes.

"Hey, little man, go under the bar," says a voice. "Put your head down and come out." It's a man of about thirty-five, a case of beer under his arm.

His coaching confuses Jonah, but I can tell he finds his words interesting.

"Put your head down. Go under the bar," the stranger says.

Jonah lowers his head slowly. With a careful duck, he emerges. He comes to my side and points. "Mommy, what is that?"

"It's a revolving turnstile," I tell him. "It goes around, and you got stuck."

"I got out!" he says.

The stranger smiles and is gone.

Back at the cabin, Jack has cleaned nearly the entire refrigerator. "Wow. Are you still alive? I brought you some food," I say.

"I'll wait. I haven't had my head out of there long enough to have an appetite."

"Does the reeking thing still work?" I ask.

"Yes, it does." It was already turning cold again. "There's a little button on the front where you can turn the power off and on. Somebody turned the switch off," he says.

"Who would have done that? Come in just to turn off the refrigerator?"

Jack's eyes narrow and he smiles. "I know who did it."

"Who?"

"Who do you think? He was fooling with the buttons last time. I bet he reached right in there and turned it off before we left."

The little rat! I knew he loved the cabin's dishwasher, and the sink, and the stove. We'd had to remove an oven control knob—he'd turned it once as we left for the day and we returned to a gas-filled house. But I didn't know about the refrigerator.

"Had to be him," says Jack. "No doubt about it."

---

Jonah and I go for a walk while Jack rests. "I'm hiking," Jonah calls, padding down the road in his sock feet. "Mommy, hike with me!"

I run down the road, and convince him to turn around before he reaches a mean dog's house. "What's that?" he asks. He's pointing to a dark impression in the ground, stuffed with browned pine needles. "It's an animal hole," I say. "An animal lives there."

"What's that?" he asks, pointing to a blackened hole in a split tree trunk.

"I think that's an owl hole," I say. "Where baby owls live."

He cranes his neck toward the hole. "I don't like that!"

"Why not? I like it."

"I don't like that. I don't want to be there."

"Hey, Jonah, I want to be there. I like to pretend I'm a baby animal and I can curl up warm and cozy in the little hole, all safe."

"I don't want to go there," he says decisively. "That's not good."

As a girl, I'd spent days in the woods. I carved my initials in trees like Daniel Boone, over miles of Virginia forest, watching white green curls of birch and tough chunks of pine fall away under my pearl-handled knife. I gathered lady's slipper plants for replanting, their delicate silken pouches like a shoe to fit a fairy's foot. In the woods, I never felt lonely, just part of the open-skied world. So Jonah's animal-hole distaste was not going to stop me from teaching him to love nature.

"Look, there's a squirrel. What does he eat?"

"Squirrels eat peanuts," he says lazily.

"But do you know where a squirrel lives?"

"In the trees," he says.

I point to the high branch of a tree. "Would you like to climb up there?"

"Yes," he says. "I want to go up in the trees. I can live in the sky!"

"If you get bigger and you're not worried about animal holes, you can go up there like an animal. You can climb and eat nuts all day."

He points again. "Mommy, what's that?"

It's the tip of a drainage pipe, peeking blackly from a heap of pine needles. An adult could never spot such a thing, but he's managed to find an old friend in all this nature. "You found a pipe, Jonah. Are you happy?"

"Yes, I'm happy. I like that pipe."

"Do you like trees too? And sky?"

"Yes." He walks uphill, past the cabin. "Mommy, what's that?" he cries. It hits me that he's entering the verbally inquisitive stage he missed. Jonah, who couldn't ask a question until diet, medication, and therapy entered his life, is now standing on the steps of a neighbor's cabin asking, "Where are we?" The dry leaves skitter around us from the slight breeze.

His young brain is expanding like a lucent cloud.

Jonah asks and points and makes notes to himself all the way back to the cabin. In the warm bathroom, he takes off his road-dirty socks to wash his feet. I reach for the water faucet, but he stops me with, "I will do it."

"Oh, that's too cold," he says. "We need some hot." After he's adjusted the temperature, he sighs happily. The water is running down the drain but his bare feet are still on the blue rug. "I love this," he says.

"What, honey? What do you love?"

"The drain."

"Why do you love the drain?" I ask, wondering if this is the magical day when I find out why he loves pipes and drains.

He pauses. "Because it's good."

I watch the smooth clear tunnel of water run into the sink. It is wet and somehow pleasing. I cannot argue with him. Entire continents have been settled by the efficient construction of drains, pipes, and water systems. Civilizations have fallen to disease due to their lack. How can I quantify their value?

"Put your feet on top of that good drain, buddy," I say. "Show me how you can scrub those feet clean."

"Mommy, I need some help. Lift me up," he says. I hoist him atop the small vanity and plop his dirt-striped feet into the sink.

"I love you," I tell him.

"I love you, Mommy," he says absentmindedly.

He lifts his feet up and watches the water run into the drain beneath them.

# 28

# A Real Boy

*Let Jonah Be Jonah*

The last meeting with Hank had upset me. The next day, I'd located a psychologist, Dr. Kyle Pontius, who runs an Asperger's syndrome support group; now, after a long drive, Jonah, one of our therapists, and I climb the stairs to his office.

Dr. Pontius enters the waiting room. He is a tall, gentle man with a beard. We greet one another. "This is my son, Jonah," I say. He turns to Jonah, on the couch with the therapist and a pile of library books. "Hello, Jonah," he says.

"Hi," says Jonah. He makes good eye contact, then eyes the doctor's imposing build and beard, so different from that of his lean, clean-shaven father.

I fill out a form, then enter his private office as Jonah and his therapist wait outside.

"So, you're here for issues involving your son's treatment program," he says.

"Yes, I am." I tell him about the CARD program, its forty-hour structure, the success we've had so far. How we've hit a road of resistance, and of the resulting recommendation of Luvox. I tell him everything about Jonah, about his insatiable energy and curiosity, how I must constantly keep him from making big messes or doing dangerous things. I detail his rising anxiety about me, how he says, "I want Mommy to be happy" when he's done something wrong and I look at him sternly. How he's begun to drag his feet at any order, to fight the therapists who make him sit in his chair where once he loved to sit.

I wonder if all my autism talk has overwhelmed him.

"Do you understand what I'm describing?" I ask.

"I have an autistic son. He's thirteen. I have a great deal of familiarity with the spectrum." I've found that most professional people involved with autism have some personal interest. That's why they're able to transcend the outdated paragraphs in the medical school textbooks that say, "Autism is a severe lifelong disorder with no cure or treatment," and look for solutions.

"How's he doing?" I ask.

"Well, we never did the whole behavioral therapy thing. But he's had ten years of speech therapy and now he gets social skills training. His speech is almost normal."

"Is he mainstreamed in school?"

"Yes. He's in the gifted and talented program. He's great at math. The teachers wish they had a room full of kids like him."

"That's great," I say.

"Anyway, back to Jonah. First of all, I want to tell you that with the remarkable progress he's made at such a young age, he is not going to be affected to a great degree."

"He's three, almost four," I say, leaning forward.

"Certainly, there will always be quirks, or an issue to deal with, but from the sound of it, nothing in his future will interfere with his functioning. Relationships, work, anything that one might expect in a man's life."

I sit back, relieved.

"As for his other behaviors, certainly we need to address those. Anxiety and oppositional behavior come when a child isn't getting his needs met. When that happens, you might see opposition or depression. Depression can make a child very hard to reach." He shakes his head and looks past me, as if reflecting. "In his case," he continues, "give him something to do with his skills and drive. If he likes mechanical things, give him some he can play with. If he wants to make messes, give him a place and time to really go to town. Let Jonah be Jonah. Then, you won't end up saying no so often, and his anxiety will decrease."

It is the sentence I have been looking for.

Let Jonah be Jonah.

"That's all I want," I tell him. "I *want* to respect his personality, let him be himself. I know we need the behavioral stuff, no question about it. But now that we've broken through, and taught him so much, he's past sitting in the chair and hearing *no* a lot. I want to make sure he's okay emotionally, as we start the higher social-type drills."

He sighs. "The behavioral stuff is powerful stuff. It works very well. But behaviorists don't concern themselves with the soul."

"They love him and have been very good to him. But no one really knows his depths like we do," I say. "I want to watch out for his little psyche."

"Behavior covers a lot," he agrees. "But this little corner is not really attended to."

"I can get him a sandbox. Then he can create castles and engineering structures in the backyard."

"How about an Erector set?" he says.

"He prefers real things to toys. But I'll get the metal kind, with nuts and bolts. He might like that."

I sit on the couch, thinking hard as he says, "Our time is up."

"Sorry," I say. "Whenever people talk about autism, they can go on forever."

"A behavioral program can cause great stress on the family. How is that going?" he asks. His eyes look gently into mine.

"Well, we've had it hard, in lots of ways."

It's so unusual for someone to ask about us, the people we used to be, that I'm embarrassed. Part of me is grateful that someone is concerned about me. It makes me want to cry, extend the session cost-be-damned and let it all out. But my other, more instinctive half is afraid to let it show. Maybe he'll say, yes, that ABA stuff is too hard, and tell people not to do it, using me as an example. Or he'll make me pity myself, which is counterproductive. So I decide to cherish the tiny glow his question gives me and move on. "But I would pick the stress of a program over the stress of no program. So, anyway, messes, finger paints! A sandbox! I'll do it right away."

The Christina who took emotional help from strangers was softer than I, nicer, younger, and more naive. She's gone.

I go to a movie with a friend and get back around ten. "Jonah's still awake," says Jack from his big leather chair. "You could say hi to him if you want."

I touch Jack on the head as I pass him and go into Jonah's room.

"Hi, bug. Are you awake?"

"Yes," he says in the dark. I sit down, feeling for him under the yellow madras-trimmed sheet. He's sleeping in a shirt and underwear instead of pajamas, a clear sign that Dad put him to bed.

"What happened today?" I ask.

"I went to see Dr. Pontius. Barney went on Saturday."

He's talking about the big purple dinosaur Barney, who's become an alter ego over the last two days.

"I want to go see Dr. Goldberg."

"We won't see him for another month or so. You sure know a lot of doctors, don't you? Dr. Goldberg, Dr. Pontius."

"And Dr. Gupta," he adds.

We've never mentioned Gupta since our single visit months ago, during the Landau-Kleffner scare.

"Yes, Dr. Gupta. Can't forget him."

"He's a real doctor," Jonah says in the dark.

"Yes, he is."

"He's not a pretend doctor, he's real. Barney's a real purple dinosaur."

"Uh-huh."

"I'm not a pretend boy. I'm a real boy."

My hand lies lightly on his angled thigh. His skin is cool and underneath it the muscles are taut, strong.

"The closet is a real closet," he says. "You can go over and get toys out of it. A Busy Bee, books, an airplane."

"Yes, you can," I say.

"Mom, I'm not a pretend boy. I'm a real boy."

"You are the most real boy in the whole world," I say. "Now go to sleep, baby. Sleep well."

"Leave the door open just a little bit," he calls to me. "Just a little bit," he says, copying himself, a whisper in the dark. "Turn the air conditioning on," he adds.

I stand in the hall and listen as he weaves a story for himself. He will not be silent, will not surrender to a capricious, invisible realm.

He's a real boy, in the world at last.

————————

In the dark that night, I see many boys. The faraway look in their eyes speaks of molecules, rainbows, shiny spinning metal, bees that buzz in the flower gardens of their minds. In the pond of humanity, they swim with silent arms toward us, or float alone on their backs. Though they may not speak, they are also real. We can feel their vibrations, and find them before they disappear in the depths.

# 29

# Happy Anniversary

*One Year In*

Today is our one-year autism anniversary.

I'm exhausted, but I get Jonah ready for school. Jack drives him, and I stay home in my nightgown. Fortunately, the exhaustion isn't from trying to control an out-of-control kid, like it was a year ago. Like any suburban mom, I did too much yesterday and am dizzy and tired.

Jonah's afternoon pool party featured nine kids under the age of five. There were seven adults: three moms, two therapists, our sitter Mayra, and a neighborhood nanny. I thought that would be plenty of supervision; I even turned away a mom who offered to stay. Then suddenly the house was flooded with kids pulling at the pool fence, and waving fried chicken legs and juice boxes.

When they were changed into their swimsuits and hit the water, we all lined the pool like nervous hawks, counting and recounting wet heads to make sure none of them slipped from our sight. There was no time to eat, or have a cool drink. The adults gnawed at chicken legs, tracking heads, until the next child grabbed our legs, or cried, or spilled food on the patio, or stood in the ready-to-pee position and had to be rushed to a potty. Then the oldest boy shrieked, "Watch me!" from the deep end until his screams took us all hostage and forced us to look. When everyone left, Mayra, Jonah, and I collapsed with a video. Jonah was so tired he watched *Blue's Clues* two times, with a big sleepy grin on his face.

So it was a traditional, harried pool party.

Jonah talked to the adults, tussled over toys with the other kids, and generally had as nice or nicer manners than most of the children present. Jonah and I fit right in, except for the therapists on standby.

---

Jack and I have a phone consult with Dr. Goldberg this afternoon, the NIDS (neuro-immune dysfunction syndrome) specialist who is turning out to be the most helpful of all the doctors. I've sent him a list of nine questions. After those are answered, we report on how well the antiviral drug (along with the antifungal Diflucan) is working.

"If you put him in a group of typical three- and four-year-olds," Dr. Goldberg asks, "does he have the same bright alert look as they do? Or is he still spacey or zoney?"

I think of Jonah at preschool. The way he takes a moment to recognize me when I walk in, the way he seems not to be able to place me until he focuses his eyes and looks hard. Then I remember the pool party, the great way he observed and imitated the other boys' kid-calls and chest-thumping perfectly.

How he turned to a little girl and asked, "Do you want some watermelon?" as he held out a dripping, fresh-cut slice.

"Most of the time, he's pretty on. Sometimes he spaces out."

"The question I have is, are all the pieces there, or are we still missing some?" Dr. Goldberg asks in his staccato, pointed manner.

"I guess we're still missing a few."

"I'd like to check a few things I didn't last time." He rattles off a list of blood tests. We raise the fact that CARD wants us to consider putting Jonah on Luvox; then I tell him what Dr. Pontius said about meeting his needs.

"It is true that a child has to get his needs met. Especially for good development of the child's brain. But before we try anything like Luvox, I want to clear up his underlying medical issues. We might consider Kutapressin. He's borderline in age, so we might choose either that, to boost his immune system, or the right medication to bring him up to speed."

"What is Kutapressin?' Jack asks.

"It's a series of shots. A shot a day for a month, then maybe every other day for the next few weeks."

I gasp. "A shot a day for a month? There's no way."

"I could administer the shots," Jack says. "I used to shoot my father." When Jack's beloved father was diagnosed with diabetes at thirty-six, the doctor told him he might live another five years. He died at seventy-two, having gone on to father Jack and another son, largely due to the good care of Jack's mother and all six boys, who often carried snacks for their dad in their pockets, in case his sugar swung out of control.

"I can't imagine putting him through that," I say. "Monday, when we visited our local doctor for an ear infection, he started showing his first fear of the doctor's office."

"Well, if we went with a drug, it could be a shorter way to clean him up," says Goldberg. "But I would choose from these SSRIs: Paxil, Prozac, Zoloft, or Celexa."

"So you think it's an appropriate thing to do," I say.

He sighs, a small sigh I barely pick up. "It might help bring him up to where he needs to be. Let's run the tests, stay on current meds, and let me see him in a month. We'll take a look at it then. I would say we would look at Paxil as the most likely."

The call ends, and I load Jonah in the Jeep. We hum down the Friday afternoon freeway to the regular pediatrician's office.

Briefly, I raise the issue of anxiety medication. Although the doctor has no autism expertise, he's a good mainstream pediatrician and I want him to understand. I wait for him to frown at me, as he did when I told him about Nystatin months ago, but he doesn't. "I would recommend Zoloft instead of Paxil. It seems to have fewer side effects, and can be used for children over the age of two."

So far, I've asked three different professionals, and gotten three different answers.

"He's doing remarkably well, as always," says the doctor. "Whatever you're doing, keep it up."

# 30

# Reclamation

*Everybody Knew*

"Everybody there in France knew Jonah was autistic except you."

Jack's brothers Ross and Guy have come for dinner, bearing some new wines to share. As we sit around the table, talk turns to last year's trip to France, and Ross, a gentle, insightful man, makes this statement to me. Jack has alluded to the possibility, but no one's ever come out and said it. "We tried our best to get you to leave him alone with Jane so she could look at him," he continues.

I choke my unexpected anger with a sip of wine. "Oh, really?"

"Yes," he says. "You didn't want to let anyone watch him, though. All of us tried, but you—didn't think we could handle him."

"I didn't know who could," I say, thinking of the large unfenced pool, the high castle terraces from which he could have fallen, the many man-high fireplaces, the vast grounds, the rooms of delicate gilt furniture.

"I remember when Jane came in that day," Ross continues comfortably. "It was the most amazing thing. She hadn't even seen him yet, and she looked across the room and she knew."

"What do you mean?"

"She'd come to the door, saw him across the room, and told me right then, Jonah's autistic."

"What was he doing?" I ask, masking my frozen heart. "Was he hand-flapping, or anything like that?"

"I don't think so. It was instinctive."

He goes on to describe how well she handled the phone call a year ago, how proud he was of the mature way she handled it, how professional she was.

True, she had the straightforward manner of a good clinician.

I'm proud of Ross and Jane, and I love them for their concern, but I'm angry as I sit at the table, sick at being the last to know. I feel like a cheated wife.

But I'm glad they didn't tell us during the trip. I think I would have fallen apart right there in France. They probably would have had to bury my crumbled bones on the castle grounds, under the ancient arbors.

My emotions, unreasonable but painful, are under wraps by the time the last bottle is tasted. I set Jonah up in his little red chair by the fireplace and watch a video with him.

"I love you so much," I tell him, as the three brothers enjoy themselves around the table. "Do you love me?"

"Yes, Mommy. And the drain."

Some perverse impulse makes me test him. "Jonah, who do you love more, Mommy or the drain?" I wait for his answer in slow motion.

"I love Mommy more. Mommy loves the drain."

———————

"I've said it before, but I'll say it again," says Ross, preparing to leave. "The change in him is amazing. You've given him every bit of help and it shows."

"Some people say he is going to recover," I tell him.

Ross smiles. "I don't think recovery is the right word. I would use reclamation."

———————

It's Monday, and Anh had an appointment. I sent Mayra off on a church trip today, so it's just Jonah and me.

At two fifteen P.M. I rouse Jonah from his nap, place him before the television with a Barney video, and get ready for a phone consultation with a new doctor, a neuropsychiatrist, a species I didn't know existed. Neuropsychiatrists treat patients who may have organic or physical issues with the brain, and are familiar with emerging brain-mapping technologies and medications. This one is reputedly brilliant and has an autistic son as well. We want to speak to him about the decision to medicate or not.

Jack calls with the doctor on the line. He's quiet-voiced, asking softly about Jonah's background. I listen to Jack seek the exact words, his precise legal manner of word selection slowing as it moves into medical territory. The terse intensity of a three-way conversation with a new doctor makes me want to leap in and take control. I can rattle this background stuff off like my address and phone number, but I make myself listen.

"Very well," the doctor says. "At what age did he speak?"

"Early," says Jack. "Ten months."

"Nine," I say.

Jack brings up the language testing, and I tell him about Jonah's latest Barney stories.

"Are the plots from movies," he asks, "or his own?"

"His," I say. "From his experience, or from what he's seen."

"That's fantastic," the doctor says. "A wonderful indicator of his future."

We tell him about the defiance toward the therapists. We discuss his rising anxiety over little things, his gallery of quirks, like his occasional grimaces and his hyperactivity. We describe his love for all things mechanical, his incredible memory, his sociable nature and sometimes-wonderful manners.

He mentions three drugs in order of preference. An anti-seizure, an antipsychotic, and the only familiar one, Paxil. Jonah doesn't have seizures or psychosis, so these drugs would be "off-label" usage, prescribed for conditions they're not formally approved for. Off-label medication use is fairly common, but the first two sound too experimental to me, and I'm pleased to hear him mention Paxil. "Sounds like he is growing out of some aspects of the spectrum," he says. "He sounds wonderful."

"Oh, he is," I say.

# 31

# Sand and Flowers

I know things usually concealed under society's veneer. I know people who live quietly in war zones, people who walk around with hellish problems in their heads. I know a woman, talented, wealthy, established. She talked to me as if I was a priest, my telephone a confessional booth. She told me about the worst day of her life, something she never told anyone in the autism community.

Their son wasn't diagnosed until he was five, back when ABA therapy was largely confined to scattered ivory-tower clinics. He was a pale blond child, meek as a lamb. He could talk but his other skills were limited.

The family left their palatial home in search of a school district with some kind of program for him. She and her son and daughters got an apartment, while the father stayed in the city to work and sell their house. After a long time, they moved together into a home near mine. The father drove two hours to work, and came home at night.

Kids in the neighborhood became a part of her son's life. Some were okay, she said, but others were cruel. As her quiet, compliant little boy grew older, he became paranoid, telling her that people were looking at him and talking about him. Sometimes this was true. Often it wasn't, but the boy grew to hate going out in public.

One of the pleasures of the boy's life was his food. (There wasn't much special diet information then.) He loved to go to a burger joint up the street. The problem was, he had become quite demanding about visiting his burger joint or doing other things he wanted to do. At age eleven, his rising anxiety combined with teenage hormones and turned to violence. He began hitting and shoving and clawing when he didn't get his way. His two younger sisters became frightened of their brother. His father went to work with bloody scratches on his face. Fortunately, everyone there understood the problem.

For three years, the family tried everything. They hired a young man to live with them so he could control their son. They tried every combination of drugs and behavioral management techniques to get his impulses under control. They talked to him, reasoned with him, grappled with him. Nothing worked. Then came the week the boy's maternal grandmother was dying from cancer. The boy's mother had just been visiting her, and had come home, wrung dry of tears, exhausted beyond belief. When she entered, her son asked her to take him to the burger joint. All she did, she said, was sigh. A tired, exasperated sigh.

He flipped out and attacked her.

The father was home, and he and the mother tried to control

the boy. But he broke away and ran down the street, past the elaborate flower beds and iron gates. They jumped in the car to catch up with him. A few blocks away, they did. The father managed to wrestle him into the car but the boy was still wild and violent. They wanted to bring him home to calm him down, but the new neighbors next door were having a front-yard welcome party. Not wanting to cause a scene, they drove up the curving highway and pulled into a vacant parking lot.

There they tried with all their might to get the boy under control. The father was taking the brunt of it. Bleeding, his shirt torn, he had managed to get the boy to the ground when police pulled up. Someone had been watching from an unseen window and called the cops. The parents were glad to see the officers. "What's going on here?" one officer asked the father. The mother and father tried to explain. He's our son. He's autistic and gets violent. We brought him here to calm him down. The cops didn't seem to hear them. The mother pulled a psychiatrist's card from her wallet. Here, call him, she urged. He can verify our story. The cops didn't even look at the card. Instead, one stood guard over the boy, and the other put handcuffs on the father and led him to the squad car.

The mother couldn't believe what was happening. She tried to explain the situation over and over again. The officers interrogated her husband as her son sat in the car. They ran the father's identity through their computers. They ignored his explanations and treated him like a criminal. After a long time, one officer finally did as the parents had requested and asked the boy to tell them what happened. He said, "I attacked my dad." Eventually the father was released from the handcuffs, and came back to his wife and son. All this time, she told me, he had been so strong. So patient, so calm. He had always been the one who kept her going, who could deal with it all. When they finally took the cuffs off and let him go, he started crying.

It had broken him.

She said, "It was the lowest point of my life."

After that, they knew their son would have to go. Three years of round-the-clock effort had not wrought the changes they needed to keep him home. The Regional Center wanted to place him in ominous rundown hospitals, or group homes with shattered windows, but with the help of a lawyer, they got him into a wonderful school in Santa Barbara. Sure, it cost nine thousand dollars a month, but it was safe and there were other kids like him.

The first time the mother walked into a boy's room there, she was strangely surprised. The room felt amazingly familiar. She couldn't understand it at first. After all, she'd never been there. Then she noticed the posters on the walls, the special interests reflected there, the toys and trinkets of its occupant. It was the same as her son's room at home. She went through the other boy's rooms, and they all looked exactly the same.

By the time she left, she felt better. Although she never thought the day would come when she would leave her fourteen-year-old son somewhere and drive away, she told herself he would be happier there.

And he is. He and his friends wash the campus windows for a small wage, swim in the pool, and do schoolwork. They've adopted a section of highway in town, and they clean it with care and responsibility, a line of boys working all together. For the first time since he was a child, he feels good about his life. Therapy and medication have stopped his aggressive behavior. He has two jobs, in a hospital and a store. When he comes home for visits, he speaks of his work with pride and good sense. He may even live with roommates in the community someday, with someone to check on him daily.

The only thing wrong now, besides the two hundred miles of freeway between her and her son, is what people say. How could she do it, they say to her face and behind her back. We could never send our child away. What kind of woman is able to do that? She represents the thing they fear most. The hands of fate tearing a family apart. I have no right to judge you and neither does anyone else, I told her. You did the very best you could. None of us know what you went through. I will always remember your story.

Sometimes, on the rare occasions when I call her, she is gone. I do not ask the voices of the young girls who answer where she is. I can see her driving the bright sunny highway to Santa Barbara, heading to see her son. She arrives with a heart full of worry and leaves with an ache in her soul. But he's happy. She gives him life once again, as she leaves him behind in the land of sand and flowers.

# 32

## Special People

*Normal? Not Normal?*

Anh gives notice. She wants to become a speech therapist. She was our first therapist, with us since the beginning. I ask her if she'll keep working with autistic kids. "Probably," she says. "There are a lot of them in my life."

Serena, our "shadow," comes in, and I tell her about Anh.

"I hate to rain on your parade," she says, "but I'm leaving too. My graduate-school classes conflict with Jonah's schedule. I'm going to have to cut back on all my families. I'm so sorry."

A double blow, and they are such capable, top-notch people.

The news runs through our autism-mommy community like a flash flood. Many of us rely on these two, and must scramble for replacement therapists. I red-alert all my friends and they promise to keep me in mind. Wonderfully, I know they will.

I call Jack and tell him they're both leaving.

"Wow," he says, stunned. He absorbs it for a moment. "This is not your day, is it?" he says. "They're dropping like flies."

I tell him about the temper tantrum Jonah had today. He tried to bite me in the parking lot, then threw a crying fit when I refused to play his Barney music as punishment. I fear he got too hungry because I forgot to give him a midmorning snack, but that's a poor excuse for biting. "I'm ready to try the Paxil," I say. "At this rate, it's either him or me."

He laughs. "You operate the moving equipment, so I guess it's him."

"Seriously, after all the research, this makes me think we should do it."

"I'm convinced we should try it now too," he says.

"I didn't tell you about the second tantrum he had in the bathroom when we came home. I took his hat and water gun away so he would pee, and he pitched a fit. He threw himself down and tried to throw things. It scared me." I pause. "And he's been talking about driving in an RV all day. Ever since you guys took a trip in one, he's been talking about the RV this, and the RV that. For the last three days now, it's nonstop."

"Yes, I've noticed," he says. Now he pauses. "I think," he says, as if figuring out a legal problem, "it makes sense to try a reasonably known solution. Paxil has a known effect in a body of people who have tried it. Let's see if it will help."

"Today, I feel it's the right choice," I say. "As Jonah gets better, other behaviors are coming out and intensifying."

"So when do we start it?"

"I've only got two more doctors to talk to, and then I'll know for sure."

"And how many will that make total?" he asks teasingly.

"That will make . . . six, I guess. Plus four autism moms."

I hang up, accepting the brave new possibility that this kind of medication might help him. I'd never imagined giving an SSRI to my son.

———

Before I go to the drugstore to pick up the Paxil, I search the Web for information on anti-anxiety drugs. A long list of medications pops up. Names like Ativan, Dalmane, Halcion, Librium, Valium, and Xanax twinkle on the screen. The sites are largely fronts for drug companies, or natural herbs like St.-John's-wort. When I log onto a Paxil users' site in search of honesty, it contains questions like, "I'm Steven, a depressed seventeen-year-old about to start taking Paxil. Will it make me impotent?"

My world has narrowed so much I don't even have time to pity a poor teenager worried about his erection. I have a little boy whose needs change with every developmental surge, and I'm starting to realize that for the rest of his life, we will be worrying and watching over him. *Dumb,* I think. Did you believe if you hugged autism close enough to squeeze the life out of it, only the simple traumas of childhood would be your prize?

I don't live in the "normal" world anymore.

People use the word *special* to describe people with disabilities. But they ought to use it for their parents too. The loss of an envisioned child is pervasive; money, career, beauty, hobbies are no longer as desirable or absorbing when disability affects your child. We parents are twinned to our children, in love and struggle. An unhealthy connection, experts might say, but they are ignorant. Just let us try acting like "normal" parents and see if we truly can, if our friends, the schools, the doctors, really let us. *Medicate him, change him, change your life, change yourself, do what I say or you are out of here* . . . I sometimes want to tell them: I used to be like you. I did once live in the normal world.

As the early years of my sweet pea boy bend toward closure, I must examine him with a careful eye. I must decide if it's normal for him to watch a favorite video twice a day, or three times a day, or to wake up in the morning speaking lines from the video. *Every child does that,* regular people say, but they don't witness the peculiar intensity of our children. Is there room for a child like mine in the concept of "every child?" I don't know what normal is. Normal is a shore we see from our bouncing, battered dinghy in the harbor. Sometimes we pull up and play on the sand, but as soon as we spread a blanket, we get evicted. I feel as far from normal as you can get.

––––––

Paxil starts on a Sunday morning. Just a quarter of a ten-milligram tablet.

"He seems to be much calmer today, not so hyper," whispers Jack that evening.

"Let's wait and see," I say. "Don't want to fall prey to the placebo effect."

The week moves by in a blur of semi-crises, our normal state. Another therapist gives notice. I tussle with two pharmacies and a doctor's office to get hold of Emla, a numbing cream for the skin, so Jonah won't feel the needle during his next blood draw (to check his food sensitivities and his white blood cell counts and ensure the antifungal isn't affecting his liver). The new CARD schedule arrives, just as we've finally worked out the old one. Worst of all is Jonah's new obstinance. His defiance is quiet, but it is automatic, deeply ingrained, where it wasn't before. I remember in months past when I asked Hank,

"Do you think he might be getting burned out?" Now, I feel like they've created a child who won't even put on his socks without a battle, and I'm furious. Mostly because of the wear and tear of Jonah's present defiance on us, but also because I'm tired of having my intuition ignored when it's often correct. I know nearly as much as the rest of them. The schools, the doctors, the behaviorists, the whole carnival of people who help me raise my child, they remind me of the fable of the group of blind men describing an elephant, each convinced the part they touch is the entire problem.

At times like this, I never want to see any of them again.

———

Within a week or two, we note a drop in anxiety.

The Paxil is working.

No longer does a whirlwind of emotion seize him over a tiny matter like whether he puts on his own shoes or not, or if he must set aside a ball while eating at the dinner table. His language has loosened too; it's easier for him to craft and release words. His face is brighter, he's more present, and he's speaking longer sentences. This drug has been a good choice.

But the therapy problem remains. After a month of struggles and fights, during which therapists emerge with tense faces from a room with a crying child, my cries to Hank are finally heard: pure table-time is a thing of the past. Jonah can now learn from the environment, come up with his own ideas. The challenge from here on out is to treat him like a regular kid, who needs extra guidance.

Hank clears out our current team because we need to "stay one step ahead" of Jonah at all times; novelty, anticipation, fresh challenge, is what engages him. But the new team is unprepared. Honed on table techniques, used to harder-to-reach autistic kids, they show up at the door and some of them actually look over my shoulder for another child: surely this can't be the autistic one?

The bright, articulate boy who opens the door, warily says, "Hi," and asks them to leave causes cognitive dissonance. When they proceed to the schoolroom, or the trampoline, and he eventually smiles and lets them play with him, giggling with delight at a new word or idea, they get even more confused. *Normal? Not normal?*

Hank tells the new team of eager young women they must develop a special relationship with Jonah, win him over, because that's the only way he'll let them work. Park trips, library trips, picnic-blanket talks. Swim lessons, field trips, playdates. Neighborhood walks filled with questions and answers, like, Why is the driveway wet? Because the owner watered it. How would the owner feel if you picked his flowers? He would be upset. Why-because equals cause-and-effect. This is the foundation for reason, for curiosity.

I hope he'll start to ask *why* questions soon, it's my big pie in the sky. They're the hardest kinds of questions for autistic kids to ask.

---

In his bed, Jonah asks, "What would happen if I had a baby in my belly?"

Beside him, I think hard. "It would grow bigger," I say, "and come out. But ladies have babies in their bellies, not boys."

"What would happen if the baby came out of my tummy?"

"It would laugh and cry and play, and drink milk."

"Where were you born?" he says.

Surely I didn't hear him right. Again he asks, "Where were you born?"

"I was born in Washington, D.C.," I say.

"Where was I born?"

Carefully I give him the name of our town.

"Where was Jordan born?"

"In New York."

He is quiet again. Thinking, thinking.

"Do you know where Daddy was born?" I ask.

"Where was Daddy born?"

"Oklahoma."

It's the most amazing conversation we've ever had. A week passes as I think about its implications. I watch the new therapists come in and out, struggle to engage Jonah, win the gaze of his averted face. I call Hank. "Jonah doesn't fit the mold anymore," I tell him.

Hank says he's known only two or three kids like Jonah in eight years of supervising programs.

As flattering as it sounds, I know of many autistic kids who've done as well or better than Jonah. One mom told me her son was still "totally clueless" at five, and now at seven he's recovered. This child, who still requires some diet and medical maintenance, is now in an exclusive private school. That's what I want for Jonah. Not an exclusive private school; I don't care about that. Just a bit of success, a piece of normality.

———————

Weeks fly by with the new team of therapists. Some are tentative, and can't get a handle on his personality. Some aren't intimidated by his resistance and respond with intrigue of their own. This works. After a few weeks of refusal, we sail into a lovely clear patch of great therapy. He is so happy, greeting each person by name, deigning to answer their elementary questions ("What color is this?" "What are you eating?"). He lets them teach him (although some have to learn how to teach a bright, stubborn child who seems so typical). But he ends up teaching them.

He tells them how a motion detector works ("Things come out and they see you and then the light comes on"), how to travel on a plane ("Put your ticket in the airplane machine at the airport, then walk down the jetway, then go on the airplane and put your seatbelt on."). "He used some strange word today," nearly all of them report over the next two weeks. "We went for a walk to the library, and he kept saying he wanted to go see the culvert. I don't know what that is."

I tell them that he still loves culverts, which can take the forms of pipes, runoff ditches, concrete-lined creek beds, or other forms that furrow through the earth. The girls smile with appreciation and delight, and say they'd never have learned that word without him.

---

It's the middle of October again, time for the annual check-in with CARD.

Just as we did a year ago, we drive to Woodland Hills, and wait in the playroom. Doreen comes in. She looks younger than I do this time; this year has aged me.

"Look, Mommy, I'm on the airplane!"

Jonah straddles a long red airplane teeter-totter. "This is a city bus," he says. I note the pretend play while I listen to Doreen and Hank. "I see he is working at the intermediate and advanced level of the program," she says. "He has made very good progress. I think we could go even faster if we were to restore the discrete trial format by working at the table. He might finish up more quickly."

Unlike last year, I am no longer the acolyte.

"I think that's true," I say, "but it comes with a high price tag. The risk is that he will fight us and become very oppositional again, and that it will instill a hatred of teachers and school. Faster progress isn't worth it to me."

She nods. We go on to language scores, the social approaches he is making to other kids, and his happiness at preschool. I tell her of his witty laughter, the way he can learn things so quickly, his most recent question, "Where does the sun go when it sets?" I mention how he pretends to be a flight attendant, complete with trays and glasses and water pouring, how he polished my nails and toes last night. His love of rhyming, and his emerging gift for music.

I look over in the corner and I see him laughing. "As far as his progress, how about crystal-balling it for us?" I ask Doreen.

"I think he will be completely done with the program within two years," she says.

I'm surprised. I thought it would be a year and a half. He's already come so far in such a short time. "Why do you think it will take two more years?"

"We are working with a lot of higher-level kids like him. They show some problems at the higher levels with executive function—the ability to plan a task and carry it out. We have a program to help with that."

This tells me she doesn't know my son. I've been told that she reviews his program every month, but she really has no understanding of where he is now. A three-year-old who can take a shower, wash his hair, try to shave, make coffee, and do a perfect pretend car wash and interior vacuum after seeing it once doesn't lack for executive function . . .

But soon there will be homework. He'll need to get organized, bring assignments home from school. As Doreen talks, I see lost books and papers, a constant stream of nagging, social lessons from the playground, the need to sensor his words and activities in a quiet classroom. Again her prognosticating ability has pegged it right. He'll need all the help he can get.

---

Jonah's fourth birthday crowns the month. The October day is soft, the backyard balmy as the late afternoon glows. I fetch Mexican food from a small Latin strip mall, the pavement peppered with craters reminding me of a bumpy Costa Rican road trip with Jack before we were married. For one hundred dollars, I get enough chicken, beans, rice, and pork carnitas for forty people, and spread it out on the backyard tables.

Jonah is thrilled. He doesn't care about the food, just the long-promised cake. He's wild for the jump house, a birthday party fixture, especially for families with jump-crazy autistic kids. Earlier in the day, Jonah helped me plug in the inflatable house's motor and muffle the sound with a cardboard box. As friends ring the doorbell, he runs to the front, smiling and saying, "Hi! You came!"

The kids, typical and autistic, run through the long hall and back to the yard. Today you can't tell them apart, jumping, eating chips with salsa, and happily circling the gluten-free cake. The party is filled with people I didn't even know a year ago. True, there are three neighborhood moms of typical kids I've known for a time, and some non-mother, non-autism friends, some of my oldest and most vital connections to the world I seem to have left. But it's the new friends, families with autistic kids, who form a unique circle. Some of these families no longer attend typical birthday parties. It's too painful to watch their kid run along the backyard fence, stimming on its linked pattern, or maybe they've had a dairy or gluten infraction that caused days of bad behavior and sleep problems. But everyone I've invited is here and talking. Mothers meet and fall into a torrent of words within seconds. I introduce the autism moms to the regular moms, and they meet graciously, but the autism moms pull back together and their talk continues, tense, knotted, and relieving.

The dads are talking too; there's more conversation between newly introduced men than I've seen at any birthday party.

Jonah is running in and out, playing in the jump house, going from group to group. The food is eaten, and darkness falls. We turn on the outdoor lights and it's piñata time. As the birthday child, Jonah's the first to strike a glancing blow.

"Okay, it's someone else's turn," I tell him.

Then a voice bellows, "JO-nah! JO-nah!" Soon all the kids take it up, and the lightning ripple of the cry swells through the crowd. The mass recognition electrifies Jonah's face. He stares at the kids, then hits the piñata. The kids cheer and chant, and he whacks again and again with a showman's excitement.

My friends and I are almost crying, we are laughing so hard. Finally, Jack breaks Jonah from the magic circle, saying, "Come on, give the bat to someone else." Hands of all ages and abilities shoot into the air. A two-year-old girl with the dark beauty of a Poe heroine is encouraged to bat. Her autism is lessening since she began IVIG, the immune-system blood transfusion. She hits the air beneath the piñata, drops the bat casually and leaves. Others are quick to pick it up and take their swing.

After the piñata's destroyed, the mothers give us tight hugs and the other guests extend best wishes and take their leave. We loll alone on the carpet, looking at presents. Jack turns on the television news and begins to assemble toys. Jonah and I wander the littered backyard as the empty jump house floats lightly above the grass, its motor running hollow in the darkness.

"Tomorrow they're going to take away the old jump house, and then bring me a new jump house, for my new birthday. And I will have a new cake, and new presents."

"What do you mean, pal, a new birthday? You have to wait a whole other year."

"No, my new birthday is tomorrow."

"Honey, no, it isn't."

"Yes, it is," he says gracefully. "And I'm going to be ten years old. I will have a new black jump house, a new cake, and a piñata."

"Maybe for your next year's birthday . . ."

"My new birthday is January ten."

"It is?"

"Yes. I'm going to be ten years old."

January tenth? It's a date emerging from the dark autumn air, with no significance or pedigree. "You are?"

"Yes. I'm going to be ten years old at my new birthday."

I can visualize the coming winter, a cold brightness lit by a conjured birthday, a ten-year-old lounging in a sleek black jump house like a sports car. How fast his years will run away from us, are running even now, with him at the wheel.

# 33

## Fast Forward

### *Another November*

As November progresses, Jonah becomes more like a regular child, a companion, than a dervish of inquisitive movement. I am feeling good, so good, that when Melanie tells me, "We've done all we can do one-on-one in speech. He doesn't need it anymore. Now's the time for speech in groups of three or more," I feel like the sun is splashing all over me.

One night at our mountain cabin, he stands on his toes and manages to open the freezer door atop the refrigerator. He points to the dairy-free ice cream and sends his gaze around. "I want that ice cream please."

Jack tells him, "No, you don't need that. You've had too much sugar today."

"Actually," I say softly, "he hasn't. So he could have it, if you want him to."

Jonah says, "I want it."

"No, I just don't like it," Jack says, shaking his head.

Jonah looks at me, then back to Jack. His finger points at Jack, like condemning Puritan minister Jonathan Edwards, delivering the sinner to the hands of an angry God. "I don't like you, Jack," he says.

"Jonah!" I say, sitting upright on the blue plaid sofa. "He's your father and you will not talk to him that way."

"Okay. I like you, Jack," he says, "but I don't like what you're doing."

We laugh, trying to be serious. "That was well said, honey," I tell him.

"Jonah, since you said that so well, you can have some ice cream," Jack says.

We look at each other across the small cabin kitchen, comedy-hour parents watching the wisecracking little kid confidently eat his treat. Like always, I calculate the meaning of his statement; does it reflect a new cognitive milestone? Is it age-appropriate? Jonah, just a month past his fourth birthday, at this moment seems the child of his original birthday, the child who raised his head from my shoulder at the moment of birth and looked into my eyes, now foxing his parents out of ice cream.

---

It's time for our second IEP. A whole year has passed with no word or contact from the school district. I'd called the special ed administrator, and asked, "Will we need legal counsel this year?" although I was frightened to bring it up.

"I don't think so," she'd said, adding that they planned to renew our program if needed.

Jack wanted to come, but he had a court date, so he told me to bring the documents home for his review. "We are so lucky,"

I'd told him. "Lucky that we know the law and have the resources to make sure it's applied for his benefit," he replied.

I'd heard so many bad stories—people spending twenty thousand dollars to fight for home programs. A woman told me she'd spent nearly thirty thousand fighting her district, and said it broke her marriage and her health.

Memories float around me as I walk to the school district building. This time, there's no feeling like I'm going to war, no worries about losing our home. I greet the special ed coordinator, who's accompanied by a woman I don't know. The coordinator tells me, "We need a special ed teacher in the IEP, the law requires that we have one." I suppose someone last year had qualified; I don't remember the issue being raised.

In the conference room, we go over the documents. It's not even the same room as last year; this one is smaller and warmer.

"Now let's talk about FastForWord," I say.

"It seems Jonah might be ready for it," the coordinator tells the special ed teacher.

FastForWord is a computer program designed by a neurologist. It can increase connections in the brain to quicken auditory processing, which is the way language and sound is analyzed, translated, and understood by the brain. Jonah has a slightly slowed rate of speech, something adults do not yet notice but that Melanie says other kids will. He might be left in the social dust if it doesn't improve.

"Did you get the price?" she asks

"I did." I take a deep breath. "It's four thousand dollars. Including the pre- and post-testing to measure his progress." The coordinator grimaces. "I know. It's high," I say. "CARD offers it for less."

"No," she says, shaking her head. "If we're going to do it, I want it done under the supervision of a speech and language pathologist."

"I think that's fine," I say.

"Isn't he too young for FastForWord?" asks the special ed teacher. "He's only four."

"Most kids don't do it until they are five or six," concedes the coordinator. "But in some ways, he's actually advanced, and he may be ready for it."

"FastForWord is a major commitment," the teacher cautions. "It's every day for six weeks, two hours a day. You have to get him there. He can't miss it if he doesn't feel like it. It's a lot of responsibility."

"I would think running a forty-hour-a-week home program would demonstrate our ability to manage FastForWord," I say. It goes right over her head.

We go through the papers, all the required legal warnings about my rights during the process. I stack them up and prepare to take them home. "Dad's an attorney," the coordinator tells the teacher.

I'm lost for a moment, remembering the mothers who call me for advice, who've never connected the word *attorney* with the innocence of *school,* some of whom have very little money, or no experience in understanding a bureaucratic system. It's not fair that my husband is an attorney, that I worked in huge institutions and learned how to work with people at the top. It's also not fair that my son has autism. Yet many people who do not have my advantages share something else with me, something possibly more important: a fire in the heart. I've seen this drive in all kinds of mothers, those who clean houses for a living, who speak little English, mothers without partners, and mothers with their own illnesses. When they seek

help for their autistic child, often they strike a chord with
those who can offer it. Getting help calls for creativity. Some
parents take second jobs, or spend their savings and get second
mortgages. We've recently sold our cabin. Some parents bor-
row from the grandparents, or hold church fund-raisers. They
may barter their services in exchange for professional evaluations that can help win school district funding at an IEP, or
they beg a day-care center to let the child get his ABA program
there so they can hold down a job. These are desperate mea-
sures, humbling and painful, but desperation is what autism
treatment is about. I've also seen mothers with solid marriages,
money, and time who spend little effort on their kid's special
needs, who refuse to try the diet because, "We love our pizza
and ice cream," who feel it is the school's job to salvage whatever parts of the child can be salvaged. I try to be tolerant, to
remember I don't know what kind of pressure each individual
family can bear. But after everything, for me, there is this:
"Even if the treatments fail," as one mother said to a friend of
mine, "you won't look back and say, if only we had done more."
That mother still regrets that her severely autistic daughter got
fewer hours of ABA early on, because now she knows some
kids improve with forty hours per week instead of twenty-five.
So my friend, after hearing this and watching her own son
change for the worse without his CARD program, convinced
her husband to sell their cherished home, move to a better
school district, and hire a lawyer, while they struggled to pay
for CARD themselves. Now he's got an IQ in the 140s, is reading and talking, and their program is funded.

I take the papers and stand up.

"Your guy sounds interesting," says the teacher, the words
coming from compressed lips. "Good luck."

"He's one of a kind, that's for sure," I say.

No matter why they've *really* agreed to it, because Jack's a lawyer or they remember our determination of last year, they've given me the go-ahead to do the three-hundred-dollar pretest for FastForWord. If he does well, we'll tackle the program. Also, our entire special ed package from the previous year is intact. I'm walking out with a bank robber's amount of money with no gun, no threats, just a sheaf of unsigned papers.

I feel good, but I hate taking money from the public trough. Taking money humbles me. It hurts my pride, contradicts all my family traditions. But I've been completely humbled by autism, and I'm grateful to live in a country that considers my child worthy of help.

---

We do the pretest for FastForWord. The new speech therapist who conducted it calls me in to discuss test results. "Good news and bad news," she says.

I hold my breath.

"The good news is, he tests as a regular, normal kid."

"So what's the bad news?"

"The bad news is, with results like these, the school district may not want to fund FastForWord," she says.

Oh, but I want him to have it so badly. "Do *you* think he needs it?" I ask.

"I have no question that it will benefit him," she says. "Hopefully it'll help his slower rate of speech and auditory processing delay. Even though he tests in the normal range, those things don't show up, and I think it would help fix those problems. He also tests weak in the area of reasoning. He's at a seven. We like to see an eight to a twelve."

I am relieved when the school consents to the program, despite his score.

We begin FastForWord, and every day we drive to her office.

---

After the first week, Jonah begins to complain. At preschool, he climbs into the car, and says, "We're not going to FastFor-Word today. No, we're not going there. We're going to Chuck E. Cheese's." Or the beach. Or home.

"Sayin' so don't make it so, Jonah," I tell him.

"I don't want to go to that office. Mom, I don't want to go there."

Soon he begins to fight it with childlike maneuvers we're hard-pressed to stop. Sliding under his chair while playing the FastForWord computer games. Deliberately guessing and not trying to get the right answers. (When the speech therapist tells me this, I recoil, remembering a time in elementary school when I ignored the yearly test's questions and raced to fill in the blank dots, so I could beat the boy at the neighboring desk.) Turning off the computer's hard drive. Crying and whining.

Out of seven separate computer games, he comes close to mastering the language-based tests very quickly. The others, which involve block maneuvering and spatial skills, are harder. So he simply doesn't try. Day after day, Hank, the FastFor-Word speech therapist, Melanie, a horde of therapists, and I rack our brains for ways to motivate him. I buy bags of toys he can get only for serious effort. I tote special snacks in the car for good scores. We all cheer him, hug him, tickle, and praise him. I even use McDonald's as a reinforcer, something I had once sworn not to do since I wanted to keep it as a gluten-free/dairy-free dinner option whenever I wanted.

And it all starts to work.

After six long weeks, he finally reaches his performance peak. He hits 100 percent on the three language games, over 40 percent on two less-loved games, and 20 percent on the block games. Then his scores begin to drop. He's sick of Fast-ForWord, and it's time to cut it off. I'm disappointed he didn't master them all, but the speech therapist and Melanie assure me it was worth it anyway, that the resulting changes in the brain usually don't appear until later and the benefits are long-term.

Right after this, he begins to read.

It's evening. We've eaten dinner at a favorite coffee shop restaurant. A single glass of Chardonnay is my treat while he eats ham bits, cucumbers, fruit, and cornbread from the salad bar. After dinner, we walk around the small dusty shopping center, killing time before Jack comes home. I see a laundromat and beckon Jonah to join me.

"Mommy used to use a laundromat, Jonah," I tell him, remembering a time when I was young and broke in Washington, D.C. That place featured men with drooping butt-crack pants and women sharing a cat-food can ashtray, but this one is nice, with a fifties theme. All the washers and dryers have old-style three-letter names, like Viv, Rod, Irv, Flo, Van, Sid, Max, and Jon.

"What's in here?" Jonah asks, tentatively putting his head in the door.

"It's a laundromat. It has washers and dryers."

"Do you put money in it?" he asked, pointing to the coin slots.

"Yes."

"I want some money."

"No. We don't have any clothes to wash."

"Let's wash my shirt." He begins to pull it over his head.

"No, honey. Come on, let's look around." The names would provide good prereading practice, I thought. I had been asking him, "What does that word say? What letters do you see?" for over a year now.

"What does that say?" I asked him, pointing to a name on a washer.

"J, o, n. Jon," he said. "Like little John," a boy he knows.

*He must know how to spell the name* Jon *somehow. It's just a fluke.* "What word is this?" I ask, pointing to another washer.

"S, i, d. Sid," he said slowly.

"And this one?"

"V, i, v. Viv," he read.

"Jonah! You can read! You read those words!"

He looks at me, startled.

"This is great. What does that one say?"

"F, l, o. Flo." And then he read Ron, Irv, Mac, Sal, even Max.

"You can read! Jonah, you can read! I am so proud of you!"

He looks at my face, deciphering my expression. He sees the happiness.

"Let's call Dad and tell him," I say.

It's late, but we catch Jack at the office. "Jonah, tell Dad what you can do." Jonah takes the cell phone. "Dad, I can read. But you can't. Good-bye." Then he removes all his clothes and jumps into an industrial-size dryer. Fortunately, no one else is at the laundromat. "Did you hear that?" I ask.

"Yes. Can he?"

"Yes!" I tell him the story, how he even pronounced the *x* of Max correctly.

"That's great!" he says, wonderment and joy in his soft voice.

My mom has to be included, cell phone bill or not. It's after ten in Virginia, but she's awake and just as happy as I am. "I had been worried, you know?" I tell her. "That he'd have problems reading. And now I know he won't. This shows me he can do so much, because as long as you can read, you can learn almost anything!"

"Well, honey, why did you think he might have trouble?"

"Well, I guess I just expected it. You know, after everything else."

She is quiet. "He's doing so good, try to think about what he can do."

"I know, Mom. But it's hard. One day, I'm convinced he's going to college, and the next, I think he'll never get through a regular class."

"Well, honey, you can't know any of that right now. And he's so smart . . ."

"I feel so much better! He's only four and three months. And he's comprehending! Getting the meaning, not just sight-reading."

"Well, honey, thanks for letting me know." She sighs. "Weren't you four when you started to read too?"

"From what you've told me."

"I wish I could see his little face, you know?" she says wistfully.

I look at his small white butt as he grasps the dryer's inside ridges and tries to make it tumble him around. "Right now, you'd see more than his face."

A man and woman enter, so I grab his clothes. "I've got to go, Mom. Bye."

"Bye, honey. I'm proud of him, and all your work to help him."

"Jonah, get dressed," I order him, pulling clothes over his prancing little body.

We pass the man and woman, who keep their eyes to themselves. "Bob," Jonah reads off the dryer near the door. "Like Bob the Builder," he adds, his latest cartoon favorite.

"Yes, honey. Let's go."

"Pull," Jonah reads from the door handle.

We pass a liquor store behind the coffee shop. "What's that say, Jonah?" I ask, pointing to the lottery stand outside.

"Jack. Pot. What's that?" he asks.

"Jackpot. A treasure."

"Like Jack, my father?"

"Like your father. And like you too."

# 34

## Blood Oaths

*Another Winter, Another Spring*

In January, eighteen months in, we have a blood-draw problem when an ex-Marine lab tech with no kids and no humor fails to hit a vein. His harsh manner and insertion difficulties send Jonah into a round of crying, and he refuses another try at the needle. Since we have to do these tests every two or three months, I discuss our situation with the lab manager, and he offers to send someone to our home.

So today a supervisor has come, a tall man with boys of his own, who holds Jonah aloft promising not to scare him. A thin blond nurse with an honest face draws him, filling four color-coded tubes. The nurse marvels at his bravery as he counts to forty along with me. Later, he calms and watches the blood enter the final tube. He's happy when it's over, holding the cotton ball to his arm. "Add another piece of tape," he tells the supervisor. "Did you forget it?"

The nurse packs up her medical kit. "Do you want to walk our guests out the door?" I ask. "Yes," Jonah says, bopping and dancing down the hall.

"He is a blessing," says the nurse, her eyes fastened on him. "He was an angel, compared to most kids."

"Thanks."

"I hope I have a child just like him."

I do not know if she knows his diagnosis. It doesn't matter.

"Good-bye, guests," says Jonah. "Good-bye, doctor, good-bye, nurse."

---

Jonah gets sick in early April, a high fever taking over. Fever-reducers and cold baths help him feel better, but by day three, he's back on the couch again after a morning of easy play. His local pediatrician advised only Tylenol and Motrin, but the fever has returned. Shaking, chilling, and giving little kitten-moans, he lies under a throw. "Oh, he's really hot," I murmur, feeling his forehead. "Too hot."

"Mayra?" I call. She comes in from the kitchen and I hand the Motrin to her. "Would you give it to him for me, so I can call Dr. Goldberg?"

"No, no! I want Mom to give it to me. I don't want you to give it to me."

As I move to the kitchen phone, he cries, louder and louder, as I speak with Dr. Goldberg's staff. I hang up and go to the sofa. "What's going on, Jonah? You have to take this," I say. "I don't want her to give it to me," he protests. "I want somebody who speaks English." Mayra and I giggle. "Jonah," I tell him, trying not to smile, "Mayra speaks English." Lately he wants only me. He's sick, and I can't blame him. "Baby, let Mom hold you while you drink this," I say.

He shoves the medicine cup away. "I don't like this kind, I want the red kind!"

He won't drink orange Motrin, preferring red Tylenol instead. I get out some red food coloring (trading dyes for fever reduction) and tinge the Motrin, then bring the little cup to him. He drinks it. I put a wet washcloth on his head, and he moans until he falls asleep. I call Dr. Goldberg again, and he says bring him in. Jack wants to come too, so he picks us up and we drive through heavy Friday afternoon rush hour, over the hilly curve of the 405 freeway, passing Bel-Air and the Getty Museum, and into the San Fernando Valley. There, Dr. Goldberg says he needs blood work to check out the fever's source.

"Not blood work!" cries Jonah. "I don't need blood work! I'm not sick. I don't have a fever, I just have a little cold."

Jack and I exchange glances. "You have to be careful what you say, doctor," I whisper, "because he understands everything."

"Check my ears, doctor! Listen to my heart. But don't give me blood work!"

"I can see that," Dr. Goldberg says quickly, as regretful as a doctor with an international nine-month waiting list can be. "You don't need a shot, but you do need blood work. Just this one time, guy, okay?"

"No, not okay. I don't need any blood work," Jonah says several times.

The doctor calls in a magically fast phlebotomist who slips the blood out of Jonah so easily he barely has time to finish his tear-stained count to ten. Quickly, the results come back. "I have to take back my word, Jonah," says Dr. Goldberg. "I know I said you wouldn't have to have a shot, but this time you have to. I'm sorry."

"No! No shot!" cries Jonah in a high worried voice, starting to cry.

Several books I'd read written by autistic authors advised, "Never tell an autistic person you are going to do something and then not do it." In this case, it's the inverse, a promise that must be revoked. I feel like we're breaking some important rule, and there's nothing I can do.

Soon it is over, and a round Band-Aid dots his butt. "I want the grape-flavored sugar-free sucker," he says. He sags in the chair on his dad's lap. "Will you get it for me?" I'm struck with how poorly he must feel, not running for it himself.

We step out of the doctor's office and walk down the sidewalk together. Jonah says, "I want to be done with medical people!" He starts to cry again. I tell him it's over, but his chorus picks up speed and velocity, narrowing into a repetition of crying statements against medical people. A clutch of skateboarders, each about fifteen, is jumping over nearby curbs. They're different only to their mothers, nearly identical in black backward baseball caps and baggy pants. Jonah stops sobbing immediately as I point them out.

We're nearly in their space, and they start jumping again, showing off for our little audience. We watch and watch. Finally, I'm ready to move, but Jonah doesn't budge. The boys seem not to be finished either. After five more minutes of hurtling skateboards, I urge Jonah along.

He walks away longingly, his feet in small black sneakers pointing backwards like their hats as he turns to look behind him.

# 35

## Fairly Asparagus

*Are You Sure You're Not an Asparagus?*

We (the noun implying mother and child in mom-talk) had a hard night last night. Nothing unusual, just a few close calls with glass bottles and hard floors. Around eight, Jonah took flight off the sofa as I was reading about a paraplegic teenager. I led him, protesting, to his bedroom, and found toothpaste hieroglyphics sketched all over the sink. So I'm lying in bed today, with Jack and Jonah at law office and preschool, respectively, trying to rest, to stop thinking about autism.

The television is on, the newspaper is scattered around me. A text about autistic trends in film catches my eye. Oh, wait, that was *artistic* trends. In another section, a new clothing designer is autistic. No, my mistake, he's "audacious." The health section mentions the autism nerve—oh, wait, it's the au*ditory* nerve.

The double-lettered *au* is a monophthong, a vowel sound that strikes one pure note and doesn't change during use. To me it's become a bullfighter's cape, a flash that elicits an unconscious response. After a year and a half in the lowlands of autism, it's clear that large pieces of the experience are never going to go away. They lie buried in me as if in a desert, their great rusted shapes rearing out of the ground if the wind gets too unrelenting and the covering sand is swept away.

The root word *Au* means self in ancient Greek and Latin, I remember, and it's also the symbol for gold on the periodic table of the elements. I close my eyes and see a tiny golden child turned inward, whispering the words of a mysterious language.

Autism, the rare element no one has yet discovered.

Last week, I took three new-diagnosis calls. One was from a woman who had blocked out the impending knowledge her son was autistic for over a year. His first diagnosis was sensory integration disorder, which in many cases is shorthand for "probably autistic but we don't want to say so." Over the phone, as her child screamed every sixty seconds or so, she told me he was nonverbal, violent, and only three. I suggested she look into the special autism school in her town. She was a single working mother and I suspected she couldn't obtain or run a home ABA program. "But I've heard that's for severe cases," she said as he shrieked in the background. "I wouldn't want him to pick up bad habits there."

Another call was from a woman whose husband couldn't tolerate being alone with their newly diagnosed daughter, so she had to watch the challenging four-year-old *and* a baby boy alone. The dad was in denial about the autism. I felt a slow-rising uneasiness for her marriage and, by extension, her health, mental and otherwise.

The third call was the typical tragedy: the pediatrician's discounting of the mother's worries, the child's loss of language, his inability to toilet train promptly, the lack of any treatment information or medical direction from doctors.

As I lie here, trying to clear my mind, I seem to be inside a gauze bandage, muffled by layers of autism stories like a mummy; I can't hear the outside world anymore. Or maybe I'm the red liquid inside the wax candy lips I got as a kid, occupying a small niche inside a giant mouth that blabs a garish, silent story no one wants to hear.

———

In March, I travel to an autism conference in Pasadena.

I don't find many traditional conferences useful, as most offer the same dour, dated litany. At one, I asked a famous Ivy League researcher about the diet, and he answered, "Some parents are injecting sheep's brains into their children. Stay away from diets and alternative medical treatments." But it's rumored that many adults with autism will attend this gathering, and I want to meet them.

Some of my closest autism-mom friends don't want to see the adults. They've either got too much to handle and can't look that far ahead, or they fear that seeing the adults might make them too depressed. But I've immersed myself in the spectrum since diagnosis day, and I want to meet people whose lives embody its challenges and rewards. I've already met a wonderful man named Stephen Shore, who wrote an autobiography called *Beyond the Wall*. We met at a fund-raiser after I read it, and I felt instant tenderness for the gentle, brown-eyed man with a master's degree in music and a doctoral degree in education. Pronounced "autistic, atypical, and psychotic" as a child, and nonverbal until four, Stephen is a married author and international lecturer who also teaches music to spectrum kids. We will meet again in Pasadena, as he's a featured speaker.

The conference is held in a vast hall. The standout among the sessions I attend is John-Paul Bovee's rousing, funny presentation on the myths of autism. John-Paul, a blond thirty-three-year-old with thick glasses, demolishes many misconceptions about autistic people, drawing on his own and friends' lives with humor and sarcasm. He glances at his watch and uses an outline to keep on track, flowing easily from topic to topic. Diagnosed as autistic at three and again at six ("early infantile autism and childhood schizophrenia"—his mother fended off an additional mental retardation label), he became the captain of his school's history quiz bowl team, and went on to earn two master's degrees, one in history, the other in library science. He's one of the best speakers I've ever seen. There's no hesitancy to his language, which shifts from thoughtful to incisive and funny. "You typical people are talking to me? Fine," he says from the stage. "I'll give you great conversation. You want eye contact, I can give that to you too. But then you tell me you want both at the same time! Well, you need to choose which it is you want."

When the Q&A begins, I ask him when he became aware of the social differences between himself and other kids. He pauses, then says, "I don't think I really became aware of being different until fifth grade." But most people didn't treat him any differently, he adds, and that was a key to his success.

After the sessions, hundreds of parents and educators mill about the reception area. I spot a table with six men and one woman leaning forward to hear the talk going on between two men, one of whom is John-Paul Bovee. With my new autism instincts, I can tell it's a table of high-functioning adults. Stephen Shore comes up to me as I wonder how to approach.

"Hi, Stephen. Can I buy you a drink? A beer or something?"

"No," he says kindly. "I don't drink alcohol."

"Okay," I say, feeling foolish.

"But I would like a soft drink."

We chat as I order drinks. "I want to meet John-Paul Bovee," I tell him. "Do you know him?"

"Sure. I'll introduce you."

We walk toward the table. Most of the men wear glasses, Members Only jackets, and short-sleeve shirts. They look like engineers or radio dispatchers—or like any group of hobbyists at a convention.

Stephen seats me next to John-Paul, and waits patiently to introduce me, for a debate is raging between John-Paul and a solid, dark-eyed man named Jon. "You say there shouldn't be a cure for autism, but you can't stand to be around him," says Jon, naming a mutual acquaintance.

"I don't like him," says John-Paul. "I don't like what he does, or how he acts. Last time I saw him at a friend's house, he left and was roaming the neighborhood, bothering people. I don't like him and I don't want to be around him."

"But maybe his behavior is part of his autism. Here's somebody you can't stand to be around, but you don't want a cure that might change him?" says Jon, his body pitched forward in the plastic chair.

"It isn't all about his autism," John-Paul says. "Just because someone is on the spectrum, doesn't mean I have to like them if I don't like their personality."

"But what if he could be cured? Then maybe he'd have a chance to act differently. And you'd be able to tolerate him."

"Autism is not something that needs a cure. There is nothing wrong with me. God made me the way I am. And God doesn't make junk," John-Paul says passionately.

"But you have two master's degrees. You're really high-functioning," Jon says with distress. "Look at me. I hate my disability." He begins to rock a little. "If I could be cured, I would."

Stephen whispers to me, "I was trying to find a time to introduce you, but just go ahead and jump in when you can."

When the debate pauses, I introduce myself. "I saw your lecture today, John-Paul, and it was fantastic," I say.

"Thank you," he replies. "I thought it went well, but it's nice to hear it from the audience's perspective."

"Are you a parent?" asks Jon.

"Yes," I say. "A four-year-old boy." They nod. "What do you do?" I ask Jon.

"I'm an at-home medical transcriptionist," he says.

"That's great," I tell him. "Along with librarian, it was my mother's fantasy job for me in high school."

"Why? I'd think you could do better, with your social skills," Jon says.

"Well, she always said my memory and spelling skills would help. I can read really fast too."

"I'd rather have a job with more social contact," he says.

"But the mothers I know would be thrilled if their child

could do what you do. You should be proud." The only other woman has left the table. The men sit silently, their eyes alert as owls. The tension from the argument still hangs in the air. "What about the rest of you?" I ask.

Someone points at a silent, round-faced man smiling at the end of the table. "See him? He's got three PhDs." One of the degrees is in Operations Research, a field that requires extraordinary mathematical reasoning skills.

"When I worked in the Pentagon's Army Human Resources office, I hired people with Ops Research backgrounds," I tell the man. "Those resumes were fascinating. They were some of the smartest people in the world."

He smiles.

"When did you get diagnosed?"

"Last year," he said. "I was thirty-six."

"Are you married?" Jon asked him.

"No," he says.

"See, I want a cure, because it's very hard to have relationships," says Jon. "Women find my disability repulsive." His hands, down by his knees, begin to flap a bit. He looks at me. "I'm sorry, but this is part of my disability."

"That's not a big deal at all," I tell him. *My God,* I think, *if he can't do it here, where can he?*

"Operations research at the Pentagon?" asks a black-haired man at the table. "What do you know about it?"

"Just that they worked in war games and theories. Not much else."

"Why were you working at the Pentagon?" asks Stephen.

"It was hard to find a writing job when I graduated from college, so I moved away from home and went to Washington, where we lived when I was a child. But I've always been interested in weaponry, tanks and stuff, ever since I was a kid."

Stephen looks at me, smiling. "That's fairly asparagus of you."

"What?"

"Asparagus. That's what some of us Aspies call ourselves. Asperger's, asparagus. Are you sure you're not an asparagus?"

"Yes, I'm sure. I have a few intellectual traits, but I'm not," I say. "Sometimes I wish I was, so I'd be more like Jonah. But I never had any language problems or social impairment."

"Operations research. What else do you know about it?" asks the black-haired man again.

"Not much. That's it." Once again he's disappointed.

"Most of the world rejects autistic people," Jon says passionately.

"When do we stop trying to change people? I'm perfect the way I am. People are perfect the way they are," responds John-Paul with equal passion, and the debate starts again. Stephen is getting tired. "This is interesting, but it's taking all my energy," he murmurs.

"Are you okay?" I ask. I'd read that he didn't like fluorescent lights and I'd noticed a bank of conference-sized lights overhead.

"I'm fine. I need to go back to my room and relax soon."

"When I read your book, I loved reading about your interests," I tell him. "I had some of the same ones when I was a kid. Geology, music, psychology, dinosaurs, and natural disasters."

"Oh, yes?" he asks.

"I decided to read every book in the old county library. I got to L, but then they moved the collection into a giant library, so I could only do sections then. That's when I started reading all the books on one topic. The World War II section, the penal system section, world religion, witchcraft, the Civil War and slavery, stuff like that."

"That's a pretty asparagus thing to do. Are you sure—?"

I smile again. "Stephen, I'd tell you if I was."

To my left, John-Paul is quiet. I ask him, "On stage, you said you have a girlfriend now."

John-Paul's face lights up. "Yes, I do," he says. "She's a wonderful girl, a good person."

"I agree with so much of your argument, we need to accept who and what people are. But the only thing I wonder is . . . do you plan to have children?"

"I do want to become a father, hopefully."

"When your child can't speak," I say, hesitating, "or is hurting himself, does that make you think about why some people want a cure?"

John-Paul sighs heavily. "Yes, I can imagine that would hurt," he says. "That would be tough." He looks away, his face sagging. "I don't have an answer to that. And I'm not saying they shouldn't get all the help they need." He asks about Jonah.

I describe him and all the men at the table listen silently, their quiet acceptance so simple and perfect it catches me short.

"He's lucky to have you for his mother," says Jon. John-Paul agrees. The black-haired man smiles warmly at me. "Thank you for sitting with us," he says.

"You guys are all great success stories to me," I say.

"Yes, we're so happy you came over," says Jon. "It's really nice that you don't mind talking to us."

"Mind? I'm the lucky one," I tell them. "I can't imagine why everyone isn't at this table."

John-Paul departs, and as the others make plans for the evening, I say good-bye to Stephen. He's been smiling for a while now. "You may not be a true Aspie," says Stephen, "but I'll consider you an honorary asparagus."

"Thanks, Stephen."

He lifts his fingers in what looks like a *Star Trek* sign and salutes me.

———————————

I drive Jonah north to an office building for his kindergarten screening. The woman who is seeing us today has decades of experience in regular and special education, including a master's degree.

As we enter the waiting room, I see an older child W-sitting on the floor, his knees flat on the ground, feet flattened behind him. The feeling of recognizing an autism spectrum person sweeps over me—but he's playing imaginatively, greets us and asks Jonah to play. I must be mistaken. The mother emerges from the office and sits down. "You know," I say, in a friendly voice, "it's not good for kids to sit like that. It's called W-sitting, and it can hurt their knees in the long run. I thought you might want to know, because my son did it and I never knew it wasn't good until someone told me."

"Oh," she says, but she obviously doesn't want to hear more.

"Hi, you must be Jonah and his mom," says the tester.

"Hi," Jonah replies.

"Come on back," she says, beckoning to him. I rise too.

"No, you wait out here. We'll be just fine," she says. She shuts her office door, and I sit silently, wondering what's unfolding out of my reach.

After thirty minutes, the door opens. "Hi, Mom," says Jonah. "I'm done."

"Won't you come back?" she asks me.

"I can't leave him out here," I say. "I need to watch him."

"We'll crack the door. He'll be fine."

I sit down before her desk, and she settles in her chair and looks over the papers. "I'd like to go over the results of his test today," she says.

*Here it comes,* I think, *everything I don't want to hear.*

She turns the thick score sheets toward me. "On the tests, he scores above his age level in language, things like answering questions about a story, and in general knowledge, like knowing his colors, shapes, letters, and numbers. Here"—she indicates the fine motor section—"he's a little behind on his fine motor skill, about two months or so. But that's not unusual. He caught a ball just fine, hopped, stood on one foot, all in the age-appropriate ranges. I had to shift his attention a couple of times, and he did okay. But I'm going to recommend you hold him back for kindergarten a year, due to his late October birthday. Kindergarten is more like first grade these days, because of the state mandates for testing, so he'll be more successful with that bonus year."

"So that's the only reason you recommend we wait?" I ask.

"We usually recommend a wait for boys born in late summer or after."

I stare at the list of scores. They're listed neatly, presenting a solid picture of a developing kindergartner. "Is that all?" I ask.

"Yes. Everything's within the age-appropriate range. So you *could* send him if you want to. I just recommend you wait."

Tears fill my eyes. She looks at me, puzzled and kindly. "I know you don't understand," I say, groping for words. "This is *great* news."

She waits as I try to stop crying.

"He was autistic. He couldn't do anything like this before."

"Oh!" she says, startled. She attempts to recover her poise. "Maybe I can see that. A little bit of Asperger's syndrome. I work with a group of Asperger's boys—"

"No. He was *autistic.* Couldn't ask or answer a question, hit his head, bit people. His speech was almost all echolalia."

Her face reveals shock. Intrigued, she leans forward. "How did you do it?"

"A thirty-to-forty-hour-a-week home program, diet, three hours a week of speech therapy, some medicine," I say. "And we work with him constantly."

"You should go to work as an advocate," she says, and names a local child disability agency. "This is really remarkable. I've got many years in teaching, including special ed, and I didn't see it. He's doing *well.*"

I dry my eyes, too stunned to be embarrassed. She hands me the test sheet.

"I wish you could help the child who was out there when you came in," she says. "He's on the spectrum, and I've tried to tell the mother, but she refuses to listen."

"But he was playing so well," I say.

"He's fine one-on-one, but he falls apart in a classroom. But anyway, congratulations. You should be very proud. He's quite remarkable."

She shows me out. Jonah stands up politely and hugs me.

"Are you done with the meeting, Mom?" he asks. "Look, I'm playing with the train!"

In the parking lot, I call Jack. "He passed his kindergarten screening undetected. She didn't see *anything*. All his skills are within age range!" I tell him everything, and we marvel over the details. Jonah's in the backseat, playing with a toy. "I'm hungry, Mom," he calls. "I want a hamburger and french fries. Let's drive to a restaurant now."

I take him to a burger place, where he eats hungrily and plays in the outdoor play structure. I stare at him, my self-directed, miraculous son. Blue-eyed and happy, he's sweet-faced and free.

And so, for a time, am I.

# 36

## Being Reasonable

### *Another Spring*

A year and nine months later. Where are we now? We have a four-year-old child who can make up funny lines and laugh. Who asks *what* and *where* and *who* questions. We get many "What would happen if . . ." questions, no *hows,* and just a few *whys* so far. I've heard *why* questions come around age five in many cases.

They're still a bit abstract for a more angular mind.

We have a companion now, someone you can take places, who can participate and learn. We have a child who will listen to our commands or requests, although he obeys them as the dictates of his personality allow. He can approach people on the sidewalk, greet them, ask the name of their dog, and pet it without too much fear. He pulls heavily, repeatedly on my hand as we walk inside a shopping mall, despite my warnings and "hand time-outs," probably to get a feel for where his body is in all that glittering space. We have a child who cannot eat dairy products without regressing. A few months ago at Chuck E. Cheese's, Jonah helped himself to a cheese pizza slice before I saw him. I let him finish it, to see what would happen. I told no one at pre-school the next morning; three hours later, two teachers and the aide met me. "Is something going on at home?" Shari asked. "We totally lost him today. He ran around and wouldn't listen to any of us. He seems upset, so I wondered if everything is okay?"

It took about three days for him to bounce back. The same thing happened when he got hold of some buttermilk pancakes. But he seems totally fine with light wheat and gluten now, although some kids regress. I've found organic breads and tortillas with low yeast and whole wheat for fiber, and these keep him on a more even keel than white bread, but they can mildly affect his blood test allergy results, so I rotate them with the processed breads. Still, if we let him eat the carb-heavy, low-protein diet he loves, his yeast grows and he gets spacey and hyperactive.

Jonah perseverates on topics. He can happily pretend the car is an airline over and over, ask the same questions about the seat belt sign for weeks, the no-smoking light, what would happen if he lit a cigarette and the air marshals took him to jail (why did I ever explain that?). He calls himself American Air-lines. I'm dubbed Delta Airlines, Jack is United Airlines, and Mayra is LA Airlines.

"How long will this go on?" I ask Melanie after a speech session.

"Typically developing kids are able to self-monitor their talk around eight years of age. Using that as a yardstick . . ." She shrugs. "He's so smart, when he learns this kind of talk isn't going to get him what he wants, he'll regulate it. But for now, expect this to continue for a few years."

Melanie is leaving soon. She and a partner are starting their own ABA and speech company to serve the ballooning number of autistic kids in our area, and we'll have to start speech with someone new. She knows Jonah's behaviors and interests like few others, and still she expects him to eventually lose his diagnosis.

He can go to sleep now on his own, although he never wants to. "Come sleep with me, Mom. Let's cuddle," he says, beckoning me. He looks disingenuously at his dad. "Good-bye, Jack." Jack shrugs and smiles at me. I turn out the light and lie atop the covers. "You know, Jonah, you're four years old now. Pre-K boys—all the boys at school? They go to sleep by themselves."

"I want you to stay. I don't want to sleep by myself."

"I know . . . but it's a skill. A skill is something you learn how to do, so you can do it when you need to."

"I don't need to have a skill. I need you to be here with me. Stay with me, Mom."

Something about the softness of his *M*'s in *Mom,* how beguilingly he uses it instead of a childish *Mommy,* wins me over. And the way he widens his eyes earnestly to make eye contact in the dark.

"I'll stay for a short time, so you better go to sleep while I'm here."

"Okay," he says liltingly. He pulls my arm around him tight, like a magic blanket, and very soon, he falls asleep.

If there'd never been a word, a *label,* attached to him, he wouldn't have gotten the help he needed. But another power of a label is that it becomes the child's name. Why not name him *rare,* or *secret, loving one.* Not *autism,* not *delayed,* not *Asperger's.*

Because he is *not* those things.

He's not even *Jonah.* He is himself.

———————

Reason is where some children with autism fall down. Not just social reasoning, but abstract reasoning. I've begun to worry about this. The *why* and *how* questions aren't coming at the rate I hoped for. Jonah rarely asks *why* about anything. His way of tackling a new topic is either to state his logical assumptions about it, or execute a plan of action immediately, asking for help only if he can't do it alone. And I still think about the low reasoning score on the pre-FastForWord test.

At a birthday party for a three-year-old, Jonah spots a machine with a thick electrical cord. I'm not quite sure what it is. He grabs the cord, finds a nearby electrical outlet and tries to pry open its cover. "Help me, Mom," he says breathlessly. "Help me plug in the bubble machine."

"How do you make it work?" the three-year-old asks, looking straight into my eyes. At a loss, I point to Jonah. "Watch him," I say. "He can show you."

Sometimes, when I ask him *why* something happened, as in, "Why are you being punished?" he'll give me a snake-mouthing-its-tail answer. "Because I'm in time-out."

Other times, he gives me exactly the right answers. "Why can't we go outside right now?" I ask. "Because it's raining and we'll get wet."

Somewhere in this limbo, I realize he's still only four and a half, and I know some kids with autism spectrum disorders who didn't ask *why* and *how* questions until they were five and six. Now they're in regular-ed classrooms and have friends.

*Hows* and *whys* are hard. They're abstract questions, pertaining to unseen processes and non-concrete ideas. But one of the major problems is that questions require social skills. To formulate a question, one must first assume that another person might know the answer.

For a child with mild to moderate autism, it can be easy to understand that Mom, who is driving the car, knows *where* she's taking you. *What* questions are basic labeling, and can be satisfied with child-friendly one-word answers, like *truck, building, washer, dryer, drain*. *Who* also is concrete and can be attached to a real being who enters your space. *When* is a bit more difficult, since a sense of time is required and that isn't easy for young children in general. But *how* and *why* calls for the child to assume there are complex motivations behind actions. This requires a theory of mind, an assumption that other people know things that are different than what you know, things that can't be seen or touched or counted. That's why *how* and *why* questions require a combination of reason and social finesse, plus the ability to ask and wait for an answer.

But, I reassure myself, the lack of questions doesn't mean that reason isn't whirring away in the back of a busy mind.

———

Thunder and lightning are among Jonah's favorite topics lately, along with tornadoes. "Mom? Do you know the sky can break?"

"Oh, can it?"

"Yes, it can."

"Tell me about that," I say.

"The sky breaks open, and lightning comes out of it," he says. "There's a door in the sky. It opens and the lightning comes out."

"That sounds great. I bet you're right."

"Yes," he says.

# 37

## Splayed Wings

### *Big Deals*

I make a second visit to a school for children with ADHD, attention deficit hyperactivity disorder (which was once called minimal brain dysfunction). The school administrators also accept a smattering of kids with other behavior problems, attention issues, and communicative disorders, but they do not consider their school a "special ed" school. Their school district curriculum is considered one of the hardest in the nation.

Melanie comes with me. We stand in a dark observation room and view the kindergarten-through-second-graders in their social-skills hour. Kids are rewarded for being "Cool Craigs" at home and obeying their parents. They earn "Big Deals" for "accepting" the fact they didn't win a game (they hold their hands in a shield to signal their acceptance) or ignoring a troublemaking neighbor. They are praised for being "on-task" and discouraged from teasing classmates. The children, mostly boys, are immersed in a reinforcing, positive atmosphere and still allowed to be fidgety young kids.

I want this for my son. The question is, will they allow him in?

We take the packet and follow the PhD-in-charge out to the front porch. "My son has Asperger's," I say, because that's one of his labels and I don't want to drop the "A-bomb" yet— it's too hard to explain the recovery process to PhDs. "But he's doing really well."

He hesitates, as he gathers his words. "We have a couple of them here, but they were originally misdiagnosed as ADHD. He would have to be really, really high-functioning."

"He is!" I say, like a Girl Scout touting a major cookie sale.

Melanie says, "With his language scores, he won't have any problem."

"Yes, and he's able to read three-letter words already," I add.

"But his behaviors," says Melanie, bringing me back to reality.

"Yes, he has some of those," I add. "He has a mind of his own, and his attention span is either too long or too short. He's squirmy and headstrong."

As the director walks back inside, I fall in step and tell him Jonah's story about how lightning comes from a broken sky. His face changes to visible surprise, and he nods. "Take the application and turn it back in," he says.

"When should we apply, if he won't be coming for another year?" I ask.

"As soon as your decision is made," he says.

I walk away on clouds, and remain there all day. There's a smile on my face and a softness in my spirit that I'm not used to.

Jonah is in a martial arts class now, twice a week. Jonah spied the class in session when we passed by it one day, plus it turns out that Dr. Goldberg recommends the sport. The instructor, a national winner who's taught thousands of kids, probably thinks he is a hyperactive kid with not enough home discipline whose nice mother neglects him by using a wide assortment of babysitters. The dutiful father who helps out with the class probably shares that view. This is an image I bear willingly. It is a "parent-optional" class, and I let the therapists go along with him. When I go, he's too happy to have me there. Dressed like the other boys in a red uniform, he keeps smiling at me, and calling "Mom, look at me!" when he does his kicks and shouts. This lessens his focus on the "Master." And I want him in that class. So what if he's a beat slow to get into "crab walk" position? I had to model a basic jumping jack with his arms and legs for him, to make him feel how the feet spread out and the hands clap together at the same time. After a few awkward jumps, he did it just fine, and clumsy jumping jacks are age-appropriate. If I hear later that he ran off to yell, "Hello down there!" into a big barrel stationed in the corner of the studio, or picks up the mats he isn't supposed to, I shrug it off. When I see him run around the room with the other kids full of glee, mouth and eyes wide open, hair lifted like splayed wings, I think, *If only they knew.*

Before class started last week, Jonah and another boy got the idea to take turns using the padded-thing-on-a-stick to block each other's blows. The boy rained blows on Jonah, and awkwardly, he blocked them with his arms as he had been taught. Then, he took the stick in turn and softly hit the other boy on the head and shoulders as I stood alone and watched, before I headed out the door.

"Now let's kick," said Jonah, and ran to get the shield-like kicking pad.

He held it and the boy kicked hard, shouting "Ya!" each time. Jonah held his ground, excitable and happy.

"Now it's my turn," Jonah said. He handed the pad to the boy, then kicked it with his strong little feet. "Ya!" he yelled. "YAA!"

There is no norm like normality.

# 38

## Turning Around

*After Eighteen Months, the End Is in Sight*

Jonah is 80 percent through with the CARD program, and will be done next year. Hank said this, although he never wants to say exactly when, so I can't him pin him down to any promises. Anyway, after dozens of bright-faced therapists, after thousands of dollars in games, toys, art supplies, exercise balls, and sports equipment, after seeking out food and play reinforcers, and hauling ourselves to exhausting clinic meetings, the end is in sight. When a child can greet his therapist, tell him that he wants them to leave and why, when his playdates have to be interrupted for his therapy, he's borderline in need of it.

Still. He needs the remaining lessons.

How to listen to a story and tell it back, focusing on *who* and *what* happened, instead of what color car appeared in it. How to moderate his impulsivity, to refrain from handling everything in the grocery store checkout line, then edging behind the register to run the conveyor belt. How to tell another child "I don't like that" when a toy is snatched from his hand, rather than simply grabbing it back or giving in. His social skills are still somewhat askew, and he needs practice. There are too many rough patches in the social world, and the role-playing is a way to prepare him. Happily, he loves his "social stories" now.

"Come on, Mom. Get out *To Bite Is Not Right,*" he says, dragging me to the therapy room and releasing the "social story" from its ringed binder. "Read it to me, Mom."

Even though he almost never bites anymore, he's been known to feint open-mouthed at the sleeves of the few therapists he dislikes, staring right into their eyes to see how his challenge affects them. And I still worry, needlessly or not, that childish excitement like getting pushed in a jump house might activate the old impulse.

Obediently, I read, "Sometimes, when I am playing with a lot of kids or I get really excited, I feel like I want to bite someone. Biting is not fun and it hurts other people. Also, I don't get to keep having fun if I bite. A better choice would be for me to offer a high-five or a hug when I am excited, or use my words to say how I feel. Then, I get to keep having fun with my friends and family."

"Good job, Mom," he says. "Now read *Standing in Line* to me. In your booming voice."

I drone on loudly about how he should stand patiently in line at the store so maybe he will get a treat when he is finished, and Mom will feel happy.

"You did a good job, an excellent job, Mom." His round blue eyes, a mixture of ingenuousness and prankster, stare at me. "What will happen if I don't wait very well at the store?"

"You know what will happen. No fun for you, no treats, very unhappy Mom."

"When will I get treats?"

"Maybe later. Maybe never."

"Never? I want treats, Mom. Don't say never."

I've had enough of social stories. "Let's go out," I say.

"No, stay and play with me. I'll be the teacher, you be the student. You have to sit here, in this blue chair. Now, tell me what you are thinking about."

"I don't know, honey."

"I know. You're thinking about Volkswagen Beetles." It's his new preoccupation, ever since I showed him an old orange one on the street. "Tell me about an old Beetle," he instructs.

"Well, it's kind of round, and the engine make a strange whiny rattle."

"Okay. That was fine, Mom. You can take a break now."

———

Between preschool and therapy one day, I take him to the grocery store. He pulls out a large cart, humming, until an older lady tells him there are kid-sized ones inside. I follow him to the checkout stand, and before I can stop him, he finds a switch to the conveyor belt and flips it. I notice a row of switches, one for each bagging stand, and wonder, *How come I never saw those?* He finds a kid's cart.

"Look at my cart, Mom! It's the right size for me, and it has a flag on top of it!" He wanders down the aisles, singing a song I don't recognize about going up, up into the atmosphere.

"Is he always that *on,* eager to get involved in everything?" asks a young woman.

"Yes, he is," I say, grabbing a big box of sugary cereal and a huge tub of yogurt from his hands.

"It's okay," he tells me. "Someday when I'm older I can try the yogurt, but not right now."

"Rad!" says the woman.

"You might say that," I say with a gritty smile.

His cart's moving so fast I fear for the legs of other shoppers. He reaches for his favorite products—dairy-free crescent rolls to bake, a green organic cucumber, a sausage and pancake concoction on a stick I decide to toss because it contains eight grams of sugar.

At the checkout stand, the cashier asks, "Do you want to add an extra dollar for Jerry's Kids?"

"Yes," I say, watching Jonah struggle to lift a water container half his body weight.

"It's for disabled kids," she says, pushing a paper balloon to me along with a pen. "You could write his name on it, and we'll hang it up. From one kid to another."

From one tweaked kid to another, I think, as Jonah helps the bagger load groceries. I sign his whole name, feeling close yet distant from the mother who's represented behind the balloon, like a cousin or a kinswoman one sees only at family reunions.

After Jonah fingers the credit-machine keys and tries to buy a magazine, he plucks a black "over the hill" balloon from a stand, almost causing me to trip over him at the store exit. Watching our antics, the bagger who's pushing our loaded grocery cart is unsure whether to follow us to the parking lot or not. "Come on," I say, motioning to him. "Join the party."

———————

It strikes me one morning in the kitchen: the pattern's broken.

Jonah's no longer regressing and coming back. All these long months, he would advance for two or three weeks, then have one or two lesser weeks. It was forward three steps, back two. A roller coaster of hope and failure. After more than a year, I'd gotten used to it. But in the stillness of the kitchen it's clear; there's a smoothness I haven't recognized until now. He's been gaining and never losing ground for a long while.

He walks in, barefoot in his blue pajamas. "What are you doing, Mom?" he asks me.

"I'm reading the paper."

"Let me read the paper too."

I hand him a section with a photo of a hilly brush fire menacing a toy-strewn backyard. "What's happening there? Is the fire going to burn up the boy's house? What is the fireman doing? Is the fire right behind the kid's house?"

"It's far away," I tell him. "Newspapers tell stories about things that happened yesterday, in a city or a country."

"Is that fire coming here? Is that north, in the mountains?" The four directions are a recent interest. "No, it's very far away. The fireman will keep it away from the kid's house, and the kid will be safe."

He picks up another newspaper section and stares at a photo of a soldier with a rifle. "That's a soldier, Mom. What's that? A gun?"

"That's a rifle." As I look at the photo, the rifle outlines itself in newsprint blocks before my eyes. I can feel him see it too.

"This is a clip, where they keep the bullets, and this is the stock, which goes on his shoulder when he lifts the gun to shoot," I say, the language coming slowly but surely. As a girl I shot pistols and cleaned rifles with my father, although I would never have a gun now. But I always found the mechanics interesting.

He keeps leafing through the sketch ads of furniture and bras. "I'm reading the newspaper, Mom. I can look at all these things."

I begin to worry about newspaper content and then I remember. Only eighteen months ago, I worried he'd never read. Now I was concerned about newspaper content. It suddenly seems a light, luxuriously free topic.

"Mom? I don't have to do what you say, Mom. I can do what I want." His voice is so pure and lilting, filled with boyish will.

"Really, Jonah?" I say mildly.

"Yeah. I can do the things I like. I don't have to do what you say."

"Well, everyone has to do what they don't like. Even grownups. But you have choices."

"What are my choices?" he asks quickly.

"Your choices are, do what you don't like for a short time, and have fun the rest of the time. Or don't do the hard things, and you will miss all the fun."

"I'll do the right thing. Mom, do you want me to do the right thing?"

"Yes, I do."

"I'll do the right thing, *then* I'll do the wrong thing!" Jonah says exuberantly.

Now he can decide for himself.

———————

At the end of June, after much hesitation—after all, he's doing so well—we agree with Dr. Goldberg to switch SSRI medications from Paxil to Celexa. At worst, we'll lose ground, or get some unpleasant side effects, waste maybe three weeks testing a medication. The doctor routinely changes medicines if he thinks they might advance the child and get at some of his underlying medical issues. For instance, he plans to switch Jonah to milder antifungals once he's ready to come off stronger medications like the Diflucan. Now he thinks Celexa might bring Jonah to new heights.

We start the Celexa, an oval pink pill, on a Friday morning.

I left that night with some other moms on a retreat; Jack thought the weekend with Jonah had gone smoother than usual. I didn't put much stock into it, but Monday began, and the week started to flow with positive reports from the therapists and preschool teachers.

"This was his best session ever with me," said Laurie.

"He was fantastic today in class . . . stayed on task, didn't have to be hushed in circle time," said a preschool teacher.

"I don't know what you're doing, but I have to tell you today is a miracle. He's like a different boy. Compliant, wants me to play with him, striking up conversations, great questions," said Hector, poking his head into my office while Jonah banged on the white piano. "I know you guys do things without telling us; whatever it is, keep it up!"

"He had no problems today in tae-kwon-do," said Cory. "He got an extra stripe on his belt."

"But he just got one last week. Now he has four?" I asked.

"Yeah. He did great. The Master was really pleased."

By the end of the week, when he stands next to me patiently while I search for a toy, or follows me around the house without dashing off to grab what he wants, I think: *Maybe this is what other kids are like?*

And the conversations! After I told him his grandmother was coming to visit, he asked, "Mom, when you were a baby, what did you do? Did Grandmother feed you a bottle, and did you cry?"

"Yes, she did."

"And who took care of Grandmother when she was a baby?" He faces me patiently, his eyes looking into mine.

"Your Great-Grandmother Franklin did. She took care of Grandmother. Because Grandmother is her daughter."

"Am I a daughter?" he asks.

"No, you are a son, because you are a boy."

"Dad's a son. I'm a son, I'm not a daughter. Are you a daughter, Mom?"

"Yes, I am Grandmother's daughter. She's my mom."

"And who spanked you when you were a little girl?"

"If I hit someone or broke something," I fumble, "Grandmother spanked me." A doctor told us to swat Jonah's behind if he does something aggressive, like purposefully breaking something or hitting someone. Jack and I have done this on occasion.

"Did Daddy get spanked when he was a little boy?"

"He did," I say.

"When I grow up, I'm going to be a woman."

"You can't, honey. You're a boy, so you will be a man."

"No," he says thoughtfully. "I'll be a woman."

"Why do you want to be a woman?"

"So I can spank softly, not hard."

Now the legacy of spanking has been passed and shame flushes my face. So this is a conversation. He's told me he'll remember everything I say and do.

---

I'm entering a new plane of motherhood. I can feel a calmer presence and awareness surrounding him like a halo. His preschool teachers are happy, happy. Laurie, one of our longer-term therapists, comes to me in the garage and says, "So, I know you did something. What is it?"

I tell her about the change to Celexa, but ask her to tell no one. I want the others to keep their own trains of thought.

On the Fourth of July, we have a house full of kids. Jonah and the other kids watch the firework displays erupting within sight of our backyard. I pull out some illicit sparklers. They are forbidden in this town, but the kids love them. They trace smoky sparks in rings and arcs above the damp grass.

"This sparkler color is green. That's barium!" shouts Jonah. He calls out each firework chemical unfailingly, as he has been "reading" a Time-Life Science book for kids about it. He's a great host, leading the other kids in "oohing" and "aahing" to each sky-born display.

"Here, do you want some water?" Jonah asks, offering his cup to his friend. "Are you okay?" he asks a little girl as she trips on the grass. He worms his way under the community blanket covering all the kids as colors arch and stream into the sky.

The next day, one of the autism mothers calls me. "My husband was blown away," she says. "He didn't see a trace of autism in Jonah. He couldn't understand why he would have been called autistic."

"Does your husband know all the work it took to get here?"

"I'm sure he couldn't understand it," she said. "But it's obviously worked."

# 39

# Survivor's Guilt

*What Is Recovery?*

The week after the Fourth, Jonah takes a post-FastForWord test to see what effect the program might have had. There's good and bad news.

The bad news is auditory processing is still slow. It still takes him extra time to process incoming words and formulate his answer. It's still only a seconds-long delay, but that may be too long for conversing quickly with impatient kids at school. Also, in a quiet room, he tests at 80 percent of all kids in auditory discrimination—the ability to distinguish sounds and words. But in a noisy room, it falls to 20 percent. This is why classroom noises are often distracting. "Across the room, he can hear what the other kids are saying in a corner," his preschool teacher told me. "It must be like hearing a radio and listening to all the stations at once." Now we have test results that support her observation.

But the good news is very good.

His scores in reasoning, previously at seven on a scale that ran from seven to thirteen, are now off the charts. I see the numbers fourteen, fifteen, sixteen. His memory skills are as high as seventeen, eighteen, and nineteen. "Jonah now has above-average expressive and receptive language skills, and above-average reasoning skills. He is a very bright boy," reads the speech pathologist's summation.

Perhaps I can dream again. Perhaps the gifted boy I once had is back.

Perhaps it doesn't matter, since intellect has nothing to do with love.

————————

I read a book that says autistic kids can't pass the Sally-Anne test. This is a basic theory-of-mind test. The book's declaration that typical four-year-olds can pass this test, but that autistic children cannot makes me mad. I stew about this all day and part of the night. I decide to run a Sally-Anne test on Jonah.

It is a three-step test that goes like this: Sally comes into a room. She places an object, like a marble, into a particular basket or box, then leaves the room. Anne comes in and moves the marble into another basket, then leaves. When Sally comes back into the room, the test asks, in which basket will she look for her marble?

Autistic people think Sally will look into the second basket, because that's where the marble actually is—according to the book, and others I've read. The reasoning is autistic people are unable to take Sally's perspective. Being able to assume the perspective of another person is called theory of mind. It's assumed autistic people do not have it.

I enter a therapy session in Jonah's bedroom. I take Laurie outside and whisper what I'm about to do. Then I pull Jonah aside and tell him we're going to watch Laurie read a book. Then I select two boxes, one white, one blue, and set them side by side in his room. "Laurie, read your book," I tell her. Laurie sits on the floor and reads a book while Jonah and I watch. "I'm tired of reading this book," she says. "I'll stop and go outside for a break." She puts the small book in the white box and leaves the room.

"Jonah, we're going to play a trick on Laurie," I say. "I'm going to move the book from the white box to the blue box." I put the book in the blue box and cover the tops of both boxes with a towel. Laurie enters the doorway. "I'm ready to read again," she sings and walks toward the boxes. "Stop!" I say. "Jonah, which box will Laurie look in? Where does she think her book is?" He looks at the boxes, then at me.

"The white box," he says easily.

"That's right!" I say. "You did a good job, Jonah!"

I can't explain to him exactly what he did, but he's proud.

Jonah gets the book from the blue box. "Is she going to read now?" he asks.

*The first try,* I think. *The first try.*

I call Hank and explain our test to him. He confirms I did it correctly, and says there are many other CARD kids who can do it.

"Then why don't the books say so?"

"I guess they never asked us," he says.

---

Whizzing down the street, I spot a shiny royal blue Volkswagen Beetle. "Look, Jonah . . . that's a great color Beetle!" I say.

He looks, then returns to the fast-food action figure in his lap. "Yeah, it is."

The next day, we pass BMWs, Volkswagens, and Mercedes. Since he taught me to notice them, I see them everywhere. "Hey, Jonah, there's a beat-up old Beetle."

"Okay," he says.

Days later, it hits me. No more airplane talk, no more car talk. Since we started the Celexa, his perseverative talk has disappeared. Like a chatty, noiseless ghost, its absence leaves the room mysteriously brighter.

------

I beg my way in to see a busy, skilled pediatric endocrinologist, to cover all Jonah's metabolic and dietary bases. His patient bulletin board is covered with pictures of children with Down's syndrome, metabolic disorders, and diabetes.

We go over the medications and the sugar-free, dairy-free, high-protein diet. He says, "He's on a very healthy diet. We'd all be better off if we ate this way.

"I see this other diagnosis in his chart," he says, after he's examined Jonah, the two of them chatting away. "I don't understand why it's here. It was obviously incorrectly made."

"No, it wasn't," I say. "He was, is, that way."

He looks away in the tactful way I recognize.

"I don't know who would have made that diagnosis," he says.

"Several people did. Three child neurologists, other autism experts." Then I remember. "The pediatric neurologist you share this office with was one. He saw him."

He still doesn't believe me.

"He called him Asperger's," I said.

"Oh, well. Okay, Asperger's, maybe, then."

"But he saw him later than the other doctors, after four months of diet and treatment. Before then, he couldn't use original language, just echoed all the time. He banged his head into the wall, couldn't ask or answer a question, got kicked out of two preschools."

It's useless. His kind face is closing down. Then my frustration gives way to an odd, exhilarated mix of confusion and delight. The moment I'd dreamed of is here.

"I'd always hoped this day would come, that a doctor would doubt his diagnosis," I say. "Congratulations, you're the one." I smile at his smooth, professional face. "Thanks for not believing me."

"At any rate," he says, rallying, "he won't have the bleak future you were told he would. You're very lucky."

---

"Mom, where did you first go to school?" Jonah is sitting at the table as I fry turkey burgers. "You mean, the name of my school?" I ask, surprised.

"What was the name of it, and where it was."

"Well, my very first school was St. Mark's Kindergarten, then my next school was Yorkshire Elementary."

Jonah will be going to a mainstream classroom in a regular school next year; it looks like he won't need the ADHD school. Everyone recommends it, takes it for granted: Dr. Goldberg, the FastForWord speech therapist, Hank, and the other professionals. I remember the hopeful words of Doreen Granpeesheh, eighteen months ago: "Regular kindergarten at five, with a shadow. By age six, you may never know he had anything." A shadow won't bother me—since Jonah is doing so well, the person will serve as a general classroom aide while smoothing out his exuberance, helping him with the body language of child's play, and repeating words he may not hear in the buzz of a busy classroom. I've heard that many high-functioning, Asperger's, or near-recovered kids need a shadow through second or third or even later grades, and that's something I can live with too. But there's no sense in worrying about it now.

---

I saw an acquaintance and her son, a largely nonverbal child with a high IQ. He's no longer a two-year-old with shy intelligent eyes, but tall and restless at three. I overheard the speech therapist's words to his mother: "He's getting those *D* and *G* sounds," and "There's still real difficulty with his oral motor skills." I looked at him and wondered, what kind of agitation would be the price if his speech never catches up with his restless mind?

It isn't fair. Why should I get the great gift of recovery?

"It's happening to me," I tell Greta. "Survivor's guilt. I'm feeling terrible that all these other people aren't getting—"

"Stop it!" she says. "You worked so hard for this. I would love to get recovery, and if I did I wouldn't feel guilty at all. Enjoy this!"

"But look at how hard *you've* worked. And you didn't get it."

"I know. But any mother should feel happy for you. We can have hope, that some of our kids can recover from this awful thing. You earned it. And you know I'd tell you if you hadn't!"

My path would have been far more despairing without the ease and comfort of having Greta close. Her son Mark is the first child with autism I ever saw, my touchstone. The achievements of this child are a testament to sheer will. If I could climb a mountain and bring recovery home for her, I would.

And for the hundreds of others I've met.

And for the ghosts of mothers who never got a chance.

---

What is recovery in the global world of autism?

When I started this journey, I read that recovery is defined as having a child in a regular classroom with no aide. As I read more, that clear-cut line wavered like smoke. An Autism Society of America publication stated that *any* progress a person with autism makes is categorized as part of recovery. A lovely, inclusive definition, but not one that sits well with outsiders—or people who want a definition of the goal.

As we've sought recovery, I've seen children with varying degrees of "autism."

In light of present-day methods, many who fit the classic Kanner definition of severe isolation and extreme impairment may not achieve substantial degrees of recovery, no matter how long or hard their parents work. However, they *can* make important improvements in behavior and comprehension. This progress is just as important to their families as recovery is to mine.

I've also met children who are impaired in cognition, speech, and sensory integration but who are affectionate, communicative, and able to play. They too are autistic, and some could reach far greater goals of independence and quality of life if they had intensive intervention. Without it, their chances will never be known.

Kids in both of these categories can and do recover. My first great hope was a four-year-old boy who could only jump, tap his head, and say "coconut" when he started ABA. He grew into a Boy Scout who attended regular school, and became a gifted artist. After intervention, his major "fault" was he asked women and girls if they wore one-piece or two-piece bathing suits. When I told Jack about him, he laughed and said, "That's the question we'd all like to ask."

I've also met kids with speech and a sort of quick visual or mechanical intelligence, or great pretend play, who have physical or mental stims. They have a huge shot at recovery, but without proper intervention they will remain in a social and developmental limbo, their strange-seeming unchecked behaviors defining them.

Many kids have malfunctioning immune systems, and some can bounce back from autism when they're treated for their multiple food allergies, skewed blood cell counts, eczema, and rashes.

And there are children who aren't labeled at all because they're so intellectually gifted—but who are quickly identifiable to parents experienced with the spectrum.

Any child may be a combination of these types. So how do you move to "recovery"? There's no way to know what will work—until the immune system is cleansed, various educational therapies are implemented, diets are tried, supplements are given, medications are consumed. Against this vast backdrop of interventions, there is one truth: You can't will your child to recover, but if you don't, he probably won't.

Some people I've spoken with don't use the word *recovery*. There is a wonderous autistic culture beginning to flourish now, and many autistic adults reject the idea that autism or Asperger's syndrome is a disorder; they insist it's simply a different way of being, a concept I agree with in many ways. Few of these adults received intensive early intervention. Autistic magazine columnist Franklin Klein wrote, "Recovery from

autism is a wishful-thinking fantasy," but that the child, given
the right tools, can have a bright future. John-Paul Bovee, who
"doesn't have a negative connotation of autism," says he makes
the changes he needs to make, but it's not his job to do all the
changing—that society must change also. I believe these men
may very well fit the definition of adult recovery that medical
professionals have provided me: the ability to live alone and
hold a job without support. I find this a rather good target,
since it is a goal most individuals without autism also strive for.
This makes the autistic person part of the majority, which to
me is a great definition of recovery.

Recovery from autism is different from recovery from
everything else, and one can split hairs endlessly. If Jonah has
ADHD traits, some social weaknesses, some adult-type interests, can he really have recovered from autism? If he has to take
medicine and be on a diet to stay healthy, is that recovery? I
will give a qualified, partial yes. Can one even recover from
autism *entirely*? If we stick with diagnostic criteria, Jonah no
longer meets the criteria for autism or PDD. Asperger's syndrome? He wouldn't meet the criteria in a formal diagnostic
setting, but he does have elements of the syndrome: choosy eye
contact, a certain awkwardness with spoken language along
with an excellent vocabulary. He has mild fine motor weakness
in his handwriting, although he can unlock any door, use electrical equipment, and manipulate the interior of a car like no
one else. He's socially immature in peer groups, but that's
improving. Since the SSRI took his verbal perseveration away,
we no longer have obsessive airplane or Volkswagen talk.
There's his tendency to monologue a bit when he is thinking
aloud, but he always draws my participation into his story or
thoughts, asking questions and looking straight into my eyes.

Will he have friends? Yes, he already does.

Will he be a popular child, blend well into cliques and social groups? He already wants to fit in, telling me one morning that he's afraid to wear pajamas to Pajama Day at preschool in case the other kids don't. But I know things may be difficult for him.

Will Jonah have friends when he starts "real" school? Or will he be teased, harassed, isolated? This fear licks at me like a small fire. Any child who's different from the pack is at risk. But Jonah's path is too early to predict. He's already an occasional classroom leader, making up novel games and encouraging shy children to play. Who knew we'd be here in only two years?

———

"What's love?" Jonah asks one night at the kitchen table, after his medicine and snacks. "It's when you feel really good about someone, and you like to be around them, and you feel warm in your heart," I say.

"I love you, Mom. Do we love each other?"

"Yes, we do, very much."

———

I never dreamed that two years after the diagnosis, my son would be back at Kid's House's graduation party, awarded an end-of-year certificate describing him as a future emergency medical technician/doctor. That he would perform a tumbling routine before the audience with his preschool classmates, a tall blond boy raising his hands in triumph like the other boys to indulgent applause.

That he would once again be the architect of his free-flowing future, not a smooth or common one, but a beautiful challenging river of its own, replete with all those hard questions I never thought I would hear. I know that I'll have to explain his journey to him sooner than I wish, because he will figure it out before long.

"What's God say?" he asks, driving home from speech therapy.

"About what?"

"Anything. What's he say?"

"Well, first, many people think God is a man, but God might be a man or a woman. But I say he's not a man or woman, that if it exists, God is a spirit that you can't see. But he or she says that we should be nice to each other and make the right choices."

"Where is God?"

The blossoming continues. He is still only four, and the elusive "how" and "why" questions are coming at last.

"Why did those ants get in our house, Mom?" he asks, bending over a line of small sugar-ants climbing over the doorsill.

"I guess they were attracted to something sweet and marched right in."

"I'm gonna get rid of these ants." He runs to the kitchen, and I find him atop the counter rummaging in the cabinet above the microwave. "I have to get medicine for these ants." He pulls out the old leftover bottle of Nystatin.

"Are you going to put it on the ants?"

"No, I'm going to put it in them. So it will kill their germs and then they will feel better and they can go home."

"Why do they want to go home?"

"So they can relax." He soaks a paper towel with Nystatin, races down the hall and pats down the line of ants with it.

"Mom, did the ants die?"

"A few got squashed."

"Where did they go? Will we see them again?"

This was getting hard. "No one knows where you go when you die. Everyone has a different opinion."

"Why?"

"Because everyone's different. Some people would say they were in heaven. Other people would say they were just not alive, or maybe they're someplace else."

"What's your opinion, Mom?"

"I have an opinion, but what really matters is your own opinion. What do you think?"

He tilts his head, sky blue eyes gazing off. "I think their bodies aren't hurting anymore."

And one night as he goes to bed: "I love you, Jonah," I say.

"I love you too Mom. I don't like to leave you, but sometimes I have to go be with my friends."

"That's fine, honey. Just fine with me."

"Will you be there when I come back?"

"I'll always be here when you come back."

# 40

## Miracle Journey

### *A Celebration*

In August, there was another big family trip. Everyone gathered at a ranch in the Canadian Rockies to celebrate Jack's birthday. Jonah entered the airport pulling his own piece of rolling luggage, loaded with books about the solar system, the human body, fairy tales, and birthday parties. On board, the flight attendant announced the day's snacks, and he quickly called for "the oatmeal cookie, so we can see if it's okay for me, and push the red call button, Mom, to get the flight attendant, because I'm not tall enough to reach it." He sat patiently, happily, studying the emergency procedure card for twenty minutes, asking questions about smoking and windows and stair exits. He watched the movie and the flight attendant's doings, sang songs in his piping, tuneful voice, and made up stories about everything in sight.

At the ranch, nearly two dozen relatives awaited. Most of them had not seen Jonah since France. He learned their names in a flash, asked the balding uncles, "Who took your hair?" and fell quickly in love with his twelve-year-old cousin Kelly. He rode a pony, learned how to hold a pool cue and jab at balls, and played Foozball with the ranch kids day after day. Every night, he sat through three-hour dinners, perched at the "kids" table, insistent that Kelly sit by his side.

On the night of Jack's birthday dinner, Jack drew Jonah onto his lap and spoke of how proud he was of his child, and how glad he was that his wife had made it to this milestone birthday with him. Few of the people at the long wooden table really knew how much we had been through, how hard Jonah had worked to rejoin the world. How somehow we had pasted together a miracle.

At that moment, I knew the worst of the problems Jonah had faced were over. What lay ahead could be very difficult, or easier than expected. The only thing Jack and I could count on was what we had been given.

The strange, powerful journey that preceded this birthday trip had changed me. I'd soaked up so much knowledge about the spectrum, and the unpredictable shocks and glories of just being alive, that it was hard to carry. I'm a different person than I was in France. I'm still laden with faults and limitations, but now I have the heavy, freeing knowledge that life is just an opportunity to live, and that the dependency of a child is the most precious thing a person can have.

# Epilogue

I couldn't leave the autism world if I tried.

It's growing as quickly as spring grass, spreading over this country every day. Before my son's diagnosis, I had never heard of a child with autism. Now, most people know of someone on the spectrum. Two years ago, we knew four neighborhood kids with autism, including Jonah. Currently there are eighteen boys and two girls. My friend's local support group had a dozen families three years ago; now her rapidly growing e-mail list reaches nearly two thousand families.

The sad neglect of the medical establishment is astounding, unbelievable until you've lived it. Out of the dozens of doctors, psychologists, and specialists we've seen who supposedly knew autism, only five offered useful help. It's a strange postmodern medical battlefield, where the fight starts after the war's declared over, after doctors have left the scene and the school personnel are mopping up.

People with autism spectrum disorders are different, whether wonderfully or sadly so. The autism spectrum threads humanity with its many essential gifts: exceptional insight; revolutionary ability to envision; devotion to ideas and work; focus leading to great achievements. These are not traits society wants to lose. Some of the greatest names of the past and present are increasingly being linked with the spectrum; inventors, artists, poets, novelists, philosophers, musicians, even a golfer, among others. I've met many accomplished, outwardly typical teens and adults who manage their challenges while living satisfying lives. But the voices of many affected people are muted—or even obliterated—by their problems. We must value and respect the differences in our spectrum children and the adults they will become. And communication is essential. Depending on where a person falls on the spectrum, achieving it may call for a hundred medical, dietary, and educational tools. But it is worth it; autistic people, soon to be millions of them, *deserve* the chance to speak for themselves. "Are you happy you can communicate now?" a reporter asked a mute, severely autistic nine-year-old who'd learned to spell out words.

"Yes," he wrote.

"Why?" pressed the reporter.

"Now I can tell my family how I feel."

At a conference I attended, Tito Mukhopadhyay, a gifted Indian teen writer and poet with autism so severe he flails about and cannot speak, was asked the single most important thing he could tell parents.

He typed: "Believe in your children."

# Recommended Reading

The tangled paths through the woods of autism have yet to be drawn on a universally reliable map. But certain books can be guideposts as the traveler stumbles through the forest. Each of these books illuminates certain aspects of the condition and offers valuable knowledge. They also endear the exceptional people at their centers to us.

I recommend the many autobiographic and educational books of the following authors with autism spectrum disorders: Temple Grandin, Donna Williams, Stephen Shore, Liane Holliday Willey, and Jasmine Lee O'Neill (who is sometimes mute and writes wonderfully about nonverbal people).

For an overall guide to early intervention, read Lynn Hamilton's *Facing Autism*. Chantal Sicile-Kira's *Autism Spectrum Disorders: The Complete Guide* is a comprehensive resource book useful for all ages. *Behavioral Intervention for Young Children with Autism,* edited by Catherine Maurice, Gina Green, and Stephen C. Luce, offers a detailed look at applied behavioral analysis (ABA). For dietary intervention, go to Karyn Seroussi's *Unraveling the Mystery of Autism and PDD*. For the high-functioning child with an ADHD profile, read *Reweaving the Autistic Tapestry: Autism, Asperger Syndrome and ADHD* by Lisa Blakemore-Brown. For medical insight, try *Biological Interventions for Autism and PDD* by William Shaw, PhD, and *What Your Doctor May Not Tell You about Children's Vaccinations*, by Stephanie Cave, MD. Always carry out medical or dietary treatments under the care of a doctor specializing in autism.

And for the extraordinary wisdom and love that a disabled child can bring, seek out *Aidan's Way* by Sam Crane and *Changed by a Child* by Barbara Gill.